Prescott Holmes

The Battles of the War for the Union

being the story of the great Civil War from the election of Abraham Lincoln to the surrender at Appomatox

Prescott Holmes

The Battles of the War for the Union
being the story of the great Civil War from the election of Abraham Lincoln to the surrender at Appomatox

ISBN/EAN: 9783337224882

Printed in Europe, USA, Canada, Australia, Japan

Cover: Foto ©ninafisch / pixelio.de

More available books at **www.hansebooks.com**

THE BATTLES

OF THE

WAR FOR THE UNION

BEING THE STORY OF THE GREAT CIVIL WAR FROM THE ELECTION OF ABRAHAM LINCOLN TO THE SURRENDER AT APPOMATOX.

BY
PRESCOTT HOLMES

With Eighty Illustrations.

PHILADELPHIA
HENRY ALTEMUS

CONTENTS.

CHAPTER I. THE SECESSION MOVEMENT . . . 9
Lincoln Inaugurated—"Confederate States" Government Formed—Jefferson Davis Declared President of the Southern Confederacy—Fort Sumter Bombarded—Its Surrender—The Rush to Arms—Richmond Made the Capital of the Confederacy—Harpers' Ferry Evacuated by the Union Forces—The Norfolk Navy Yard Evacuated and Burned—Robert E. Lee Placed in Command of the Confederate Forces in Virginia—Massachusetts Troops Fired Upon in Baltimore—General Irwin McDowell in Virginia—Battle of Big Bethel—The First Union Defeat—The Shenandoah Valley—General George B. McClellan's Campaign in Western Virginia—Rich Mountain—McClellan Commands the Army of the Potomac—English Government Confers Belligerent Rights on the Confederates—Confederate Privateers—"On to Richmond"—General Beauregard—Battle of Bull Run—Joseph E. Johnston and "Stonewall" Jackson—The Union Forces Defeated—Stampede to Washington—Battle of Ball's Bluff—Another Defeat for the Union Troops.

CHAPTER II. THE CAMPAIGNS IN THE WEST (1862) . 47
McClellan Made Commander of the Union Forces—Formulates Plans of Campaigns—General Halleck in the West—Fort Henry Attacked by General Grant and Commodore Foote, and the Ironclads—"Unconditional Surrender" of Fort Henry—Operations Against Fort Donelson—Generals Floyd,

Pillow, and Buckner—Donelson Taken—Johnston Abandons Nashville, and Retreats to Murfreesboro—Grant and Buell Advance—Island No. 10 Attacked—The Position Surrenders to Commodore Foote—Battle of Pittsburg Landing, or Shiloh—Albert Sidney Johnston Killed—Success Crowns the Union Arms—Fort Pulaski, Near Savannah, Bombarded and Captured—Fall of New Orleans—The Submission of Natchez—Butler Superseded by Banks—The First Attack on Vicksburg—The Siege Abandoned—Bragg Succeeds Beauregard—Guerilla Warfare—Movements in Kentucky—Union Troops Surprised and Defeated by Kirby Smith—Bragg Defeats Buell—Rosencrans Assumes Command of Buell's Army—Battle of Corinth—Confederates Defeated—Joseph E. Johnston Commands the Confederates in the West—Attacks Rosencrans—Battle of Stone River, or Murfreesboro—Confederates Repulsed—Morgan and Forrest's Guerilla Depredations—Sherman Attacks Vicksburg—Haines' Bluff.

CHAPTER III. THE "MONITOR" AND THE "MERRIMAC" 116
The Naval Engagement in Hampton Roads—Shot-proof Vessels—The *Merrimac*—Her First Successes—Destruction of the *Cumberland*, and Others of the Wooden Fleet—Description of the *Monitor*—The Great Combat Between the Mailed Vessels—The *Merrimac* Disabled—The Blockading Fleet Saved.

CHAPTER IV. THE PENINSULA CAMPAIGN, FROM YORKTOWN TO GETTYSBURG 128
The Union Army Crosses into Virginia—McClellan in Command—Forward Movement—Winchester—Yorktown Captured—Williamsburg Occupied—Norfolk Evacuated, and Burned by the Confederates—McClellan's Reverses—"Stonewall" Jackson in the Valley—Banks Surprised—Fremont and Shields Attacked—Jackson Escapes—Battle of Seven Pines, or Fair Oaks—Confederates Defeated—Jackson Re-

inforces Lee—The Seven Days' Battles—General Pope Supersedes McClellan—Cedar Mountain—Second Battle at Bull Run, or Manassas—Union Forces Retreat to Washington—McClellan Reinstated — Lee Enters Maryland — Harper's Ferry Surrenders—Battle of Antietam—Lee Repulsed and Retreats to Virginia—McClellan Removed and the Command Conferred on General Burnside—Battle at Fredericksburg—Burnside Defeated—General Joseph Hooker in Command — Battle of Chancellorsville — Hooker Defeated—George G. Meade Commands the Union Forces—Lee Plans to Conquer a Peace Upon the Soil of the Loyal States, and Invades Pennsylvania—Battle of Gettysburg—Confederate Successes the First Day—Generals Hancock and Longstreet—Confederates Repulsed — Pickett's Famous Charge — Lee Defeated—Northern Invasion Abandoned.

CHAPTER V. VICKSBURG, AND THE OPERATIONS IN THE WEST (1863) 192
The Reduction of Vicksburg Determined Upon by Grant—Porter, and His Iron Clads—Haines' Bluff Abandoned by the Confederates—General Pemberton Shut Up in Vicksburg—Vicksburg Bombarded—Its Siege and Surrender—Sherman and Johnston—Port Hudson Taken—The Conquest of the Mississippi—Operations in Tennessee—Rosencrans and Bragg—Battle of Chickamauga—Union Forces Retreat to Chattanooga—Grant's Arrival—Battle of Chattanooga—Bragg Removed from Command — Longstreet Before Knoxville — Sherman Relieves Knoxville.

CHAPTER VI. CHARLESTON AND FORT SUMTER. . 235
Expedition Against Charleston—The Ironclads Seriously Injured—The Attack Abandoned—A Third Attack Begun by Lincoln's Orders—Forts Wagner and Sumter Bombarded—Sumter in Ruins—Charleston Bombarded—The Attack Abandoned.

CHAPTER VII.   SHERMAN'S MARCH TO THE SEA   . 250

Sherman Against Johnston—Generals Hardee, Hood and Polk—Operations of McPherson—Thomas and Schofield—The Siege of Atlanta—Sherman Captures Atlanta—Jefferson Davis Visits Hood, who Assumes the Defensive—Confederates Repulsed—Beauregard Assumes Command—The March to the Sea—Atlanta Burned—Savannah Occupied—Hood in Sherman's Rear—Hood Surprises and Defeats Schofield—Hood and Thomas—Battle of Nashville—Hood Defeated—Sherman in the Carolinas—Columbia (S. C.) Captured and Burned—Charleston Evacuated by Hardee—The City Burned by the Confederates — Wilmington (N. C.) Taken—Schofield Moves to Goldsboro—Battle of Bentonville—Sherman Reaches Grant's Headquarters.

CHAPTER VIII.   THE CLOSING BATTLES IN VIRGINIA   297

Grant Commands all the Union Armies — Battles in the Wilderness—Meade and Hancock—Longstreet Wounded—Confederates Repulsed — Battle of Spottsylvania—General Sedgwick Killed—"I propose to fight it out on this line"—Battle of Cold Harbor—Attack on Petersburg—General Early Advances into Maryland—Washington Narrowly Escapes Capture—Early's Retreat—Burning of Chambersburg, in Pennsylvania — Sheridan Against Early—Battle of Cedar Creek—Sheridan "thirty miles away"—Early Defeated—Hancock Attacks Lee's Forces—Siege of Richmond—Fort Fisher Assaulted—Butler Superseded—A Second Assault—Fall of Fort Fisher—Peace Negotiations Opened by the Confederates — Lincoln Insists on Absolute Submission—Lee Strikes at Grant with the View to Unite with Johnston's Forces—Attack on Fort Steadman—Battle of Five Forks—Confederates Retreat to Petersburg—Petersburg and Richmond Taken—Lee's Army Surrenders—President Lincoln Assassinated—Surrender of Johnston and Others—Jefferson Davis Captured—The Cost of the War in Blood and Money.

THE BATTLES FOR THE UNION.

CHAPTER I.

The Secession Movement.*

On March 4, 1861, Abraham Lincoln was inaugurated President of the United States, surrounded by soldiers under the command of General Scott. During the campaign preceding the election, the Southern leaders had threatened to secede from the Union if Lincoln were elected. Charles A. Dana puts the case in the following succinct way:

"The election of Abraham Lincoln was brought about by a dissension in the Democratic party. It was divided and the Republican party was united, and the consequence was his election. The great question at issue in that election was this: Shall the owners of slaves enjoy the right of taking their slaves into the Territories of the United States that are now free, and keeping them there? The slave-owners claimed that right. Slaves were property. They were like other property, and why should their owners be denied the right of taking their property into the Territories, when a Northern man could take his property, his horses, his oxen, whatever he possessed? The slaves were their oxen; they were their chattels, and they insisted that they ought to have the right of taking them into the Territories and keep-

* The history of the events leading up to the Civil War will be found in the "Lives of the Presidents," in *Altemus' Young People's Series*.

ing them there as slaves. That was the fundamental question of the election. And when Mr. Lincoln was elected, the South said: 'Now we are denied this right, we will break up the Government; we will secede; we will withdraw.' That right, too, they claimed as a constitutional principle. No Northerner had claimed it, though some ardent partisans had threatened it; but several of the Southern States now set it up as an original, inalienable right. They claimed that the refusal to them of the right to take their property with them when they went to live in one of the new Territories, was sufficient occasion for the withdrawal from the Union of the slave-holding States, and for the breaking up of the Government."

The South had been contemplating rebellion for years, and had only refrained from attempting it because hitherto she had pretty generally had her own way. The choice of Lincoln immediately determined their resolution. John B. Floyd, of Virginia, the Secretary of War under Buchanan, had quietly contrived that the arsenals of all the Northern States should be stripped of their arms and ammunition, and those warlike materials concentrated in the Southern section of the Union.

South Carolina naturally led off in the Secession movement, her Ordinance of Secession being adopted on November 17, 1860; Georgia came next, and the remainder of the border (or planting) States quickly followed. Virginia joined two days after the fall of Sumter.

On February 9, 1861, Jefferson Davis, of Mississippi, was declared President, and Alexander H. Stephens, of Georgia, Vice-President of the CONFEDERATE STATES OF AMERICA. On March 4, 1861, the Confederate flag was unfurled from the State House at Montgomery, Alabama, and the Confederacy was inaugurated.

Of moral justification for the disruption of the Union

JEFFERSON DAVIS.
(*President of the Southern Confederacy.*)

there was absolutely nothing. The South separated themselves from the Union from motives of transparent and avowed selfishness. Stephens declared that "the corner-stone of the new Confederacy was slavery." In

MAJOR ROBERT ANDERSON.

a few years that corner-stone was pulled out, and the whole fabric came toppling down in irremediable ruin.

War between the new Slave Power and the Old Union was so certain to ensue that the South made instant preparations for the worst. The Southern Congress authorized Davis to accept 100,000 volunteers for

BOMBARDMENT OF FORT SUMTER.

twelve months, and to borrow fifteen millions of dollars. And so great was the faith of most foreign nations in the permanence of the Confederacy that the bonds were circulated in Europe, and principally in England. This was one reason why English opinion, among the wealthy classes, was so largely enlisted in favor of Secession. The bondholders felt they had an interest in securing the triumph of the Southern aristocracy, and they brought every possible pressure to bear on their Government to force a recognition of the Confederacy, and the raising of the blockade. When the rebellion collapsed, great was the regret of these investors that they had relied upon the ability of a Slave Empire to stand up against the might of freedom.

When the Lincoln Administration came into power sixteen forts were in possession of the Secessionists, who had thus acquired 1226 heavy guns to turn against the Federal authority. It should be remembered that the North was left, at the very commencement of the struggle with comparatively few educated officers. The greater number of those who graduated at the Military Academy at West Point, and continued in actual service, were Southern men; and these, with comparatively few exceptions, although trained at the expense of the nation, and bound to loyalty by the most solemn oaths, at once joined the Southern forces.

FORT SUMTER (April 12, 1861).—The first gun was fired by the South on Fort Sumter, in Charleston harbor. The fort was commanded by Major Anderson, with but 70 men. It was bombarded by the forts and batteries under command of Peter G. T. Beauregard; and for 34 hours this little garrison of 70 men contested with 7000 rebels, no one being hurt on either side. The shells set fire to the barracks, and the garrison, worn out, suffocated and half-blinded, were forced to surrender on April 13. The effect of this event was electrical. It unified both the South and the North; the American flag, the symbol of Revolutionary glory and of national unity being unfurled thoroughout the North.

If there had previously been any doubt as to the necessity of taking serious steps against the rising rebellion, it was now evident that pacific measures were no longer possible. Until then, the shrinking from civil war had been so great that men were willing to compro-

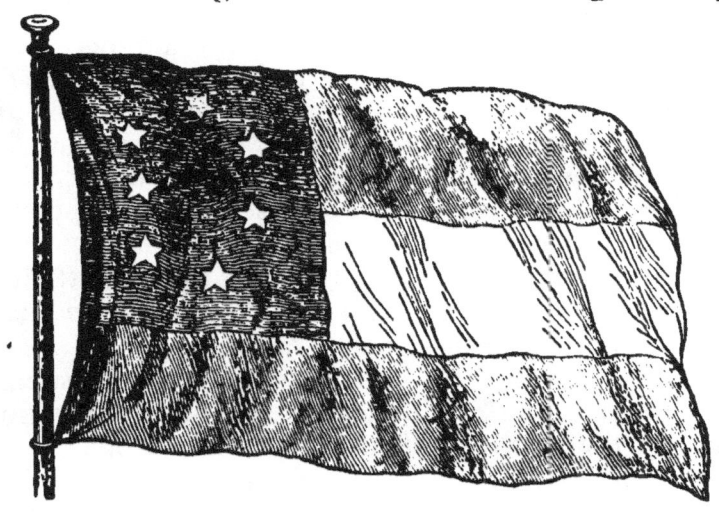

THE CONFEDERATE FLAG.

mise matters with the South, even at the cost of not inconsiderable sacrifices. But now a spirit of determined resistance to Southern aggression was aroused in every one of the Northern States. It was seen that a bloody struggle was inevitable, and men nerved themselves to meet the terrible demands that would be made upon their patriotism. A national fort had been seized; a body of Federal troops had been defeated; the flag of the Union had been lowered at the demand of traitors. The time for hesitation had gone by, and the Government understood its duty. Lincoln issued a proclamation on April 15, declaring that the laws of the Republic had been for some time, and were then, opposed in the States of South Carolina, Georgia, Alabama, Florida, Mississippi, Louisiana, and Texas, " by combinations too powerful to be suppressed by the ordinary course of judicial proceedings, or by the powers vested in the marshals by law." The President accordingly called forth the militia of the other States of the Union, to the aggregate number of 75,000 men. He appealed to all loyal citizens " to favor, facilitate, and aid his efforts to maintain the honor, integrity, and existence of the National Union, and the perpetuity of popular government." This was responded to by 300,000 volunteers. The resolution of the North to fight for the existence of the Union has never been surpassed by any popular movement in any account of the world's history.

The Secessionists audaciously thrust their capital into their northernmost State, and on April 20, made Richmond the Capital of the Confederacy.

Troops were pushed into Virginia, and threatened Washington. The Sixth Massachusetts Regiment, hurrying to the defence of the National Capital, were attacked in Baltimore, and several men were killed. Thus, the first blood shed in the Civil War was on April 19, the eighty-sixth anniversary of Lexington and Concord.

Harper's Ferry, in Virginia, was attacked on April 18. The commander, whose force was small, observed symptoms of dissatisfaction all around, and fearing that he could not withstand the attack that he knew was to be made, blew up the fort, crossed the river with his men, and retreated towards Pennsylvania.

It was resolved by the Secessionists to seize the Navy Yard at Norfolk, Virginia, to prevent which it was determined to set fire to all the ships, together with all the public buildings, and national property. The loss to the Government was estimated at seven millions of dollars. Eleven vessels were thus destroyed. The *Merrimac* was sufficiently uninjured, to be afterwards repaired by the Confederates, and to render service to their cause.

Pennsylvania and Massachusetts were among the first to answer President Lincoln's call for troops. Fortress Monroe, situated on the point of land between the James and York Rivers, at the junction with the Potomac, was the only place now held by the Federal Government in Virginia. Those rivers were blockaded by what remained of the fleet, and the vessels were concentrated at Hampton Roads, near the fortress.

Baltimore refused to allow foreign State troops to pass through her soil on the way to Washington. Lincoln, feeling his weakness, suggested that the troops pass round Baltimore instead of through it. He finally declared that troops must be had for the defence of Washington, and as they could come by no other route but Maryland, the people of Maryland must be content to let them pass.

On April 20, Robert E. Lee, a Virginian, and an engineer officer of much distinction, connected by marriage with the family of Washington, separated himself from the Federal service, considering the claims of his State paramount, and went over to the Confederacy, and was made Commander of all the military and naval forces in Virginia.

Maryland was reduced to submission before the end of April by an expedition of Massachusetts troops under Benjamin F. Butler, and New York's famous Seventh Regiment, under Colonel Lefferts. Butler was a lawyer, not trained to military life, but possessed of spirit, resolution, and audacity. He was placed in command of the Department of Annapolis, which embraced the country 20 miles on each side of the railway from Baltimore to Washington. Lefferts went on to Washington to guard the capital.

General Scott, the Commander-in-Chief, said the occupation of Baltimore was made without his knowledge or approbation, and required the Government to recall Butler from his post; and this was done. The President, however, was satisfied with the operations of this active leader, and immediately commissioned him as a Major-General of Volunteers, and the command of a large military district, including Eastern Virginia and the two Carolinas, with his headquarters at Fortress Monroe.

Every day the movement in the South was becoming more formidable; every day the sympathizers with Secession in the border States were growing more dangerous and irreconcilable. It was now seen that the President's call for militia would not be sufficient to meet the attack which was evidently meditated by the South. Lincoln accordingly, in a proclamation issued on May 3, called into the service of the United States 42,000 volunteers for three years; ordered an increase of the regular army to the extent of 22,714 officers and enlisted men, for not less than one year, nor more than three years; and directed the enlistment of 18,000 seamen for the naval service. The response to these demands showed how thoroughly in earnest were the people of the loyal States in their resistance to Secession. The number of volunteers exceeded the demands of the Government, and money, amounting to more than forty millions of dollars, was subscribed for the various purposes of the war.

The Capitol at Washington was by this time changed into a great citadel. Troops occupied the legislative halls, the rotunda, and other chambers; the basement galleries were converted into storerooms for the army;

and the vaults under the terrace on the western front of the edifice were used as ovens, where 16,000 loaves were baked every day. Before the summer had fairly set in,

BENJAMIN F. BUTLER.

the Federal capital had been protected by a line of fortifications and entrenchments, distributed along the neighboring heights on the Virginian side of the Potomac, and presenting a formidable front to any hostile force coming from that direction. Major-General McDowell, an officer of the regular army, was placed in command of the troops on the south side of the river, and the greater portion of the district recently under the orders of General Butler was transferred to him. The Northern forces had now reached a total of about 95,000 men, divided into eight distinct bodies, which were stationed in various parts of the country. Several of the men, however, were not yet armed, and but few of the regiments had acquired anything like efficient discipline. The chief rallying-place of the Confederate Army was at Manassas Junction, situated on the Orange and Alexandria Railway, about 25 miles west from the city of Alexandria, and thirty in a direct line from Washington. The position was important, as commanding the great Southern railway route which connects Washington and Richmond, and also another line leading to the valley of the Shenandoah, beyond the Blue Ridge. Butler had at an early period recommended the occupation of that locality; but Scott, whose measures at this time were marked by the extreme caution of old age, took a different view, and the result was that the Confederates, acting with greater enterprise, seized the position, which they found of service as a menace against the Federal capital.

BIG BETHEL (June 10, 1861). After fortifying Newport News—a point of land at the junction of the James River and Hampton Roads—Butler formed a design of attacking a Confederate force which had been stationed at Big Bethel, about 15 miles off, on the road to Yorktown. This force was the advanced post of a rather considerable array of Southern troops under the command of Colonel Magruder, formerly an artillery officer in the U. S. Army. The main body was at Yorktown, whence expeditions were frequently sent out, with the object of harassing the Union Army in the vicinity of Fortress Monroe. From observations, it became evident that Magruder was preparing to seize Newport News and Hampton, so that he might confine Butler to the fortress which he had made his headquarters. It was therefore resolved to take the initiative. The Confederate detachment at Big Bethel consisted of 800 North Carolina Volunteers, and 360 Virginians, with a battery of five howitzers and one Parrott rifle-gun. Some field-works had been erected, and the position was naturally strong, owing to the surrounding forest and the presence of some swampy ground which protected the Confederate flanks. In front, at a place called Little Bethel, was a small picket of cavalry; and the whole detachment was under the command of Colonel D. H. Hill. The attacking force sent forward by Butler was composed of four regiments, under the direction of General Peirce. These started on the night of June 9, and their plan of operations was to send two regiments directly to the front, along the Fortress Monroe and Yorktown roads, while the other two were to endeavor to outflank the enemy. An unfortunate blunder deranged the execution of the scheme. The supporting regiments coming within sight of each other in the obscurity of the early morning, mutually mistook their forces for those of the enemy, and at once opened fire. The advanced guard, hearing the firing, and supposing that the enemy had got into their rear, fell back upon their supports; and by the time the mistake was discovered, and the forward march resumed, all hope of surprising the enemy was at an end. The cavalry at Little Bethel had pressed on to Big Bethel, and nothing remained but to make a direct attack upon the latter position, in the hope of carrying the works at the point of the bayonet. Big Bethel was reached by ten o'clock. To take an entrenched position is a trying task even for well-seasoned troops: for raw and undisciplined volunteers it is almost an impossibility. The men were led up to the charge, but failed to make any way. Though supported by the artillery, the Union regiments flinched before the Confederate batteries. What was wanting on their part was not courage—for they remained in the field nearly three hours, making scattered and desultory attacks—but coolness, knowledge, and concentration. Their losses were severe, and during the engagement two additional regiments from Fortress Monroe arrived on the spot, while four others were held in readiness to march to the front. On the right of the attacking force the Vermont companies distinguished themselves by great perseverance, gaining a position in the rear of the enemy, and silencing one of his batteries. About noon the Union troops were withdrawn. The retreat has been described as a rout. Doubtless it was somewhat precipitate. The Confederates boasted much of their own valor at Big Bethel, and were unsparing in their denunciations of the cowardice, as they described it, exhibited by the Union troops. It must always be recollected, however, that it is one thing to hold a fortified position, and quite a different thing to attack it.

THE SHENANDOAH VALLEY.—The Federal authorities determined to send a body of troops up the valley of the Shenandoah, in conjunction with a movement of McClellan from the neighborhood of Grafton. It was necessary to the protection of Washington that the Confederates should be driven from Harper's Ferry, their possession of which would at any time enable them to execute a flank attack on the capital. To effect this purpose, an army of 20,000 men, under the command of General Patterson, was pushed forward from its camp in the neighborhood of Chambersburg, Pennsylvania, to Greencastle and Gettysburg; and at the same time troops were marched up the north bank of the Potomac to Rockville. These

HARPER'S FERRY, VIRGINIA.

movements rendered it prudent for General Joseph E. Johnston to withdraw to some safer locality. His force was about 7000 in number, and he feared being overwhelmed by the gathering hosts. He therefore began his retreat on June 16, but, before doing so, he blocked up the railway and canal near the ferry by blasting the overhanging rocks. He destroyed the great bridge on the Baltimore and Ohio Railway by blowing it up. Whatever guns he could not take with him he spiked; and, having burned another bridge a few miles higher up the Potomac, he marched along the valley, and encamped for a time near Charleston. Patterson immediately afterwards crossed from Maryland into Virginia; and was met with a demand from Scott to send him all the troops he could spare for the defence of Washington. In consequence Patterson was left with so small a force that he found it necessary to withdraw them at once across the Potomac. The explanation of this untoward event is, that there had been a panic at the capital. Immense Confederate forces were believed to be at Manassas. And as they had been placed under the vigorous control of Beauregard, it was feared an attempt would be made on Washington before Congress could meet on July 4. The danger was probably exaggerated, but it was not imaginary. Washington swarmed with Secessionist sympathizers, who were ready to abet any treason that might be plotted from without. Still, Patterson's forward movement had had the effect of driving Johnston to a more remote position, and he made no attempt to reoccupy Harper's Ferry. He established his headquarters at Winchester, and entrusted the task of watching the Potomac to Colonel Jackson (the officer afterwards known as "Stonewall" Jackson, one of the most heroic of the Southerners), in combination with the cavalry under the command of Colonel Stewart. On July 2, Patterson's force again crossed the

Potomac, and occupied Harper's Ferry. Shortly afterwards, Johnston moved his army to the relief of Beauregard at Manassas, and nothing of importance took place between himself and Patterson.

Attention was now directed to McClellan's operations. He had been in command of the military district which included Ohio, Indiana, Illinois, and Western Virginia. He was a soldier by education, and, was joint-commissioner with Lee to report on the warlike operations in the Crimea. Retiring from the service after that date, he became manager of the Illinois Central Railway, but resumed his original profession on the outbreak of the Civil War. Having by midsummer organized a force of 15,000 soldiers, principally recruited in the Western States, he advanced against the Confederate troops in Western Virginia. These did not count more than 6000 men, with a small proportion of cavalry and artillery; the whole under the command of General Garnett. The country occupied by the Southern commander was well adapted to defensive operations, being traversed by the main body of the Alleghanies and by several minor ridges running in the same direction, which is from the north-east to the south-west.

RICH MOUNTAIN (July 11, 1861).—General Garnett—an officer of experience and talent—took up his position on an eminence called Laurel Hill, situated west of the chief line of the Alleghanies, and covering the highroad leading from Philippi to Beverley. He threw forward a detachment under Colonel Pegram, which was to station itself upon an isolated and forest-clad hill named Rich Mountain, a few miles south of Laurel Hill, from which it is separated by woody country and a creek. The force numbered about 2000, and his duty was to obtain a command over the road leading in a north-westerly direction from Beverly to Weston.

Against these positions McClellan advanced from the north, and on July 11 halted at a short distance from Rich Mountain. Fighting began on the following day, when four regiments, commanded by Colonel Rosecrans, were sent forward by a circuitous path through the woods, to turn the left of Colonel Pegram's position. Under a drenching rain, they climbed the steep side of the mountain, and, undeterred by a heavy fire which was opened on them as they neared the summit, completely routed the defenders, and drove them down the opposite side of the acclivity. All this while McClellan himself, with the main body, was in front of the position; but no occasion arose for his immediate services. Pushing on towards the east, Rosecrans, arrived within three miles of Beverly, in which direction Garnett, who abandoned Laurel Hill on finding his position turned, had himself proceeded, until, discovering the perilous proximity of the enemy, he struck northward through the mountains, in hope of gaining St. George, on the Cheat River. Pegram had by this time surrendered, with 600 of his men; the remainder joined their comrades under Garnett, who was actively pursued by General Morris. The line of retreat was rendered difficult by rocks, thickly intertangled woods, and streams swollen by the summer rains. Here and there, in narrow gorges, the fugitives had cut down large trees, and turned over great boulders of stone, with a view to baffling their pursuers; but the forces of General Morris dashed on through every obstruction, occasionally engaged with the rear-guard of the enemy, and at other times tracking their foes by the knapsacks, camp-equipage, and abandoned wagons which they had left behind them in their headlong flight. McClellan had given orders for intercepting the retreating columns; but Morris, on July 13, overtook the Confederate general at Carrick's Ford, on the Cheat, and inflicted on

WILLIAM H. SEWARD.
(*The War Secretary of State.*)

him a severe reverse. While exposing himself with great courage, Garnett was shot dead, and the shattered remnants of the army were conducted by Colonel Taliaferro to Monterey, on the eastern side of the Alleghanies, where they arrived in a state of the utmost destitution and fatigue.

The campaign had been a great success. With the loss of only fifty men, McClellan had routed and dispersed the forces of his opponent, had taken nearly 1000 troops, and had captured seven guns, 1500 stand of arms, twelve colors, and the greater part of the equipments and baggage of the Confederate camp. McClellan was disposed to take a very sanguine view of the existing situation; and gave it as his opinion that Secession was killed in that part of the country. The Confederates rallied after awhile, and, on General Lee being appointed to the post lately occupied by Garnett, a series of vigorous operations took place on the western side of the mountains. Yet the results obtained by the Unionists were really important. The army of General Garnett was for the time disorganized, broken up, and crestfallen. The Union forces had certainly made a fortunate commencement of the war, and a fortunate conclusion lay before it; but between those two extremes many signal disasters were to be endured and overcome.

On July 22, General George B. McClellan was called to the command of the Army of the Potomac.

Lincoln called an extra session of Congress to convene on July 4. He recommended that Congress should grant legal means to make the existing contest a short and decisive one, by placing at the disposal of the Government 400,000 men, and $400,000,000. The number of men, he remarked, was about one-tenth of those of proper ages within the regions where all seemed willing to engage; and the sum was less than one-twenty-third part of the money value owned by men who appeared ready to devote the whole.

The total force in the field was computed at 230,000 men, after abstracting 80,000 who had only enlisted for three months, then on the eve of expiring.

The Secretary of the Navy reported that the total naval force of the United States was 42 vessels, nearly all of them on foreign stations; while the *home* squadron consisted of but 12 vessels, carrying 187 guns, and about 2000 men.

On May 13, 1861, the English Government issued a Proclamation of Neutrality, by which belligerent rights were conferred on the Confederates. To confer this position of a belligerent was in some degree to recognize their existence as an independent Power; and this was an immense gain to the cause of Jefferson Davis. It took the Confederacy out of the category of rebels, and placed it in that of acknowledged nations. The privilege was one which the Federal Government never conceded, for to do so would have been to annihilate the justification for the war. If the Confederacy was a beligerent in the technical sense of the word, it was an independent nation; and as an independent nation there was no reason for attacking it. Only as a rebel could it fairly be made amenable to the law force. This view was sustained throughout the long struggle by William H. Seward, one of the ablest of our Secretaries of State.

The Confederate privateers (numbering about twenty) were by this time very active, and although their operations did not commence until the early part of May, they had by the end of July captured vessels and property valued at several millions of dollars.

The military position in the early part of July was such as to create great confidence in the minds of the Northern people. The cry "On to Richmond!" was raised in many quarters, and it was believed that means had been obtained for making the war as sharp, short, and decisive as the President desired it to be. The line of the Potomac was held by the Union troops from its mouth to the Cumberland, in Maryland. The adjacent seacoast was patrolled by armed vessels, and the Virginia bank of the river was carefully watched, though the troops had not been able to prevent the erection of Confederate batteries. The Union cause was represented in Virginia itself by McDowell's army (45,000 strong), and by the large force under Patterson. Between the latter force and McClellan's army was a gap in the line, indicating, of course, a weakness in that particular direction. But the Union position, on the whole, was good.

The main Confederate Army was under the orders of Beauregard, and was probably somewhat less numerous than McDowell's. It was stationed at and near Manassas Junction, a strong and important military position between Washington and Richmond, with which it was connected by rail. All around were wooded hills and frequent streams, and, in addition to the natural defences of the position, which were great, Beauregard had thrown up several artificial fortifications. A second Confederate Army was stationed in the Shenandoah Valley under Joseph E. Johnston, whose headquarters were at Winchester. This position also was strongly entrenched, and the duty of Johnston was to check the advance of Patterson, and prevent his junction with McClellan. The question now to be determined was whether the Unionists were strong enough to advance on Richmond, or the Confederates strong enough to take Washington, or whether neither was strong enough to affect its manifest intention, and could only nullify the operations of the other. General Scott, the Commander-in-Chief, was suffering from the accumulated infirmities of age. He was not the man who, 14 years earlier, had led his forces to victory in Mexico. For three years he had been unable to mount a horse; and dropsy and vertigo rendered it difficult for him to transact the ordinary business of his office. It was impossible that he should take the field in person; and accordingly the active direction of the troops was confided to Brigadier-General Irwin McDowell, a native of Ohio, who had graduated at the Military Academy at West Point, and had served under General Wool in the Mexican War. Since May 27 he commanded the Department of Virginia, with his headquarters at Arlington Court House, and had worked hard at the organization of the army.

GENERAL IRWIN McDOWELL.

He had done much, but had not had time to do sufficient. Popular clamor, however, demanded a headlong rush against the Confederates; and in this mood of uninstructed confidence, of passionate enthusiasm, and of ill-grounded hope, the nation laid itself open to the serious reverse which was about to happen.

BULL RUN (July 21, 1861).—All things being supposedly in readiness for the assault upon the Confederate lines, the forward movement of the Union troops began on the afternoon of July 16. The enterprise would have been one of grave difficulty, even had the attendant circumstances been more favorable than they really were. But there were particular facts which added largely to the perils of the campaign. Not only were the troops unacquainted with the actual operations of war, but the Union plans were seriously disturbed by the conduct of the army under Patterson. His forces were relied upon for holding Johnston in check, and preventing his junction with Beauregard, whose division was about 50 miles off, but with the advantage of railway and telegraphic lines between. Patterson, however, was unable to carry out his part of the programme, owing to the determination of his men, who had been enlisted for three months, to disband at the very earliest opportunity. They were implored to re-engage, if only for ten days; but, with the exception of four regiments, they refused. Their conduct was precisely that of large numbers of troops engaged in the revolutionary war; and the embarrassment from which Washington so frequently suffered was now once more experienced. Patterson had advanced towards Winchester, where Johnston was posted; but, on the very day when the rest of the troops moved against the enemy, he was compelled to recede towards the Potomac, owing to the unpatriotic spirit of his regiments. The force under Patterson was originally inferior in numbers to that of his adversary, besides being ill-provided with artillery; it would now, in the course of a very few days, be reduced to the most slender proportions. It therefore seemed prudent to withdraw in the direction of Maryland, where he could still assist in blocking Johnston's advance on Washington, although he was unable to fight a regular action.

Massed into five divisions, the Army of the Potomac, to the number of about 53,000, sought the lines of the enemy in the middle of July. Only 3000 of the entire number were regulars; the rest were raw and inexperienced soldiers, and in many instances the officers were not much better instructed than the troops they commanded. 16,000 men, under General Mansfield, remained at Washington, to guard the city against surprise; and the others moved forward along four roads, all converging in the vicinity of Centreville. The right column, under the orders of General Tyler, began its march at two P. M. on the 16th, and was followed, at eight A. M. on the following morning, by the remaining divisions. The Confederate force was posted along Bull Run—a small stream rising in a chain of hills to the west of Alexandria, and falling into the river Occoquan, about twelve miles from the Potomac. The line extended some eight miles, from Union Mill, where the Orange and Alexandria Railway crosses the stream, to the Stone Bridge on the Warrenton turnpike-road. The banks of the little river are steep and rocky; thick woods offered admirable covert for soldiers; and the surrounding country, from its irregularity and abundance of foliage, presents favorable opportunities for defence. Confederate reserves were held in readiness near Manassas Junction; and not far off, Beauregard had his headquarters. An outpost with fortifications, at Centreville, protected that part of the line, and strong pickets were thrown forward to Fairfax Court House, a village ten miles from the main army, in the direction of Washington. The division under Johnston, to the left of the other Confederates, gave additional strength to the Southern line of battle, and Patterson's unavoidable retreat contributed in a serious degree to the disaster which ensued.

Some obstructions on the road, in the shape of felled

trees thrown across the path, delayed the progress of the Union forces, but did not prevent the van from reaching Fairfax Court House by noon on the 17th.

Here there was a slight skirmish with the Confederate pickets; but the place was occupied by the Union Second Division, while the other divisions, with the exception of the Fourth, which was kept behind to guard the communications with Washington, were stationed between Germantown and Centreville, at two points on the Alexandria and Richmond Railway, and on the approaches to Centreville from the south-east. On the morning of the 18th, it was found that the Confederates had evacuated Centreville, which they had roughly fortified only eight hours previously. They were seen to be posted on the right or southern bank of Bull Run, and Tyler, who had command of the First Union Division, resolved on making an immediate attack. The country was thickly covered with wood, and the Confederate brigades of Generals Longstreet and Bonham took advantage of the fact. The Union point of attack was at Blackburn's Ford, situated between the Warrenton Road and the Richmond and Alexandria Railway. Tyler, however, did not attempt to cross the stream, but opened fire with his heavy guns at a distance of a mile and a half, and afterwards somewhat nearer. His adversary replied with spirit, and a brisk duel went on for some time. At length, several of the New York troops broke and fled, throwing away their arms; the other regiments retired in fairly good order. A small force of Confederates then crossed the stream at Mitchell's Ford, and, taking up a position on high ground to the east of the road to Centreville, poured a heavy fire into the retreating ranks. The object of Tyler in making his movement was to carry out a reconnoissance; and this having been accomplished, he did not consider it advisable or necessary to risk any further conflict.

It being now evident that the Confederate position was too strong to be attacked in front, it was resolved to approach the enemy on his left flank. No fresh movement, however, could be made for a couple of days, owing to the difficulty of moving inexperienced troops, with their accompanying supplies and baggage; and those two days were of the greatest value to the Confederates. Johnston, no longer having the dread of Patterson before his eyes, quitted his position in the Shenandoah Valley, and on July 20, arrived by rail at the headquarters of Beauregard with 6000 men and twenty guns, to be followed by the rest of his force. Other regiments were moved up from Richmond, and the Confederates now believed themselves equal to any attack likely to be made. Their left was on the Centreville and Warrenton Road, a little above the bridge over which that highway crosses Bull Run; their right was at Union Mills Ford, about nine miles farther down the little river, near the railway connecting Alexandria and Richmond. In front was the

GENERAL PETER H. T. BEAUREGARD.

stream, with its high and precipitous banks; at the rear were dense woods, capable of concealing large numbers of marksmen. The general character of the country was undulatory, and in parts extremely rugged. High hills alternated with lower elevations, and the gorges between were often so narrow that a small force could easily stand against one much larger. With no little confidence, therefore, did Beauregard and Johnston draw up their legions on Sunday morning, July 21. The Confederates were disposed in three lines, watching the eight fords over the stream. Beauregard stated that his entire army amounted to 27,833 men, with 49 guns for the defence of the Confederate position.

The plan of attack formed by McDowell was one unusually sensible and soldierly for that early day, and perfectly worthy of commendation at the present. It was to turn the Confederate left, and, if possible, to destroy the railway leading from Manassas Junction to the Shenandoah Valley, so as to cut off the remainder of Johnston's army. With this view, the men were served with three days' rations, and furnished with instructions as to how they were to proceed. The army was late in starting, owing to some delay on the part of the First Division; and it was ten o'clock on the morning of the 21st when the advance crossed the river at Sudley Springs. Colonel Evans, the Confederate officer on the opposite bank, disputed the ground, but the Union forces made way, and were gradually reinforced by other divisions of the army. McDowell was commanding in person, and he hurried up additional regiments, with a view to crushing his adversary. Matters began to look grave for the Confederates, and Beauregard and Johnston rode towards the scene of contest, to give immediate direction to the movements of their troops. Some hard fighting took place on an elevated plateau, partly covered with pine-woods, and intersected by water-courses. The Unionists repeatedly drove their adversaries down the eastern slope of this eminence; and at noon the Confederates, though replying with firmness to the opposing fire, and doing considerable execution with their field-pieces, had undoubtedly lost ground. During one of these charges, the Confederate officer, General Bee, observed rather excitedly to General Jackson, "They are beating us back!" "Well, sir," replied Jackson, "we will give them the bayonet." Bee turned to his men, and endeavored to rally them. "Form! form!" he exclaimed. "There stands Jackson like a stone wall." In this way did the gallant Confederate leader obtain the designation which clung to him till his death. The courage and self-possession of Jackson did wonders, but the day was still going in favor of the Union men. Towards the centre, the brigade under Colonel Richardson opened fire against Jones and Longstreet at Blackburn's Ford, to prevent their reinforcing the Confederate left; and, by order of Beauregard, Longstreet crossed the stream, and detained some of them from the more important field of conflict. The Confederate right and the Union left were hardly engaged at all

So unpromising did the aspect of affairs seem to Beauregard and Johnston that, shortly after twelve o'clock, the latter hastened to Lewis House, in the rear of the Confederate line, to see whether he could hurry forward the troops which were expected to arrive by rail from the Shenandoah Valley. During his absence, the Confederates made an approach towards retrieving their position; but they were still very hard pressed. Jackson executed a movement by which he was enabled to seize one of the Union batteries—a success due to the mistake of the officer in command, who, not feeling sure that the advancing troops were those of the enemy, abstained from firing. About this time Mc-

Dowell ordered Colonel Sherman, who occupied the centre of the Union line, to charge the opposing batteries with his entire brigade. The movement was begun with a good deal of dash and energy; but the brigade ultimately fell back. Again and again the desperate attempt was renewed, and the regiments were terribly cut up; but the Confederate batteries were admirably handled, and Sherman was unable to carry out his orders. Still, the Union troops were having the best of the encounter. The Confederates were driven down the wooded slopes, and the ground was thickly strewn with the dead and wounded. Many of the Confederate officers had by this time fallen; Jackson was struck, but refused to quit the field; and Beauregard, placing himself at the head of his troops, led the charge. Shortly afterwards he was slightly wounded, but, like Jackson, remained with his regiments, and was in time rewarded by a complete change in the fortunes of the day.

Meanwhile, Johnston was at Lewis House, commonly called "the Portico," from which he could scan the country all round. He felt extremely anxious as to the issue of the struggle, for up to that time fortune seemed likely to declare itself on the side of the Union forces. It was now three o'clock and the looked-for reinforcements had not yet arrived. "Oh, for four regiments!' he is reported to have exclaimed to one of his officers; and not long afterwards a cloud of dust was seen rising into the air from the direction of the Manassas Gap Railway, to the south of where he was standing. For the moment, Johnston was under the impression that this indicated the advance of Union reinforcements. He soon discovered his error. The strangers proved to be a body of Confederates, numbering 4000 and commanded by General E. Kirby Smith. They had come by rail from the Shenandoah Valley, and Smith, on hear-

BATTLE OF BULL RUN (JULY 21, 1861).

ing the sound of cannon on his left, had stopped the train, and marched his men across the country in the direction of the battle which was going on. At the Portico they received the commands of Johnston, who ordered them to attack the right flank of McDowell's line. He also directed Colonel Cook's brigade to join in the action. Other bodies of Southern troops likewise dashed forward to the plateau where Beauregard was desperately contending against the Union advance; and he found himself so heavily reinforced that the relative position of the two armies was entirely reversed. The Confederate ranks were now far more numerous than those of their opponents, and the new arrivals were fresh and vigorous. Beauregard, who had ordered an advance of the whole line shortly before, felt victory almost within his grasp. The reinforcements took position to the left of the onward-sweeping hosts, and the whole accumulated mass fell like a thunderbolt upon the fatigued Union troops. Very soon they were outflanked, and driven headlong down the opposite side of the plateau. Sharpshooters appeared in the woods at their back; from three sides a storm of shot poured into their staggering ranks; and the perils of the time were aggravated by panic. A portion of General Stewart's cavalry joined in the Confederate charge, and in a moment the battle was ended, and the Union troops gave way in hopeless and miserable flight. The victorious regiments, however, suffered severely in the final assault. Kirby Smith fell badly wounded shortly after he had placed his troops to the left of the main body, and Generals Bee and Barton were killed a little later. But the day, after a long and sanguinary fight, had been won, and Jefferson Davis, who had left Richmond in the morning, arrived in time to see the rout of the Union forces.

The flight of the Union troops was marked by every

sign of disorganization and military incompetence. Flinging away their arms, ammunition, knapsacks, and other incumbrances, like the Confederates after the battle of Rich Mountain, the discomfited soldiers dashed pell-mell from the scene of their crushing reverse, scattering dismay far and wide by their cries of terror. All pretence of order and method was at an end. Each man thought only of himself, and the honor of the army was entirely lost in the overwhelming consideration of personal safety. A panic once begun cannot readily be stopped. The unreasoning apprehension passes from rank to rank, and from regiment to regiment, like wild-fire; and the contagion of fear is as mysterious in its agencies and as rapid in its effects as any other epidemic. Where veterans have lost all sense of military subordination and mutual reliance, it is not surprising if inexperienced and half-disciplined troops should become totally disorganized, and even for the time unmanned. The rush from Bull Run, with all its disgraceful incidents, was in no respect surprising; it was nevertheless painful in the highest degree.

McDowell, on perceiving that his men were utterly defeated, rode off to Centreville, ordered General Blenker's German brigade to support and rally the flying troops, and directed Colonels Davies and Richardson to take up a position to cover Centreville. Johnston had ordered Ewell to cross Bull Run in force, and attack that village; but, in attempting to execute the movement, his subordinate was so warmly received that he found it necessary to retreat, his men being thrown into disorder by the heavy guns of the enemy. By sunset, most of the Union troops reached the farther side of the Centreville ridge, and it became a question whether an attempt should there be made to reorganize the shattered army. The panic had not spread to all of the regiments. Blenker's brigade, the regulars, and a portion of the reserves at Centreville, retained their military form, though nearly exhausted by thirty hours' marching and fighting. These battalions were of immense service in covering the confused retreat, and in checking the pursuit. But they could not infuse any better spirit into their demoralized comrades, and it was agreed by all the commanders that there was no choice but to fall back. The men had been fighting for hours under a blazing sun; they were tired, hungry, and disheartened; their rations, issued the day before, had been recklessly thrown away; and a large number of guns and small arms, together with stores of ammunition, had been lost. It appeared, moreover, that Blackburn's Ford was by that time in possession of the enemy, and that he was endeavoring to turn the Union left. Orders were given to continue the retreat; but the troops had taken the matter into their own hands, and, as night came on, were hurrying along the road to Washington.

In the fields and ways from the battle-ground to Centreville, the wounded lay in hundreds. Many dropped with fatigue, and were crushed by the artillery, or ridden over by the horses. A dull, deep roar, made up of many cries of rage, agony, and terror, surged along the paths by which the troops were retreating, and clouds of dust, illuminated by the western sun, revealed the several lines of flight. It was not until the early morning of the 22d that the fugitives reached Washington; and even then their fears did not desert them. During the eventful Sunday, crowds assembled round the telegraph and newspaper offices, reading with eager satisfaction the despatches that came from the field of battle throughout the morning and the early part of the afternoon. Everything, it was then reported, was going well. The Union soldiers were successful at all points. A complete and overwhelming victory was certain. But, as the afternoon wore on, the telegrams ceased to arrive. An ominous silence supervened, and men began to ask one another what it meant. Then came placards announcing, "Utter rout of the troops!" "Stampede to Washington!" "All our batteries captured!" and so on. From a city of joy, the Federal capital passed into a city of mourning.

The losses of the Union army were stated by McDowell at 19 officers, and 462 non-commissioned officers and privates, killed; 64 officers, and 947 non-commissioned officers and privates, wounded. The "missing" were very numerous; many went off altogether, and never returned to the colors. The Confederate loss was estimated by Beauregard at 378 killed, and 1483 wounded. Of prisoners, including wounded, he had no fewer than 1600 men, and among the captured were officers and men of forty-seven regiments of volunteers, and of nine different regiments of regular troops, detachments of which were engaged. The gains of the Confederates in artillery, small arms, ammunition, accoutrements, flags, military appliances, hospital stores, wagons, horses, etc., were very large, and Johnston and Beauregard were in a better position for pushing a vigorous campaign after the battle than before. It was subsequently made a ground of complaint against Jefferson Davis and his colleagues that an advance on Washington was not immediately ordered. But, to use Davis' own words, "It was a hard-fought field, and the victors were in no condition to pursue." So Washington was not attacked, and the North had time to rally.

In his report on the battle, General McDowell was compelled to make many complaints of his men, and to point out many defects in the military system. But it should always be recollected, in considering the events of this unhappy day, that the Union soldiers, for the most part, fought well for long hours, drove their adversaries before them again and again, and at one time came very near obtaining a decisive victory. It was only when they were outnumbered and outflanked that they fled in uncontrollable dismay. Many well-trained armies have done the same. Discreditable as their flight was, it was no worse than that of Braddock's regiments from the ambushed French and Indians, or that of Gage's men from Concord. Such panics are known to every service, and should not be alleged as a special reproach against any one in particular. The Sadowas of history are few.

Swinton, in his *Decisive Battles of the War*, thus summarizes the effect of this eventful action: "The victory of Bull Run gained more than a field; it won a campaign. Midsummer passed, autumn came and went, winter at last found the Union and Confederate troops in Virginia in their peaceful log-camps. The year 1861 slipped entirely away without another forward movement in Virginia; the next year opened silently there; spring came again before the spell which Bull Run had thrown was broken up. Nor was this true of Virginia alone, but of the whole West; incessant skirmishes and desultory engagements by detached forces occupied the time and strength which had been designed for grand operations; for these latter were repressed at their beginning, and the military year of 1861, from which so much had been hoped, came to its end at the battle of Bull Run."

BALL'S BLUFF (October 21, 1861).—Near the end of October, McClellan made preparations for sending out a strong reconnoissance towards Leesburg, to ascertain the movements and intentions of the enemy. About 2000 Union troops had crossed the Potomac and in the course of the 21st a collision took place in the woods covering the banks of the river. Being devoid of artillery, the Confederates charged with fixed bayonets, and the opposing line gave way. Colonel Baker, the U. S. Senator from Oregon, who

BATTLE OF BALL'S BLUFF—DEATH OF COLONEL BAKER.

commanded one of the Union brigades, rallied his men. A hot musketry engagement ensued, in which they were much galled by the raking fire which came from out the forest. Baker was at length mortally wounded, and fell; and his men then rushed towards the steep banks of the Potomac without the slightest restraint, pursued by their adversaries, who slaughtered as many as they could reach by bayonet or musket-shot. The discreditable incidents of the 21st of July were thus repeated three months later, and it became distressingly manifest that a quarter of a year had made little difference in the military character of the Union army. Some of the fugitives swam across the river; others attempted to get away in boats, which were swamped by the numbers who crowded into them. Several were drowned; still more perished at the hands of the foe; many were captured in their efforts to escape. Of the whole force, half were killed, wounded, or taken; there was an admitted loss of nearly 1100 men. Telegrams were despatched during the action to General Banks, who sent forward fresh troops; but the day was by that time irretrievably ruined. The disastrous result of the movement appears to have been attributable partly to the misapprehension of orders, by which McClellan's design of a reconnoissance was changed into a general action without proper means for supporting it; and partly to want of firmness in the men. The Confederates were superior in number to the Union forces, and were undoubtedly better disciplined and better handled.

An upholder of the Confederate cause has remarked that the victory at Ball's Bluff, like that at Bull Run, " bore no fruits but those of a confidence on the part of the South, which was pernicious, because it was overweening and inactive, and a contempt for its enemy, which was injurious in proportion as it exceeded the limits of truth and justice and reflected the self-conceits of fortune."

CHAPTER II.

The Campaigns at the West (1862).

At the commencement of 1862, the Union forces were upwards of 640,000 volunteers, and more than 20,000 regular troops. The quality of these soldiers was in many instances very indifferent; but every day helped their education in their new trade. When McClellan was made Commander-in-Chief of the armies, he prepared at Lincoln's request a memorandum in which he drew out a scheme of operations, and set forth the means by which his conceptions were to be carried into effect. The most important strategical point, he said, was in Eastern Virginia, and the struggle must be fought out there. Campaigns in other directions, however, were necessary in support of the principal movement. An advance must be made on the Mississippi, and the Confederates must be driven out of Missouri. Operations should likewise be conducted in Eastern Tennessee, for the purpose of assisting the Union men in that locality, and of seizing the railroads leading from Memphis to the east. Efforts should be made to organize and equip regiments in Western Virginia; and the importance insisted on of occupying Baltimore and Fortress Monroe, and at the same time of concentrating a large army in the vicinity of Washington. For the carrying out of these various projects, McClellan demanded 250 regiments of infantry; 100 field-batteries of six guns each; 28 regiments of cavalry; and 5 regiments of engineers: giving altogether a total 273,000 men. This was for the active operations alone. Another large body would be needed for holding Washington and the line of the Potomac, for furnishing garrisons to various towns, and for performing the routine military duties required by a state of war. A strong naval force, it was suggested, should act in conjunction with a fleet of transports; and the railway service of the country was to be turned to advantage by every available means. "We must endeavor," said McClellan, "to seize places on the railways in the rear of the enemy's points of concentration; and we must threaten their seaboard cities, in order that each State may be forced, by the necessity of its own defence, to diminish its contingent to the Confederate Army." To him it appeared possible that by a combination of vigorous movements the war might be terminated in one more campaign. He hoped to occupy Richmond, Charleston, Savannah, Montgomery, Pensacola, Mobile, and New Orleans, and in this was to "crush out the rebellion in its very heart."

Some of the earliest encounters of 1862 took place in Kentucky. The Western Military District was at that time commanded by General Halleck, who had his headquarters at St. Louis. Under his orders were Generals Grant and Buell; the first in Western Kentucky, the second in Eastern. The army under Buell occupied Somerset and Columbia, near the upper part of the Cumberland River, and was opposed by General Zollicoffer, whose camp was at Mill Springs, on the southern bank of the same river. Crossing to the northern bank, he was joined by General Crittenden, his superior in rank; at midnight on January 18, the troops began their march with the design of surprising, ere it was yet light, the Union army who were stationed about ten miles north of the Confederate entrenched camp.

The Confederate approach was discovered at 6 o'clock on the morning of the 19th, and the action commenced

GENERAL ULYSSES S. GRANT.

shortly afterwards. At first the Union forces were repulsed; but after awhile they regained the ground they had lost, and at 8 o'clock, a furious encounter was taking place between the forces, which appear to have been pretty evenly matched. It was at this time that

Zollicoffer, riding forward in front of his men, was shot dead; and his men were so much disheartened by this unexpected event that they began to lose form, and to fall back confusedly, and finally gave way in disorderly flight. General Thomas ordered a pursuit of the Southerners, who were accordingly followed as far as their entrenchments. During the ensuing night, shells were thrown into the Confederate camp, and the discomfited troops, fearing they might be cut off, and being very ill-provided with food in the situation they had taken up, determined to retreat across the Cumberland. The men succeeded in effecting their passage, but it was found impossible to carry with them the wagons, horses, artillery, and camp equipments, which fell into the Union hands. General Crittenden's regiments retreated first to Monticello, and afterwards to Gainsborough, in Tennessee. Their sufferings on the route were extreme, for they had been obliged to leave behind them all their stores, and were compelled to make their way through a tract of country so thinly populated that it could afford no adequate support for a large army.

FORT HENRY (February 6, 1862).—Crittenden's retreat placed Eastern Kentucky entirely in the hands of the Union forces; but the western division of the State still remained to the Confederates. General Sidney Johnston, the Southern commander, held a line of defence which extended from Bowling Green, on the right, to Columbus, on the left—a position rendered unusually strong by the neighborhood of the Cumberland and Tennessee Rivers, and by a railway system connecting the ends of the line, and giving a command over the adjacent country. Johnston had protected himself by the erection of two forts, one, called Fort Henry, was situated on the right bank of the Tennessee, in the State of Kentucky, while the other, Fort Donelson, was planted on the left bank of the Cumberland, 15 miles to the south-east of the other, and within the borders of Tennessee. The defences of Fort Henry were formidable, and the position was strengthened by the creeks and swamps among which the works had been constructed. Nevertheless, Grant determined to attack the fortifications, in combination with the fleet under Commodore Foote. The expedition embarked at Cairo, on February 1, and the troops were landed about five miles below Fort Henry on the 5th. The fort was to be assaulted on the land side by the soldiers, and from the river by the fleet.

All being prepared, the march of the land forces began on the morning of the 6th. The first division, under General McClernand, proceeded along the right bank of the river, with orders to take up a position on the road from Fort Henry to Fort Donelson. Two brigades of the second division under General Smith proceeded at the same hour along the left bank, so as to occupy the heights commanding Fort Henry; and to the third brigade of the second division was assigned the duty of moving directly against the fort, and assaulting the works when the proper moment should have arrived. Unfortunately the roads were heavy with mud, owing to a great fall of rain a few days previously, so that the army was not in a position to co-operate with the fleet when the latter opened fire. The first naval line was composed of four gunboats, partially protected with iron armor, but hastily adapted to their present purpose out of river-steamers or ferry-boats; the second line consisted of three wooden vessels. A vigorous cannonade was interchanged between the ships and the fort, and the gunboats, getting nearer in shore, directed an effective fire against the works; but, before the action had lasted quite an hour, an unlucky casualty occurred in the fleet. A shot struck the gunboat *Essex*, entering the starboard boiler and filling the boat with steam. Many of the crew were badly scalded, and the *Essex*, unable to do anything more, was forced to drop astern. The other gunboats, however, continued to advance; and when they had got within 600 yards of the fort, the Confederate flag was lowered, and signal was made that General Tilghman, the commandant of Fort Henry, was prepared to surrender. On his asking what terms would be accorded him, the commodore formulated the terms in two words, "Unconditional surrender." The action had lasted an hour and a quarter, and the Union success was due entirely to the naval force, as, owing to the obstructions to which allusion has been made, the land forces were unable to reach the positions to which they had been assigned. The defenders of the fort were made prisoners of war; but the derangement of the Union plans enabled the main body of the Confederates to escape behind the bulwarks of Fort Donelson. Grant's cavalry pursued for some distance, and a portion of the field-artillery was abandoned; yet the men got safely to their place of refuge. By possessing Fort Henry, the Union forces were able to take up a position in the rear of Columbus, on the Mississippi, and within ten miles of a bridge crossing the railway which connects that town with Bowling Green. The Tennessee River was now open to the Union gunboats, and the three wooden vessels were sent up the channel, with orders to destroy the railway bridge, and to capture or sink such of the enemy's vessels as they might encounter. These directions were completely carried out. Lieutenant Phelps, who commanded, penetrated as far as Florence, in Alabama, and succeeded in capturing three steamers and an unfinished gunboat. Six other river-steamers were burned by the Confederates themselves, to save them from the adversary, and scarcely any opposition was offered to the lieutenant, who possessed himself of a large amount of camp equipage and other stores, with which he returned to Fort Henry on February 10.

FORT DONELSON (February 19, 1862).—The success of the Union forces in reducing that work encouraged Grant to prosecute operations against Fort Donelson. On February 12, he set out with the divisions of McClernand and Smith, consisting of 15,000 men. Six regiments were at the same time detached, with orders to proceed by water, and under convoy of a gunboat, to the Cumberland River. Preparations for the investment of Fort Donelson were at once begun, and the operations were conducted with so much vigor as to promise a speedy success. The garrison was strong in numbers; but the troops who had fled from Fort Henry were in a mood of depression which augured ill for their steadiness. The works in themselves were not contemptible. Heavy batteries commanded the river, while, on the land side, rifle-pits and entrenchments offered resistance to the Union advance. The entrenchments, however, formed the weakest part of the defences, for on the morning of the 12th they were still unfinished. The hilly nature of the country, covered with dense oak woods, and intersected by a broad, deep valley, which almost divided the Confederate position into two distinct parts, presented opportunities of which both sides could equally avail themselves. The army within the fort, and in the external works connected with it, was augmented, on the 13th, by the troops under General Floyd, who had marched from the city of Cumberland. The Confederate force now amounted to about 14,000 men, who were under the general direction of Floyd, as the senior officer. The right wing was commanded by General Buckner, and the left by General Pillow. Among the three commanders, and in the several divisions of the army, there was but little unity of feeling or design, and a disaster was insured by the inefficient character of the troops, and the ignorant blundering of the officers. At three o'clock on the afternoon of the 14th, Commodore Foote began the attack with four ironclad gunboats and two wooden vessels. These advanced in a crescent shape, and opened fire at a distance of a mile from the batteries. The Confederates, however, did not reply until the boats had got within a distance of 400 yards. A hot encounter then ensued, and continued for nearly five hours, when the ironclad gunboats were so much injured as to be obliged to withdraw, with a loss of 54 men. Foote hereupon retired to Cairo, determining to wait until a competent force should be brought up from that place to attack the fort. The land forces under Grant had previously taken their positions in front of the works, and the whole of the Confederate left, with the exception of a strip of swampy ground near the river, was by this time invested. Some skirmishing had occurred, but to no very serious extent, and the Union troops were now suffering rather from the severity of the cold than from the guns of their enemies. The weather had for some time been unusually warm for the season; and the troops had recklessly thrown away their coats and blankets. When a change came, and they were surprised by frost and snow, an immense amount of suffering, which might have been avoided, was experienced by the troops in the open field.

The Confederates were not much better off, and their position in all respects was so critical that, at a council of war held on the night of the 14th, it was resolved to reopen, if possible, the communication with Nashville by Charlotte, and to save the greater portion of the army by abandoning the position at Fort Donelson. The plan proposed was to attack the Union right next day, in order that while the action was proceeding the rest of the army should cut their way out by the most available of two roads leading to Nashville. The operations of the 15th were embarrassed by

COMMODORE A. H. FOOTE.

delays consequent on the icy condition of the roads, and a want of sufficient preparation on the part of the men. Nevertheless, an animated encounter was proceeding by nine A. M., when General Pillow attacked the Union troops in front, and General Buckner, who was to conduct the rear-guard of the retreating army, opened fire on their left with artillery. The Union troops soon found their ammunition exhausted, and gave way with some precipitation. Pillow now pushed forward with rapidity and vigor, supported by Buckner on his right, and by the cavalry under Colonel Forrest. For a moment, the Confederates seemed to be prevailing, but their enthusiasm was short-lived, and their commanders were totally inadequate to the demands of the situation. Pillow and Buckner misunderstood one another; General Floyd appears to have done nothing; the inferior officers were left without instructions; confusion speedily supervened, and Buckner, who had full possession of the road by which he proposed to escape, was perplexed and bewildered as to the proceedings of his colleagues. In the course of the day, he received a message from Pillow, bidding him return to his entrenchment, and while in full retreat was met by Floyd, who expressed surprise at what he was doing, but afterwards confirmed the directions of Pillow. Buckner accordingly struggled back to the Confederate lines; but before the whole of his force could get within them, Smith's division attacked his right, and in a little while burst into the entrenchments. After two hours' fighting, the Confederates were completely defeated, and Smith's division retained possession of the works. Grant had lost upwards of 1000 men, of whom nearly 300 had been captured by the Confederates, placed on board steamers, and sent up the river; but he had achieved a great success, and the Southerners were now in so serious a position that it was a question whether they would not be entirely overwhelmed. The attempt to break through the lines had been an utter failure. Communication with Nashville was cut off. The troops were suffering much from the inclemency of the weather; and they had now on their hands a large

CHARGING ON THE OUTWORKS OF FORT DONELSON, FEBRUARY 13, 1862.

number of wounded, for whose necessity no adequate provision could be made. Another council of war was held on the night of the 15th, when several of the officers met at the headquarters of General Floyd, in the little town of Dover. Floyd having requested the views of Buckner and Pillow as to what should be done under existing circumstances, Buckner spoke very emphatically to the effect that another sortie would result in nothing but a massacre; and it was understood that Pillow was of the same opinion. After some further discussion, from which it appeared that General Sidney Johnston had effected his removal from Bowling Green to Nashville, and that consequently there was no longer any necessity for covering his operations, it was agreed that negotiations should be opened for the surrender of the army, together with the fort.

Floyd, speaking on *personal grounds*, observed that he " would rather die than surrender." * Hereupon Pillow remarked that there were no two persons in the world whom the Unionists would be better pleased to capture than himself and Floyd; and he proposed that they should endeavor to escape. Buckner undertaking to remain and conduct the negotiations, it was resolved that that officer should assume the chief command. As daylight was by this time near at hand, and the Union attack would certainly recommence in a little while, Buckner drew up his missive to Grant and sent it off. Arrangements, however, were at the same time made for the escape of Floyd and Pillow and Colonel Forrest, with a certain proportion of the army. In the early dawn, these got away from their perilous position—the infantry in boats, and the cavalry on the lower road to Nashville. The letter from Buck-

---

* Floyd was Buchanan's Secretary of War, who had dismantled all the Northern arsenals before the " unpleasantness." It would probably have gone hard with him if he had been captured.

ner to Grant proposed an armistice until twelve o'clock that day (the 16th), in order to arrange terms of capitulation. Grant replied by insisting on "unconditional and immediate surrender," and added that "he proposed to move at once upon the Confederate works." In responding to this communication, Buckner observed that the existing distribution of his forces (incident to an unexpected change of commanders), and the overwhelming strength of his opponent, compelled him, notwithstanding the brilliant success of the Confederate arms, to accept the "ungenerous and unchivalrous terms" which were proposed. The capitulation was then effected. Nine thousand men laid down their arms, and the stars and stripes floated over the stronghold of the Cumberland. Fort Donelson was now occupied by the Union troops, and the river by the gunboats. The Confederates had lost, during the four days' fighting, nearly 1200 men, and the blow thus inflicted on their cause in that part of the country was of the most disheartening nature. On the same day, Bowling Green, from which Sidney Johnston had just withdrawn, was occupied by the Union officer, General Mitchell, at the head of a division from Buell's army.

Floyd was at once deprived of his command. Pillow was not again employed; but Buckner, who had certainly acted in a creditable spirit of self-abnegation, was once more placed at the head of a Confederate army, as soon as he had been exchanged. The position of the Confederates was at this time far from hopeful. The Union gunboats having advanced up the Columbia River to Clarksville, General Johnston considered it advisable to abandon Nashville, and take up a position farther south. The people of Nashville were wild with rage and apprehension at Johnston's departure. Many of them took flight by any conveyance they could obtain, and crowded the roads leading southward with disorderly mobs. Two unfinished steamers on the wharf were burned; and nothing but rapacity, fear, and outrage prevailed for some days. Order was not restored until the arrival of the first brigade of the Union army on February 25. The mayor then surrendered the place into the hands of General Buell, who took measures to calm the popular excitement and re-establish the forms of government.

In the meanwhile Johnston pursued the line of his retreat without being followed, and took up a position in the vicinity of Murfreesboro'. The whole of Northern Tennessee, with the entire line of the Cumberland River, was now abandoned by the Confederates. Columbus, on the Mississippi, was evacuated by General Polk, who removed his army, guns, and stores to a line of defence situated forty miles to the south, near the small town of New Madrid, on the western bank of the great river. On March 3, the day following the departure of the Confederates—the Union cavalry from Paducah, followed by the gunboats under Foote, arrived at Columbus and took possession of it. General Beauregard was now established at Jackson, Tennessee. His army formed the center of the Confederate line of defence for the Western States. Polk was to the left, at New Madrid, and Johnston to the right, at Murfreesboro'. The Confederates had been compelled, by the recent course of events, to make a great retrogression towards the south, to give up the whole of Kentucky, and to leave the northern part of Tennessee open to attack. They had lost the command of important rivers and railway communications; had beheld their ranks thinned by fatigue and want, as well as by the operations of war; and were now dispirited, not merely by the calamities which had occurred, but by the prospect of others which seemed imminent. The Union reverses in the East had been amply compensated by their successes in the West, and the development of events placed the fortunes of Washington far above those of Richmond.

Generals Grant and Buell continued their advance, and prepared for fresh attacks upon the Confederate armies. The line of defence taken up by the Southerners, after their retrogressive movement, was one of extreme length, extending from New Madrid, in Missouri, and Island No. 10, on the Mississippi, in the northwestern part of the State named after that river, to Murfreesboro' and Cumberland Gap, in the northeast, with the center at Jackson, to the south of both extremities. The left, at Island No. 10, was supported by an outpost at New Madrid; and the defence of the island depended to a great extent on the possession by the Confederates of that small town. General Pope, therefore, led an expedition against the latter place, while Commodore Foote, with his gunboats, made a demonstration in front of the insular position. These proceedings began on February 28; batteries were afterwards erected, which were used principally against the gunboats and shipping in the river; and on the night of March 13, in the midst of a violent storm of rain, thunder, and lightning, the Confederate garrison of New Madrid retired to Island No. 10, and to the works on the left or eastern bank of the Mississippi, within the State of Kentucky. The town was at once occupied by the Union forces, who came into possession of large quantities of stores, and were enabled to cut off the island from any communication by the Lower Mississippi.

Encouraged by their success, the Union forces next brought their batteries to bear against the main body of the Confederate left, stationed on Island No. 10. But these operations, though prosecuted with vigor, were unproductive of any decided effect, and it was then determined by Pope and Foote to resort to other measures. They resolved to cross to the opposite shore, and seize the batteries which commanded the channel from that side. To do this it was first necessary to cut a canal across the narrow neck of land separating New Madrid from the upper attacking force, so as to enable the gunboats to get a greater command over the insular defences than the winding course of the Mississippi would allow, and to give increased facility to the transports engaged in carrying troops from New Madrid to the opposite side of the river. The length of this canal would be twelve miles, and its execution would necessarily be a work of prodigious labor, seeing that, if done at all, it would be indispensable to finish it with the utmost rapidity. The work was undertaken, and successfully carried out. Half of the distance was through a swampy forest, where the trees had to be cut off four feet below the surface of the water; the rest of the way was less difficult, but still such as to require a great expenditure of toil. By the first week in April, the canal was fully made, and the work had not at any time been interrupted by the Confederates, their attention having been fully engaged by the heavy fire of the Union gunboats and mortar-batteries, and by a few naval actions which succeeded in keeping the besieged in continual alarm. On the night of April 6, four steamers and a large number of transports were brought through the canal, of the very existence of which, beneath the shadow of its luxuriant trees, the Southerners were ignorant. A division, commanded by General Payne, was sent across the river in the transports, and the men, landing without opposition on the left bank of the Mississippi, drove back the defenders of the batteries, who seem to have been completely taken by surprise. The defences on Island No. 10 were at once abandoned, and the position was surrendered to Commodore Foote, together with a large amount of warlike material. Extraordinary want of spirit and resolution was shown by the Confederates throughout the whole proceedings. It was important to their position in the West that they should retain New Madrid, the island, and the batteries on the Kentucky shore; but these were abandoned almost without a blow.

BUILDING A CANAL.

SHILOH (April 6, 7, 1862).—After the capture of Nashville, Grant proceeded with his forces down the Tennessee River to Pittsburg Landing. Buell prepared to march on foot to the same locality; and the Union army, being thus divided, was exposed to the attacks of its enemy. The Confederates could now reckon on the services of two armies, both numerically strong, and commanded by officers of ability. At the head of one was Albert Sidney Johnston; Beauregard was at the head of the other. To strike a concentrated blow at Grant, Johnston united his whole force with that of Beauregard on April 1, and on the 3d the army began its march towards Pittsburg Landing. Altogether, the commanders had under their control rather more than 40,000 men, divided into three corps and a reserve; but the regiments were defective both in organization and discipline. The march was very slow, partly owing to the inexperience of the men, partly on account of the thickly wooded country. The neighborhood of Grant's position was not reached until the afternoon of the 5th, and the attack was deferred until the next day. Grant, with singular want of prudence, had omitted to throw up any defences, and his divisions were scattered about the ground without any concentration or method. Separated by numerous creeks, and covered with woods, the ground offered several facilities for a sudden attack, and made the difficulty of an improvised defence all the greater; though, with a little care beforehand, such a position should have been very awkward to assault. At daybreak on the morning of the 6th, the Confederates advanced in four lines, and the Union pickets were driven in so rapidly that their respective divisions had no time to get under arms. The division of General William T. Sherman was among the first to bear the brunt of the attack, and nothing was in readiness for such a catastrophe. Many of the officers were in bed; of the men, some were preparing their breakfast, while others were cleaning their rifles.

The astonishment and dismay of the Union troops were for a time overwhelming. A portion of General Prentiss's division struggled into order, but was speedily driven back by the terrific fire which came blazing out of the woods. Prentiss himself was soon taken pris-

AN IRONCLAD RIVER GUNBOAT.

oner, together with three of his regiments; but in a little while some of Sherman's brigades got into line, and offered a brief resistance to the advancing foe. Nevertheless, the Confederates continued to gain ground, and, pursuing the forces of Prentiss and Sherman, now in full retreat, passed through their deserted camps, and captured the greater part of their field-artillery. Presently, they came in sight of General McClernand's division, posted upon some rising ground. These troops for a time made a stand, and, though some among them gave way at the first onset, the others were sufficiently steady to check the Confederate advance, and to induce General Braxton Bragg, who commanded one of the supporting bodies, to bring his troops into action. In conjunction with a few of the other brigades, he attacked the Union troops with much animation, driving them back from their positions, and creating the utmost confusion among the opposing lines. When the Confederate left had been reinforced by General Polk's corps, McClernand's division, which formed the second Union line, was completely routed, and very little chance of retrieving the day remained to them. Two divisions of Grant's army, however, still retained their positions; and these, being well planted and amply provided with artillery, withstood the Confederate assaults from half-past ten in the morning till four in the afternoon. The attack was led by Bragg in person, and was again and again renewed, but with no other effect than to strew the field with dead and wounded, mowed down by the continual fire, both of rifles and artillery, which the Union troops kept up from out the woods where many of their number were posted. Towards the end of the engagement, General Johnston, while superintending the right of the line, was struck in the leg by a rifle-bullet; but he refused to dismount, and continued to give his directions until a feeling of extreme weakness showed that an artery had been cut, and that death was close at hand. The centre of the Confederate line was still held in check by the two Union divisions commanded by Generals Hurlbut and W. H. L. Wallace; yet victory, on the whole, lay with the attacking force. It seemed as if with one more effort the Union troops would be completely crushed; but that effort was not made. The Confederate troops were exhausted, and it is admitted by Beauregard that the men were engaged towards evening in plundering the deserted camps, and loading themselves with spoil. Beauregard had succeeded to the chief command on the death of Johnston; and, feeling doubtful whether his army was in a condition to do more that day, he ordered the several divisions to retire. The number of the Union troops was about the same as that of the Confederates, and with the natural advantages of their position they should have done better. But want of generalship had been conspicuous, and the day was lost for lack of reasonable foresight.

On the night of April 6, the disordered masses of the Union army were scattered about the immediate vicinity of Pittsburg Landing, under shelter of the ironclad gunboats drawn up in the Tennessee River. The Confederates held the greater portion of the battle-field. They had taken all the enemy's encampments but one, together with nearly all his field-artillery, about thirty flags, colors and standards, more than 3000 prisoners, several thousands of small arms, an immense supply of subsistence, forage, and munitions of war, and a large amount of means of transportation. The struggle, however, was not yet concluded. The next morning, the Union troops were again seen ranged in order of battle. Buell had arrived during the previous day on board a steamer and had at once proceeded to Grant's headquarters. Some of his troops had even reached the ground in time to take part in the final stand made by the Union forces on the evening of the 6th. Others crossed the river during the night, and four divisions marched into camp early on the morning of the 7th. The Union forces were thus reinforced to the extent of about 20,000 men, several of whom might be described as veterans. Fighting was resumed at five A. M., when the fresh troops, having placed themselves in front of their disorganized comrades, advanced to the attack. Buell was the officer in command and he made his dispositions with great ability. Grant's forces were so completely dispirited by the combat of the previous day that they were not able to render effective assistance, and on neither occasion does Grant himself appear to have done much in the way of personal supervision. General Nelson was sent forward with the regiments under his direction, and the contest was general by seven o'clock. The battle was maintained for some hours with considerable spirit, but the Confederates aimed at nothing more than holding their opponents at bay while they effected their own retreat. The Union forces continued to recover the positions they had lost on the 6th, and to repossess themselves of the guns and colors captured by the Confederates. When the main body of the Southern forces had got safely away, the front line, which had been keeping the Union forces in check, also quitted the ground, and rejoined their comrades, who had retreated to Corinth. Several rallies had occurred during the day, and there had been moments when the Confederates seemed as if they were about to achieve another victory; but they were, in truth, quite unfitted to meet the fresh and unwearied troops which Buell had brought into the field, and, notwithstanding a few temporary gains at various points, they were compelled, about four o'clock in the afternoon, to leave the ground in entire possession of the enemy whom they had van-

BATTLE OF SHILOH (APRIL 7, 1862).

quished not many hours before. No regular pursuit was attempted until the 8th, and even then but little was done. The Union loss on the two days had been 1735 killed, 7882 wounded, and 4044 missing. The Confederates lost 1728 killed, 8012 wounded, and 959 missing. The battle has been variously called by the names of Shiloh and of Pittsburg Landing. It was one of the most hard-fought encounters that had yet taken place.

Success crowned the Union arms, at this period, in other regions besides the West. At the beginning of 1862, it had been observed to be a part of the Confederate design to shut up the Union troops in Port Royal Island, South Carolina, by placing obstructions in the neighboring rivers, by erecting batteries in the vicinity, and by massing troops so as to be able to throw a large force on the most vulnerable points whenever it should be considered advisable to do so. These plans it was determined to frustrate. The river approaches to the city of Savannah are defended by Fort Pulaski, a casemated work situated at the mouth of the river Savannah, and by Fort Jackson, a barbette-work on the mainland, only four miles below the city. The left or northern bank of the river is formed by a succession of islands, which, dividing the stream into a number of creeks and bays, render navigation difficult. On one of these islands stands Fort Pulaski, distant about eighteen miles from the city of Savannah. At the period in question, it was armed with 47 guns, and garrisoned by a force of 300 men, under Colonel Olmstead. Before the invention of rifled cannon, it had unquestionably been a place of great strength; but the changed conditions of warfare had left it comparatively weak. For the reduction of this position, four regiments from the Eastern States, and some companies of engineers, were detached from the Union Army of the South.

Batteries were placed on Tybee Island, and the left bank of the Savannah River was occupied by a force sufficient to intercept communication with the city, and to prevent the Confederate gunboats from carrying succor to the fort. The batteries were not completed until April 9, owing to the great labor involved in conveying the guns to their insular position, and there erecting them. When the works were completed, however, 36 pieces of artillery were ready to open fire on the fort. During the time that these guns were being placed in position, the garrison made not the slightest attempt to interrupt the work. The bombardment commenced on April 10, and a hot artillery-duel continued during that day and the next. So large a breach had been effected in the walls by noon on the 11th, that preparations were made for storming the fort; but about two hours afterwards, before active operations could be commenced, the commander surrendered. By the destruction of the wall on the south-eastern face of the fortress, the magazine had become exposed to the fire of the batteries, so that further defence was impossible, and the only choice lay between immediate submission and instant death in the ruins of the structure. Great vexation was experienced in the South at the fall of Fort Pulaski. The capture of Savannah did not follow the exploit, as was expected, and the interior parts of Georgia were not reduced. The defences of the city were increased, and a sufficient force was stationed in the neighborhood to repel any attack that might be designed, The possession of Pulaski prevented any further attempts to run the blockade into Savannah by the mouth of the river; so that the siege was not entirely barren of results. Other expeditions about the same period were directed against various positions on the coast of Georgia, and these were attended by a degree of success which sufficiently repaid the labor expended in conducting them. In North Carolina, Fort Macon was taken on April 25, by a force sent out by Burnside from the town of Newbern. The fort was defended with great determination, but it was at length compelled to succumb to the superior fire of the Union forces. The capture of this fort gave Burnside a safe port of entry for the vessels employed in furnishing supplies to his army of occupation. The Union arms had now obtained complete command over the coast of North Carolina; but the loyal sentiment alleged to exist among the people was found to be entirely absent.

Burnside was not wanting in activity. About the time that Fort Macon surrendered, a reconnoisance was made in the direction of Norfolk, Virginia, from Elizabeth City, North Carolina. A body of Confederate troops was encountered at a distance of 35 miles from that town, and, after an indecisive action, the forces of both belligerents drew back. Norfolk thus remained untouched; but the Confederates were doubtful as to its safety, and its evacuation occurred shortly afterwards. These, however, were small results in comparison with the capture of New Orleans, which took place during the spring. It was a very important matter to secure this city, which is by far the greatest port in the Southern States of America. The people of Louisiana generally had given a most enthusiastic support to the Confederacy, and, both from diversity of descent and distinction of interests, entertained a hearty detestation of the North. The commerce of New Orleans was ruined by the blockade, and nowhere did a more intense feeling of animosity towards the Union prevail than in that fine emporium of the Mississippi which Jackson had so successfully defended against the British. The river-fleet employed against the blockading squadron had recently been increased; but two additional ironclads, commenced some time before, still remained unfinished

SCENE ON THE MISSISSIPPI RIVER AT THE PRESENT DAY.

at the beginning of April. It was believed by the citizens that the forts near the mouth of the river would be sufficient to prevent the passage of ships; and it was thought by many that New Orleans was imperilled rather from the north, by a fleet which might possibly descend the stream, than from the south, by one approaching from the Gulf of Mexico. In the latter direction, the city was protected by two lines of defence. The outer line consisted of Forts Jackson and Philip, built on opposite banks of the river.

New Orleans was in no condition for repelling an attack when the Union forces determined to reduce it. The city had been almost denuded of troops, to augment the Confederate army in Tennessee under Beaureguard. Forts Jackson and Philip (situated about 75 miles below New Orleans, and 25 from the mouth of the river), were garrisoned, for the most part, with regular troops, many of whom had formerly belonged to the United States Army; but in the city itself only one company remained. Three thousand volunteers for ninety days were raised as a substitute for the regiments that had been withdrawn; but the newcomers were insufficiently armed. Still, something had been done to meet impending dangers. A few heavy guns had recently been sent to the forts from Richmond, at the urgent request of Brigadier-General Lovell, who had the principal command in Louisiana. A boom had been thrown across the river from fort to fort, and, when carried away by the spring floods, had been succeeded by another of more elaborate construction. The river was further protected by a fleet of seven steamers, provided with iron prows to act as rams, and covered with cotton bulkheads so as to ward off the action of shot; and the steam ram *Manassas* was stationed a short distance above Fort Jackson. Yet the defences of New Orleans, though good in some respects, were on the whole insufficient to resist the extraordinary resources of the Union forces. Louisiana was so distant from the chief seats of war that the inhabitants do not seem to have very seriously concerned themselves about their safety. It was only when news had been received as to the probability of an immediate attack that any extra measures were adopted.

The combined naval and military expedition now sent forth had been in preparation for some months. The fleet was under the command of Commodore Faragut, and included 30 armed steamers and 21 mortar vessels, the direction of which was confided to Commodore Porter. General Butler was at the head of the land forces, which had been recruited chiefly from the Eastern States. The first instalment of troops arrived at Ship Island, in the Gulf of Mexico, off the coast of Mississippi, on December 3, 1861; the second instalment reached the same spot in January 1862; and the squadron under Farragut followed shortly after. While the united forces were staying at Ship Island, a reconnoissance was undertaken to determine the best mode of approaching New Orleans. It was determined to proceed by way of the river. This proved to be a work of difficulty. It took nearly three weeks to get all the ships over the bar at the south-west entrance to the Mississippi, and Farragut found the depth considerably less than had been indicated on the official maps—a difference which had been accounted for by the suggestion that the channel had been partly filled up, owing to the absence of traffic since the blockade. When at length the vessels got fairly into the stream, some of the gunboats and mortar-vessels crept cautiously up, making observations as they went, and concealing their presence by wreathing their masts, rigging and hulls with bushes, reeds and willows, which, mingling in appearance with the thick woods on the left side of the advancing squadron, would be likely to deceive any Confederate observers who might be in the neighborhood. A station for the fleet was selected 22 miles below the forts, and the gunboats were sent farther up the river, with orders to oppose any of the enemy's vessels which might be visible, and to shell the woods, so as to clear them from Confederate sharpshooters. This was in April; and, the channel having been thus surveyed and protected, the troops were conveyed in transports to a position 12 miles in the rear of Fort Philip, on the north-eastern bank of the stream. Two schooners from the mortar-fleet occupied a bayou, or creek, in the rear of Fort Jackson soon afterwards; and on April 13 several of the Union gunboats were within two miles of the latter fortification. The boom which the Confederates had stretched across the river had been damaged shortly before, partly by the action of a storm, and partly by the breaking loose of some fire-rafts which drifted against the obstruction. Everything being now in readiness, the bombardment commenced on the 18th, the mortar-vessels taking the lead, and the gunboats assisting whenever the others required relief. A terrible fire was in this way concentrated on the forts, but especially on Fort Jackson, the citadel of which was in flames on the very first day. On the following day the officers' quarters were entirely consumed and the artillerists driven from the parapet-guns. Owing to the soft and spongy nature of the soil, the shells penetrated eighteen or twenty feet into the ground where they exploded with a muffled noise and convulsion suggestive of an earthquake. The levee—that elevated portion of the river-bank which is artificially made—was broken in more than a hundred places, and the water, rushing into the fort, flooded the parade-ground and casemate.

During six days this horrible bombardment continued, and the forts could do little in reply, owing

COMMODORE DAVID G. FARRAGUT.

to the short range of their guns. Fire-barges were frequently sent down the river by the Confederates; but these, while doing no harm, inflicted considerable injury upon the Southerners themselves, by setting the wharves of Fort Jackson on fire and enabling the enemy, after dark, to point his guns with greater accuracy. On the night of the 20th, no fire-ships were sent down from the forts, and the Union squadron, taking advantage of the obscurity, despatched some of their gunboats, under cover of a heavy fire, to complete the destruction of the boom, and drag off the remaining schooners which still impeded the channel. The feat was one of much difficulty and peril, for the guns of Fort Jackson opened fire on the gunboats with great animation; nevertheless, it was safely accomplished. Attempts were made to blow up the boom by means of a galvanic current acting on petards; but the explosives failed to ignite. Lieutenant Caldwell thereupon boarded one of the hulks, slipped the chain, and made an opening large enough for the fleet to pass. His vessel was swept ashore by the current; but she was afterwards got off, in spite of the cannonade from Fort Jackson, and the river was now free to the invading force. The bombardment, however, continued three days longer, and it was not until the early morning of the 24th that the squadron moved up the Mississippi in two columns. The previous day had been occupied by preparations for passing the forts; and while these were going on, the enemy's positions were still vigorously shelled. Much ingenuity was shown in protecting the engines and machinery of the vessels from the action of the hostile artillery. The signal to get under way was given at two o'clock A. M. on the 24th, and on approaching the fort a terrific cross-fire was opened on them. The *Hartford*, in which Farragut was leading the left column, caught fire from one of the combustible rafts, and for a time got aground; but the flames were speedily extinguished, and the guns were so well

CAPTURE OF NEW ORLEANS: ATTACK ON FORT PHILIP.

worked that in a little while Fort Philip was nearly silenced. Some of the other vessels became entangled in the remains of the barrier, and were not extricated without difficulty.

Before the Union squadron had quite passed the forts, the Confederate fleet of gunboats and rams appeared in sight and took part in the conflict. The advance was much facilitated by the darkness of the night and the dense vapor from the guns; for, although General Duncan, who commanded the coast defences, had sent instructions to the naval officers to keep the river lighted with fire-barges, in anticipation of an immediate attack, nothing of the kind was done until the Union vessels were off the forts. It was now that the river-fleet did its utmost to oppose the advancing enemy. The *Manassas*, and an ironclad called the *Morgan*, attacked some of the Union vessels, one of which was run down, though not with such suddenness but that her crew were enabled to escape. The *Morgan*, being much damaged by the collision, shortly afterwards surrendered; three other Confederate ships were captured; and the *Manassas*, in aiming a blow at one of her adversaries, ran ashore, was abandoned by her crew, and finally blew up, after floating some distance down the current. All this while, the Union fleet was progressing up the river, to a greater extent even than the commanders were aware; for, when morning dawned, they discovered to their surprise that the vessels had passed the forts, and that the Confederate flotilla had been nearly destroyed. It was therefore determined to push on at once to New Orleans. A regiment of troops encamped on the banks of the river was compelled to surrender; and on the morning of the 25th the advanced guard encountered the batteries of the second line of defence, at Chalmette, which, however, was too weak to offer much resistance. As the Union vessels drew near to the grand object of their attack, burning steamers, fire-rafts, and cotton-ships in flames, came floating down the tide. It was evident that the people of New Orleans were in a mood of angry desperation, and that everything was being destroyed which could be harmed by fire.

At one o'clock on the 25th, the Union squadron anchored in front of the city. A terrible spectacle presented itself. Black clouds of smoke rose for miles along the levee, indicating that the vast stores of cotton in the neighborhood were being consumed. The river was covered with burning ships, which threatened the Union vessels with conflagration. An excited crowd was drawn up on shore, and all Union sympathizers, who ventured to give expression to their feelings, were at once shot down with pistols. For a long time, the people had believed the lower defences of the river to be absolutely impregnable. When they discovered their mistake, and plainly heard the enemy's guns engaging the upper defences, astonishment, despair, and rage filled the hearts of the citizens. The town itself was completely open to attack, and the hopelessness of maintaining it, with not more than 3000 raw troops, was so apparent to General Lovell that he retired at once to Camp Moore, on the Jackson Railway, together with a few of the volunteers, though the greater number disbanded, and returned to their homes. The civil authorities having practically resumed their control over the city, Captain Bailey, of the *Cayuga*, which headed the right column of the squadron, went ashore to demand the surrender of the place. He was at once threatened by a violent mob, but, being protected by the more respectable citizens, made his way to the mayor's office, where he demanded the submission of New Orleans to the forces of the United States. Farragut had by this time stationed his ships at intervals off the levee, with their guns pointed against the city; and the Confederates had no force with which to encounter the strength of their enemies. Farragut was aware that his own situation was not devoid of peril. He had in his rear two strong forts and some war-vessels. He was separated from all other Union forces, and was surrounded by a violently hostile population. It was therefore very advisable to proceed with caution. A sharp controversy took place between the commodore and the mayor, mainly on the question whether the city authorities themselves should haul down the Confederate flag, and substitute that of the United States (as Farragut demanded), or whether the Union troops should do it. A detachment of sailors and marines went on shore on April 26, hauled down the symbol of rebellion, and ran up the stars and stripes. By about the close of the month, the Union flag was floating from all the public buildings; but the exasperation of the people found vent in acts of insult which sorely tried the patience of the Union officers. At one time, Farragut considered it necessary to menace the city with bombardment; and the mayor replied in a high-flown communication, assuming that the commodore desired to murder women and children, though he had requested that they might be at once removed. No bombardment, however, followed; and New Orleans, conquered, but not submissive, set itself to the invention of new forms of annoyance, as the only solace remaining to its wounded pride.

Louisiana lost heart with the fall of New Orleans. If Farragut had any anxiety with regard to the forts in his rear, the occasion for such a feeling was very soon removed. When morning dawned on that memorable 24th of April which witnessed the passage up the river of Farragut's squadron, Porter, whose detachment of gunboats and mortar-vessels still lay below the two forts occupying the right and left banks of the Mississippi, prepared to engage those works, as well as the

COMMODORE DAVID D. PORTER.

remains of the Confederate fleet, with the force at his disposal. Some steps towards reducing the forts had already been taken. The army under Butler had been sent round to the rear of Fort Philip, and plans had been commenced for cutting off the garrison of Fort Jackson. But it was obviously desirable that the two positions should be taken as speedily as possible, and, on the morning of the 24th, Porter sent a demand for their surrender. This being refused, the bombardment was again opened on the 26th, and next day the demand for surrender was repeated. The terms proposed by the commodore were honorable to his adversaries. The officers were to retain their sidearms; both officers and men were to be paroled; and private property was to be respected.

The officers in the forts were desirous of continued resistance; but the soldiers were mutinous, and their superiors saw that they had no longer the means of fighting at command. When intelligence arrived that New Orleans was in the hands of the enemy, and when it was seen that Butler had cut off the garrison from retreat, the troops refused any longer to obey orders, and, seizing the guns, turned them from the ramparts. Some of the cannon were spiked, and officers who ventured to interfere were fired at. Several of the men deserted with their arms, and surrendered to Butler's pickets; and the aspect of affairs grew alarming during the night of the 27th. A capitulation was consequently inevitable, and on the morning of the 28th a boat was sent off to Porter, with a letter stating that the forts would be given up on the terms proposed. Porter went to Fort Jackson, and, while discussing the terms of capitulation, observed the Confederate ironclad, *Louisiana*, drifting on fire towards the Union ships. The Confederate naval officers had in fact towed the ram to a point above the forts, had set her in flames, and then turned her adrift with guns shotted, apparently in the expectation of her blowing up in the midst of the Union squadron. Just before the discovery of this fact, Porter had been informed that the articles of capitulation would not include the naval force; but he regarded the firing of the *Louisiana* as a breach of faith. He asked whether there was any powder on board, but could obtain no satisfactory answer. Sending word therefore, to the captains of his ships to be on their guard, he continued the negotiations. The catastrophe on board the *Louisiana* came sooner than was anticipated by those who prepared it. As the ironclad got abreast of Fort Philip, it exploded with a terrific report, and the guns, as they became red-hot with the flames, which had been burning for some time, scattered shot and shell in various directions. It is marvelous that widespread injury was not the result; but the only casualty was to a Confederate soldier in the fort, who was killed by one of the fragments. The capitulation having been completed, Porter took measures against the three Confederate steamers which were lying about half a mile above the forts. One of these had already been scuttled; the others surrendered without resistance. Considering that he had been treacherously dealt with in the matter of the *Louisiana*, Porter made prisoners of the naval officers and crews, and sent them to the North. It was the opinion of General Duncan, the Confederate commander of the coast-defences, that the ironclad was set on fire previous to the Union boats coming to anchor abreast of the fort; but the facts looked suspicious of a sinister design.

Before the actual surrender of the forts, General Lovell, the Confederate chief in Louisiana, had received an incorrect intimation that the event had already taken place. He accordingly ordered the evacuation of the forts on Lake Ponchartrain; and when this order was afterwards countermanded, the troops had left the works, and some had deserted the flag. The gunboats and armed steamers on the lake were destroyed, and the Confederate power almost ceased to exist in that region. At New Orleans Farragut observed several ironclad rams in course of building; but the principal of these soon came floating by in flames, and another was sunk in front of the Custom House. Eight miles above the city, Farragut found two forts, where the guns had been spiked, and the gun-carriages set on fire. A mile higher up were two earthworks, not armed; and at this fort a boom of enormous dimensions was discovered, so fashioned as to stop the passage of gunboats, but not yet placed in its position across the stream. The Confederates, therefore, had evidently expended a good deal of time and labor in the defence of the Mississippi, but had postponed many of their works until it was too late to complete them. On May 1 formal possession of New Orleans was taken by General B. F. Butler, at the head of the land forces of the U. S.

Butler's measures were only such as are usual in conquered cities which are evidently determined to continue an irregular resistance after a formal and hated submission. He established what was in fact the rule of martial law. In his proclamation he plainly intimated that all acts of violence against Union soldiers, and all disorders, disturbances of the peace, and crimes of an aggravated nature, interfering with the forces or laws of the United States, would be referred to a military court for trial and punishment. Other matters (including civil causes) would be left to the ordinary courts. The transmission of communications by telegraph was placed under military supervision; and in short a complete censorship over the publication of news or opinions was established together with the subordination of the civil power to that of the sword. The assembling of persons in the streets was prohibited, and the police arrangements of the city passed into the hands of the occupying force. For all this, Butler had abundant justification in the state of popular opinion, and it is clear that he could not have discharged his duties in any other way.

The submission of New Orleans being secured, the Union steamers ascended the river as far as Bâton Rouge, the capital of the State, which was given up without a struggle. The town had in fact no means of resistance and simply yielded to necessity. Its sympathies were wholly with the Confederacy, and out of a population of about 5428 it had contributed 875 men to the Confederate Army, and 240 to the Home Guard. But it was impossible to encounter the naval force by which it was threatened, and with its submission a large tract of cotton-bearing and sugar-producing country fell under Union power. Still pursuing their career of conquest up the Mississippi, the Union vessels received the submission of Natchez, and the fortunes of the Confederates in all the Western States were rendered critical by the subjection of Louisiana. The raising of the blockade of the Mississippi made it advisable for the Confederates to evacuate the forts and navy-yard of Pensacola, on the south coast of Florida; for, with the Union fleet at liberty to pursue other operations after its recent successes, it seemed very doubtful whether that exposed position could be maintained. The commandant, General Jones, had for some time been invested with discretionary power to abandon the place whenever such a step appeared to him advisable; and that time he considered had now come. He transported to Mobile whatever weapons, stores, and machinery he could manage to get off, and then resolved to fire the public buildings of Pensacola. But the act of removal was no easy matter in view of the hostile flotilla which was known to be lying off Fort Morgan, at the entrance to Mobile Harbor. The task, however, was accomplished with great ingenuity. Sham guns were mounted on the works, and other arrangements made for deceiving the enemy; many valuable materials were sent by rail, or in a small river-steamer to a place of safety; and on the night of May 9 the infantry were marched out of the town. Three companies of cavalry were charged with the duty of setting fire to the public buildings; and it was not until the flames burst out simultaneously from many quarters that the Union forces had any suspicion of what was being effected. The garrison of Fort Pickens then commenced a furious bombardment; and on Porter arriving with his vessels, the military and naval officers demanded the surrender of Pensacola. The demand was at once complied with by the civil authorities, and a force under General Arnold endeavored to save what remained of the forts and navy-yard. To some extent the endeavor was successful; but the destruction of public property was very large.

With five exceptions, the harbors along the coast of the Confederate States had now fallen. The Southerners were therefore compelled to carry on their commercial transactions with Europe in an irregular way. Nassau, one of the Bahama Islands, and a British possession, became the port of entry for the commerce of the Confederate States with England; and steamers proceeded from thence to Charleston or Mobile, running the blockade with frequent success. In this way the South was furnished with several of the necessaries and luxuries of life. Yet the blockade kept out a great many things which the Confederates wanted, and almost destroyed the export trade of the planters. During the spring of 1862, the prospects of the Rebel Government looked so black, that President Davis ordered a fast-day, and directed that prayers should be offered up on Friday, May 16, for the strengthening and protecting of the armies. In his proclamation he admitted the gravity of the situation. "Recent disaster," he observed, "has spread gloom over the land, and sorrow sits at the hearthstones of our countrymen."

Butler's position continued to be onerous and difficult. The markets were so insufficiently supplied with food, that the people stood in danger of starving. Butler gave orders for the safe conduct of cargoes of flour, live stock, and other necessaries, from Mobile and various places in the interior. He had captured a quantity of beef and sugar intended for the rebels in the field and 1000 barrels of stores, which he distributed among the deserving poor—"even though some of the food will go to supply the craving wants of the wives and children of those now herding at Camp Moore and elsewhere, in arms against the U. S."

Whatever his faults, Butler had certainly restored the State to the Union. He was superseded on December 14, by General Banks, who at first tried a more lenient mode of administration, but was soon compelled to give up the attempt, on finding that his clemency produced no other effect than riotous demonstration, cries for President Davis, and threatening language towards the military. New Orleans was like a passionate and wayward child, which mistakes generosity for weakness, and can only be kept in decent order by the use of the strong hand. Butler acknowledged this from the first; Banks preferred to buy his experience.

Beauregard's position at Corinth became extremely perilous after the capture of Island No. 10, the Confederate defeat at Shiloh, and the fall of New Orleans. The Union forces had now possession of the Mississippi, and large forces were gathering in different directions to crush the rebels. Annoyed at the discomfiture of the Western Army on April 6 (though the reverse had been repaired on the following day), General Grant was superseded in his command, and the army was strengthened by Pope's division. An advance on Corinth was commenced at the close of April, and each successive camp on the road was fortified at an immense expenditure of labor. Seven of these lines of fortifications—one of them 12 miles in length—were erected between Pittsburg Landing and Corinth; and towards the end of May the town was evacuated by the Confederates. Halleck, who commanded the Union troops, entered Corinth on the 29th; but the enemy had escaped. Pope was sent forward to pursue the retreating columns. Beauregard had suffered some losses on the road of his retreat; but he succeeded in saving by far the greater part of his army, and in establishing himself at Tupelo, about 50 miles south of Corinth. The Union forces had acquired a command over the Mobile and Ohio Railway, and were thus in a much better position than before. Fort Pillow, on the Mississippi, was abandoned by the Confederates on June 4, and the Union gunboats at once descended the river, and anchored next day off Island No. 45, close to the city of Memphis. Here the Confederate fleet engaged the naval forces of the enemy on the morning of June 6, and, after a sharp encounter, was defeated with heavy loss. The surrender of Memphis followed as a matter of course, for the city had now no means of defence. It was one of the principal places of export for the produce of those regions; but its prosperity was ruined for a time, and it was evident that there had been a great destruction of cotton before the entry of the conquerors.

The Union forces now determined to attack Vicksburg, situated on a sharp bend of the Mississippi, in the State similarly named. The position was important, as it enabled those holding it to bar the passage of the river; it was also strong, not merely by reason of its fortifications, but because of the vast swamps and forests, and the numerous creeks and tributary streams, which presented so many obstacles to a land force proceeding against it. On the present occasion, however, it was to be attacked from the river. Farragut, advancing up the Mississippi after the surrender of New Orleans, had by June 24, come within sight of Commodore Davis, descending the stream from Memphis. With the fall of Vicksburg, the river would be opened to the commerce of the Western States; but as long as the town and fortifications remained in the hands of the Confederates, the great water-highway would be effectually blocked. Siege was therefore laid to the place, and the bombardment opened on the 25th. It continued, with occasional intermissions, for a month; yet the storm of shot and shell failed to produce any serious effects. By the labor of more than 1000 negroes, a canal was dug through the small peninsula, formed by the bend of the river, which fronts the town. It was hoped in this manner to open a channel by which ships could pass up and down, out of reach of the batteries; but the work proved a failure. An exciting incident occurred on July 15. The small Confederate steamer, *Arkansas*, which had been roughly and hastily coated with iron, and had for some time been lying hidden in the Yazoo—an affluent of the Mississippi, which it enters a little above Vicksburg—issued forth from its place of concealment, drove away three Union gunboats which had been sent to make a reconnoissance, and, entering the larger river, boldly passed through the whole fleet, inflicting much damage, and finally anchored under the guns of Vicksburg. The *Arkansas* was itself a good deal injured by the fire; but a subsequent attempt to sink her failed in its object. On the 24th, the siege of Vicksburg was abandoned for a time, and Farragut's vessels returned to Bâton Rouge.

The summer and autumn of 1862 did not pass without some operations in the West, by which the Confederates hoped to recover the ground they had lost in that part of the country. A scheme of gigantic dimensions was elaborated: it was proposed to attack the Union forces at Bâton Rouge, at Corinth (Mississippi), and in Eastern Kentucky. These three localities formed the two extremities and the center of the line; and three armies were assembled under the orders of Breckinridge, Van Dorn, and Bragg, in Louisiana, in Upper Mississippi, and in Eastern Tennessee. Bragg had by this time succeeded Beauregard in the command of the West, and by far the largest of the three armies was that which the Southern Government confided to his care. He had been an officer of the U. S. Army, and was well known as a strict disciplinarian. Van Dorn had on previous occasions given signs of ability; but of Breckinridge there was not much to be said. The campaign was opened by some dashing incursions made by Generals Morgan and Forrest into Kentucky and Tennessee. Morgan had already acquired distinction as a species of guerilla chief. He was a purely amateur soldier, but had won the respect of his superiors by enterprise and skill. His force consisted of volunteers, raised principally among the wealthy classes of Kentucky and Tennessee; and their number was small.

At the time that Morgan was making his way through Kentucky, Forrest was marching with a calvary force into Western Tennessee. His methods of procedure were similar to those of other guerilla chiefs. Detached posts were attacked with success; convoys were captured; and Murfreesboro' was surprised, together with the garrison, who were all taken prisoners. General Crittenden, who had lately been appointed to the command, was one of those who fell into the hands of the enemy. Scarcely any resistance was offered to the Confederate forces, nor had any precaution been taken against surprise. Buell, who was in command of that district, reflected very strongly on the conduct of the officers and men whose duty it was to defend Murfreesboro' and his strictures do not appear to have gone beyond the justice of the case.

Breckinridge engaged in an attempt to gain possession of Bâton Rouge.

GENERAL JOHN C. BRECKINRIDGE.
(*Vice-President with Buchanan.*)

The design was to obtain some position on the Lower Mississippi, that the river might not be so much in the hands of the Union forces. The land operations were to be facilitated by the action of the ironclad *Arkansas*, which had been repaired after her engagement with the Union gunboats at Vicksburg. It was hoped that a simultaneous attack by land and water would take place on August 5, but the *Arkansas* broke down when about 15 miles above Bâton Rouge. The regiments under Breckinridge had suffered terribly from heat and scarcity of water in the sandy regions through which they had marched, and, when they reached the object of their attack, were not in the best condition for fighting. The Union forces also had been reduced by sickness; but they had obtained some information as to the movements of their adversary, and Breckinridge, on arriving at Bâton Rouge, found them drawn up in force outside the town. The invaders attacked with great spirit in the early morning of August 5; overwhelmed the first of the Union lines, captured the camp, and were proceeding to attack the second line, when a heavy fire from the batteries checked their advance. The pause, however, was only momentary. Forming their ranks afresh, they dashed forward, and drove the Union troops into the town. General Williams was killed at the head of his troops, and many other officers were stretched upon the field. The assailants had the best of the encounter, but, owing to the absence of the ironclad, were unable to maintain their position. The Union gunboats in the river severely galled their ranks, and from the houses came a continual fire of rifles. Breckinridge was therefore compelled to order a retreat, which, however, was not commenced until the enemy's camp had been set on fire. In the meanwhile, the *Arkansas* had been attacked by the opposing gunboats, but was too much disabled to offer any resistance. She was therefore run ashore, fired, and abandoned, when she blew up and reached the termination of her career after a somewhat inglorious fashion. On August 10, Farragut bombarded and partially destroyed the town of Donaldsonville, between New Orleans and Bâton Rouge; but the Confederates afterward fortified a position at Port Hudson, nearer Vicksburg, and were thus enabled to exercise some control over the great water-highway for which both parties were contending.

The campaign of Eastern Kentucky began early in August, when Kirby Smith issued from the passes of the Cumberland Mountains, pushed forward through a difficult country, and appeared in front of Richmond on the 29th. The town was defended by a force of 8000 men, under command of General Manson. They were mostly raw levies, and had been so recently supplied with arms, that it might fairly be a matter of doubt whether they knew how to handle them properly. Manson had posted them upon rising ground, crossed by the road from Barboursville to Richmond; and here they were attacked at daybreak of the 30th, and compelled, after some temporary success, to shift their position to a line somewhat nearer the town. The Confederates renewed the assault with fresh energy, and the Union troops were driven in confusion to a line of hills in the immediate vicinity of Richmond. Though rallied for awhile, and covered by artillery, they continued to lose ground, and a vehement attack of the adversary finally swept them into the town itself. At the same time, a body of Confederate cavalry, marching round Richmond, fell upon the wagons which had been sent to the rear, and captured almost the whole train. Finding themselves encountered by enemies on two sides, the unhappy soldiers of the Union, whose experience of war had in numerous instances commenced that day, saw no choice before them but to surrender. The triumph was sufficient to intoxicate the Confederates with a sense of their own invincibility. As the result of this one conflict, they had taken 5000 prisoners, and had possessed themselves of nine pieces of artillery, 10,000 stand of arms, and a large amount of supplies. The capture of Richmond was followed by that of Lexington on September 2, and that of Frankfort on the 17th. Louisville and Cincinnati were now hastily fortified by General Wright, the Union officer commanding the Department of the Ohio. Frantic endeavors were made to organize volunteer corps to meet the victorious legions of Kirby Smith. But the prospects of the Union in that Western State were extremely dark; for the main army, under Bragg, was now moving forward in prosecution of the general scheme of the campaign, and Munfordsville, with about 4000 men, surrendered to the advanced divisions on the 17th. Buell hurried from Nashville to the relief of his colleagues in the northern part of the State; but Bragg was already between him and those whom he desired to assist. By ordinarily good management on the part of Bragg, Buell might have been disastrously defeated; but he with singular imbecility, turned aside from the road by which he might have stopped his adversary, and suffered him to recapture Munfordsville, and to relieve Louisville. Bragg, who had been closely followed and in some degree harassed by Buell, seems to have been apprehensive of being overwhelmed by superior numbers. Turning to the west, he marched first to Bardstown, and then to Frankfort, where he inaugurated a provisional government of Kentucky. Thus Louisville was saved, and at the same time a Union detachment stationed at Cumberland Gap, which in the first instance had been cut off by the advance of Kirby Smith, was enabled, by the latter operations of that commander, to escape to Cincinnati.

The bad management of the Confederates, after their first striking successes, changed the whole character of the war in those parts. The Union troops now re-

CUMBERLAND GAP.

sumed the offensive, and Bragg saw that he must retire into Tennessee. Buell started in pursuit on October 1, and fell in with the greater portion of the Confederate army on the road from Lebanon to Harrodsburg. By this time Bragg had discovered, as Morgan had discovered before him, that the people of Kentucky, with a few exceptions, were not inclined to support the Confederates. He was naturally very anxious to quit the State, but thought it necessary to fight an action before doing so, in order to redeem his credit, and to save from capture the large amount of stores which he had seized during his incursion. He therefore drew up his army in a position where he considered it probable that he should be encountered by the Union troops. His forces were divided into two portions, posted on two distinct roads, distant from one another about twenty miles. Bragg's headquarters were fixed, on the 6th, at the town of Harrodsburg, situated at the point of junction of the two roads, which were being simultaneously watched. Polk, who was stationed on the road from Lebanon to Bardstown with three divisions, was directed to offer battle to the Union forces at Perryville, where a very warmly-contested action took place on the 8th.

The Union forces, who were marching from the west, appear to have been taken by surprise, not knowing, until roughly undeceived, that the Confederates were so close at hand. Bragg had already sent orders to his other divisions, planted on the Louisville and Lawrenceburg road, to march with all haste towards Harrodsburg, so that he felt tolerably secure of being well supported. Immediately on the Union forces being seen advancing, the Confederate infantry rushed forward, and a number of Buell's raw troops who unfortunately happened to be in the front line, fled in dismay. The older regiments maintained their ground; and when the

A RAILROAD BATTERY.

Union troops had been largely reinforced, the strength of the opposing parties became more evenly balanced. The Union men resolved to act on the defensive until the whole of their division should reach the field. Polk, however, renewed his attacks with great fury; the Union troops were driven back, losing several of their officers; and the action might have ended in a decided reverse for Buell's army, had not night put an end to the combat. Further reinforcements reached the Union forces during the evening; and Bragg considered it prudent to retreat. He had gained his object in fighting, and had now to consider how he could best secure his withdrawal into Tennessee. In killed, wounded, and missing, the Union troops had lost more than 4000 men. The Confederate loss was estimated at about 2500; and this large expenditure of life had resulted in no positive advantage to the one side or the other. Buell blamed the conduct of some of his officers in command of the less experienced troops; the Government blamed Buell, and he was shortly afterwards removed from his command, and succeeded by General Rosecrans. It must certainly be admitted that Buell had not distinguished himself; yet, whether owing to good fortune, or to the bad management of his opponent, Kentucky had been cleared of invaders. Accompanied by long lines of wagons, laden with plunder, by vast herds of cattle and horses, and by private carriages conveying those families who preferred to throw in their lot with the South, the Confederates retired with deliberation, and passed safely through Cumberland Gap. The Union troops were in no mood to press them closely, and, with their rear well guarded by cavalry, they gained the safer regions of Tennessee.

Mississippi, in the latter half of the year, was the scene of some important events. Sherman was in command at Memphis; Rosecrans, not yet appointed as the successor of Buell in Kentucky, was at Corinth, with directions to check the Confederate Army of the Mississippi, should any attempt be made to cross the Tennessee River and harrass Buell in the operations just described. Price, commanding the Confederates, concentrated his forces at Iuka, 30 miles to the south of Corinth, and on being attacked by Rosecrans, retreated in good order. Rosecrans had hoped to overwhelm his enemy, but, failing in his design, fortified himself at Corinth. Price waited till he was joined by Van Dorn and Lovell, and then attacked Corinth. The Union pickets were driven in on October 2, and on the morning of the 3d the bulk of the Confederate army appeared in sight. Before the Union troops could be withdrawn behind the inner line of defence, they were attacked by the Southerners, and compelled to retire. Rosecrans, in the course of the night, made such excellent arrangements, that early next morning, he was ready to renew the fight. The Confederates had approached from the south, but believing the northern side to be more exposed, they marched round to that point, only to find that Rosecrans had fortified his position with great enterprise and skill. The Union troops were now fronting towards the north, when they were attacked on the 4th. Stationed behind their works, they managed their artillery with resolution, and in a few hours they silenced the Confederate batteries. Price now prepared to storm the defences. His troops rushed impetuously forward, captured some redoubts, and drove the defenders into the town. There the Union troops rallied, and Price's division, not being supported by that of Van Dorn, which had been delayed by the difficult nature of the country, was hurled back by a vigorous effort, and compelled to abandon what it had won. When Van Dorn's columns arrived, they were too late to help their comrades. The Union troops were again in possession of their batteries and breastworks; but Van Dorn concluded to attempt to take one portion of the defences. His men advanced with extraordinary courage, making their way up a rugged ravine under a tremendous fire from the forts. Numbers dropped on that painful and deadly path; the ranks were formed anew to fill the gaps that had been formed in them; the guns still played with terrible intensity on those devoted men; but the advance continued. When the attacking force had gained the edge of the ditch, the Union troops themselves slackened fire, as if overcome by the heroism which they could not subdue. The pause, however, was only momentary; and when the guns once more opened at short range, the Confederates for the first time faltered, and reeled back. Then two regiments from the garrison leaped from the works, and rushed at their enemies with a furious charge. The exhausted Southerners staggered down the side of the hill, fol-

GENERAL W. S. ROSECRANS.

GENERAL JOSEPH E. JOHNSTON.

lowed by the Union troops; and Corinth was once more safe.

The losses on both sides had been fearful, and the disappointment of the Confederates was all the greater on account of their preliminary success. Van Dorn retired behind the lagoons and marshes from which he had issued forth, followed for many miles by the Union troops, who, however, ultimately retired to their former position. The desperately contested Western campaign had resulted in both parties reassuming, with but few exceptions, the positions they had held at the beginning. In many respects the efforts of the South had been amazing; in many respects the blunders of the North had been remarkable; yet the North was still in the position of command, and the independence of the South was still a doubtful dream.

On the defence of Port Hudson and of Vicksburg, the hopes of the Confederacy in the West now mainly depended. If the Southerners could retain possession of the river between those places, they would probably be able to hold the State of Mississippi, and in that case their position would be much stronger than if they lost every portion of the river, and, as a consequence, the vast provinces through which it runs. The command of the West was given to General Joseph E. Johnston, who commanded the Confederate Army at Bull Run, but who had for some time been incapacitated for active service by the serious wounds he had received at the battle of Fair Oaks. The Mississippi Army, which included the garrisons of Vicksburg and Port Hudson, was placed under General Pemberton, who acted in subordination to Johnston; the Tennessee forces came also under the supervision of that able commander. The Union forces were well represented in the Western States by two large armies, one commanded by Grant, and the other by Rosecrans. The main body of Grant's force was engaged during the late autumn in an expedition from Western Tennessee into Mississippi, and a detachment was being organized for an attack on Vicksburg. The army under Rosecrans was stationed partly at Nashville, and partly along the line of the Cumberland River; and in this position it was watched by the Confederates under Bragg, who was assisted by the irregular operations of his guerilla chieftains, Morgan and Forrest. Rosecrans did not at that time feel himself strong enough for offensive operations; indeed, it was as much as he could do to defend his position against the frequent incursions of his active enemies. It was found necessary to fortify Nashville, and in the month of December the movements of General Morgan were such as to excite some uneasiness. Hartsville, a small town on the right bank of the Cumberland, was taken by Morgan in the early morning of December 7, after a march of forty miles through snow and ice. The Union troops were surprised by the sudden appearance of the enemy on their side of the river, which they had considered it impossible to cross at that point. Their resistance was slight, and, in the result, about 1800 troops surrendered. After being sent as prisoners to Murfreesboro', they were paroled, and permitted to depart for Nashville, though not before they had paid a large ransom in arms, blankets, and overcoats. Shortly afterwards, Morgan was instructed to seize the railway between Nashville and Louisville, so as to isolate some of the Union detachments, while Forrest threatened Grant's communications with Columbus.

Rosecrans abandoned his defensive position as the year was drawing to a close, and on the 26th advanced towards his opponents at the head of a large and well-appointed army. Less than forty miles interposed between Nashville and Murfreesboro'; but the progress of the Union troops was rendered difficult by the Confederate skirmishers who thronged the woods on both sides of the road. It was not until the 30th that Rosecrans reached the vicinity of Murfreesboro'. Fighting took place that day, and the pickets of the Southern commander Polk, were driven in. The two armies bivouacked that night within sight of each other's fires, and Rosecrans disposed his troops for the operations of the morrow as well as the difficult nature of the country would permit. The land was broken up into a number of low hills, which concealed the positions of the enemy; and the several divisions of the Northern force were so hidden from one another in the density of the forest, that anything in the nature of general supervision became almost impossible. The adversaries were now fronting one another on the banks of a stream called the Stone River, and portions of both forces stood on both sides of the channel. The night of the 30th did not pass in perfect inactivity as far as the Confederates were concerned. A brigade of their cavalry moved round the enemy's rear during the hours of darkness, and made so vigorous an assault on the wagon-trains that stores to a large amount were captured. The movement was as daring as it was successful—the cavalry actually passing round the whole body of the Union army, so that they rejoined their comrades on the opposite flank from that which they had quitted. The action of the 31st was commenced by Bragg, who ordered his left wing to advance, when the Union forces were again taken by surprise, and driven back in so much confusion that several guns were captured before the horses could be harnessed. Two of the Union divisions were dispersed in rapid succession, and word was sent to Rosecrans to inform him of the misfortunes that had already occurred. Other portions of the army made a more determined stand, and the Confederate attack was finally checked, though it had succeeded sufficiently to compel the whole of the Union right and center to recede, and to take up positions very different from those which they had held in the morning. The right-hand portion of the left wing still kept its ground between the Stone River and the railway from Nashville to Murfreesboro'; but, on the whole, the Union forces had been seriously injured by these vigorous operations.

The Confederates had not purchased their success, such as it was, without a considerable expenditure of life. The Northern troops, driven to bay, had fought with great resolution, and their opponents had suffered terribly. A brigade of Polk's corps had lost a third of its number in attacking the division commanded by General Sheridan; and in other quarters the destruction of life among the field and staff officers had been immense. The new positions taken up by the Union forces were such as to render a fresh attack extremely difficult. Both flanks were protected by streams, with bridges and fords in the rear; and the spirit of the troops was for the most part good. The Union left was planted on a hill near the Stone River, and, as this was the key to the whole position, the partial triumph of the Confederates was not of much value. If all their efforts were not to be thrown away, the attack must be renewed; but the majority of the Confederates were in too exhausted a condition to resume the combat. The change in the Union position had been effected early in the afternoon. An hour or two later, a fresh division, under Breckinridge, arrived on the ground, and advanced against the enemy. With great spirit the men rushed up a rising ground, upon the top of which the Union forces had planted a powerful line of batteries. The contest was maintained with admirable courage; but the Confederates, notwithstanding their devotion, could make no head against the obstacles to which they were opposed. After losing many of their number, they retired to the point from which they had started; and, as darkness had now closed in, little more could be done till the morrow. A clear moonlight enabled some of the Union batteries to continue their fire, but with this exception the night passed in quiet. Owing to the right wing of the Northern Army having been driven in upon the left, the Confederates were now in possession of a large part of the field which in the morning had been occupied by the Union troops. During the progress of the battle, the communication with Nashville had been often cut off, and the ammunition-train of the Union right wing was twice captured by the Southerners, and twice retaken by their antagonists. Thus, on the hard-fought field of Murfreesboro', the old year came to an end, and on the following day—January 1, 1863—both armies were too worn out by what they had already undergone to do much more than recombine their shattered ranks. Detachments were sent out by the Confederates to threaten the Union communications, to capture supplies, and to reconnoitre the condition of the enemy's forces. Rosecrans withdrew his army a short distance to the rear, and the Southerners then occupied the ground between the river and the railway. The Union troops, who were reinforced by two brigades, entrenched themselves where they stood; the wounded were sent to the rear, and every preparation was made to dispute any renewed attempt on the part of the Confederates to get possession of the road to Nashville.

On the morning of January 2, demonstrations were made along the whole Union line; but operations on a large scale were not commenced until three o'clock in the afternoon, when a numerous body of Confederates burst upon a Union division which, at an early hour of the morning, had been sent by Rosecrans to take ground once more on the eastern side of the river. The attacking force consisted of the entire right wing, and for a time the Union troops were repulsed. On receiving an addition to their numbers, however, they pressed forward with so much impetuosity that the Confederates gave way, and, leaving many dead and wounded on the field, retired to their own lines. In this conflict, which was obstinately disputed for a considerable length of time, the Southern troops lost a battery and a stand of colors. Soon afterwards, Rosecrans gave the order for the entire line to advance, when the Confederate right wing was broken, and the flank so seriously menaced that Bragg considered it advisable to withdraw the whole of his forces. Breckinridge's division had been completely mobbed, and but for the interposition of a brigade from Polk's corps, which checked the pursuit and saved some of the abandoned artillery, the disaster might have been even worse than it was. Night fell once more upon a bloody and tumultuous plain; and next day each army held the other in such dread that very little was even attempted. Rosecrans managed so skilfully as to induce his opponent to believe that large reinforcements had arrived during the night. This finally determined the action of the Confederate general. He felt that he was no longer able to maintain his position, and that Murfreesboro' must be abandoned if Tennessee was to be retained at all. The prisoners and baggage-wagons were accordingly sent to the rear; at eleven o'clock at night the army commenced its retreat; and a new position was soon afterwards taken up behind the Duck River, some fifty miles to the south of Murfreesboro'. That town was occupied by the Union forces on the 5th, and 1500 of the Confederate sick and wounded were found there by the conquerors. It is a remarkable fact that in this series of battles the two combatants are thought to have lost about the same number in killed, wounded, and prisoners. Rosecrans, in his report, confesses to having been deprived of 8778 men. If we are to set down a similar number on the Confederate side, we reach a total loss of more than 17,000. Both armies had fought with singular determination, and, being equally matched, they had inflicted upon one another a frightful amount of injury. Such an action should have been a turning-point of the war; but unfortunately its results bore little proportion to the cost.

At about the same period, the guerilla chief, Forrest, had been unfortunate in his attempts to sever the communications of Grant's army in Mississippi. In the latter part of December, 1862, he effected a good deal of damage to the various bridges and lines of rail, and captured several Union detachments, but on returning to the Confederate lines, was attacked on two sides by separate bodies of Northern troops. After a sharp engagement, his force was utterly routed, and it was with difficulty that he and his men escaped across the river into Tennessee. Morgan was rather more successful, but the amount of damage inflicted by these two leaders was of a petty and vexatious, rather than a serious character. The general position of the Union troops in the West was not materially affected by the incursions of Morgan and Forrest, and the minor successes which they gained were accounted very poor compensation for the Confederate reverse at Murfreesboro'. Engagements of this trivial nature continued to occur from time to time; but their importance is not sufficient to merit a detailed account.

In the latter days of 1862, Grant, whose headquarters were at Oxford, Mississippi, was preparing to advance on Granada, the point of junction between the Memphis and Mobile and the Corinth and Mobile Railways. While doing so, his depot at Holly Springs was vehemently attacked, on December 19, by General Van Dorn, at the head of some Texan cavalry. The town appears to have been badly guarded; and when Van Dorn dashed into it, the Union troops were so overcome by surprise that, after the merest pretence at fighting, the garrison laid down their arms, with the exception of a few cavalry, who escaped. The torch was then applied to the vast accumulations of flour, cotton, and other stores which the place contained; the railway, the station and the rolling stock, were set on fire; and the explosion of the magazine caused the destruction of a large part of the town. Having effected his purpose, Van Dorn got safely away, and Grant, considering that his plans had been seriously affected by this disaster, abandoned his advance into Mississippi. Not many days after, Sherman, who commanded a detachment of Grant's army, was unfortunate in a renewed attack on Vicksburg. He had under his direction four divisions, commanded by Generals Steele, Morgan, M. L. Smith and A. J. Smith. His force embarked at Memphis, Tennessee, on December 20, and next day was joined by Porter, with two gunboats. The main body of the fleet was at the mouth of the River Yazoo, which flows into the Mississippi a few miles above Vicksburg. The expedition now descended the larger stream, exposed occasionally to the attacks of sharpshooters on the banks, whose assaults were revenged by the burning of houses, and the destruction of much property. The discipline of the men was extremely defective. The scene of confusion at the embarkation was such as to reflect discredit on all concerned. On the night of the 24th, and early morning of the 25th, the detachment arrived at the mouth of the Yazoo. The fleet consisted of more than 60 transports, with a number of ironclads and other gunboats and several mortar-boats. On the 26th, the expedition moved up the Yazoo, and troops were landed at various points extending over a distance of about three miles. The assailants were now eight miles from the point of attack, for it was proposed by Sherman to assault Vicksburg in the rear—that is to say, from the north-eastern side. The Confederates, however, had already erected defences and were prepared for a vigorous resistance. A battery, reared upon a bank known as Haines' Bluff, barred the progress of the Union gunboats up the Yazoo; and between that bluff and the threatened city itself a large number of Confederates were posted on a line of low hills stretching along Chickasaw Bayou, which connects the lower part of the Yazoo with a bend of the Mississippi a little above Vicksburg. Additional batteries and lines of breastworks were constructed by the Southern forces as soon as it became evident that the Union army had landed on the left bank of the Yazoo. Reinforcements were hurried up by rail from Jackson, and the defenders of the city felt so confident of success that several of the civilians, including ladies, stationed themselves on the higher bluffs, to watch any engagement that might occur.

The Union troops being now ranged in order of attack, the division under Gen. Steele was sent to a point above Chickasaw Bayou, to operate against the battery which enfiladed that point from the right of the Confederate line. Fighting ensued on the 27th, but the battery was not taken. The action was renewed on the 28th, and the Union troops then attempted to cross the bayou, so as to bring their left and center into combination. Still no impression could be made on the Confederate position, which every hour grew stronger, as fresh works were thrown up, and fresh reinforcements arrived from Jackson. Nevertheless, they held grimly to their purpose and, some military bridges having been extemporized on the 29th, two companies of the 6th Missouri Regiment crossed the bayou, with instructions to undermine the bank on which the Confederates stood.

ATTACK UPON ROANOKE ISLAND: LANDING OF THE TROOPS.

The enterprise was one of great peril; but the Missourians set to work with quiet determination, and their spades and pick-axes made an impression on the crumbling earth. The sharpshooters of the 13th Regulars opened fire on the defenders of the bank, to prevent those firing on the men below; but in some instances their aim was inaccurate, and two Union men were shot dead by their own comrades. The Missourians called out, "Fire higher!" and the Confederates above responded with the exclamation, "Fire lower!" The opposing ranks were so close together that conversation was carried on between the two lines. "What regiment is below?" asked one of the Confederates. "The 6th Missouri," was the reply; to which the Southerner responded, "It is too brave a regiment to be on the wrong side." These Missourians had had no food for several hours, and one of them called out, "Have you got anything to eat up there? I am hungry." A large loaf of bread was immediately thrown down to them. At the same time that this attempt was being made to undermine the bank, the division on the right attacked some other bluffs beyond the bayou. An advance over the center bridge was to have been made at this juncture; but, owing to a mistake, the order was not given. This error caused the failure of the whole operation. The right division, not being properly supported by the center, was repulsed with great loss, and night came on, accompanied by torrents of rain. The ground, at the best low and marshy, was converted in a little while into a muddy swamp, where the wounded dropped in their exhaustion, and, being beyond the reach of assistance, perished miserably in the ooze, dying either of exposure to the cold, or of absolute suffocation in the slough. The Union forces had lost 3000 men, and were no nearer the realization of their project than when they had begun. At one time during the 30th, it was designed to attack Haines' Bluff; but a heavy fog came on, and it was apparent that the expedition must be abandoned. The troops re-embarked that evening, and returned up the Mississippi. Shortly afterwards, Sherman was superseded in the command of the detachment by McClernand, and the force was divided into two corps, under Sherman and Morgan.

The failure at Vicksburg took place in the final days of the old year. On the first day of the new year (1863), the Union forces experienced another misfortune in the recapture of Galveston, Texas. General Magruder, having collected artillery at Houston, marched towards the neighborhood of the town which he designated to take, and occupied in force the works erected opposite the island on which that town is situated. Two steam-packets he converted into gun-boats, which he rendered shot-proof by bulwarks of cotton-bales. The boats were manned by Texan cavalry, and were accompanied in their expedition by tenders and yachts, filled with spectators and volunteers. As the troops crossed the railway bridge which connected the island with the continent, the gunboats steamed up, and engaged the Union gunboat called the *Harriet Lane*. The latter soon drove off one of the Confederate vessels; but the other, named the *Bayou City*, continued the contest with great determination. By this time, the land troops had obtained possession of the town, and the Union forces, being unprovided with artillery, surrendered at discretion. The blockade in that locality was at once raised, and the port was re-opened to commerce. The conclusion of 1862 and the commencement of 1863 were marked by serious reverses to the Union arms. The future was involved in clouds and darkness; yet the spirit of the Northern people did not fail one jot.

CHAPTER III.

The "Merrimac" and "Monitor" (March 8, 1862).

"At the outbreak of the Rebellion," says Swinton, "an enormous disparity was visible between the naval strength of the Union and that of the Confederacy. The regular war steamers of the United States, though scanty in number, contained some of the finest ships in the world. On this navy was imposed the task of blockading 3000 miles of seacoast, stretching from Cape Henry to the harbor of Galveston. The department bought up everywhere the vessels of the mercantile marine, and every floating object propelled by steam which could be converted into a war vessel.

"The Confederates had to get along with scantier means of provision. They wanted to break up the blockade, to repel naval forays on their rivers and coasts, and to send out ocean guerillas to cripple the vast commerce of the Union. For this purpose, and for most of the blockade-runners, they relied upon the English shipyards. From thence came the Alabamas, the Shenandoahs, the Sumters, and all their famous cruisers, *which were built, furnished, armed, equipped, and manned in English ports.*"

Shortly before McClellan's temporary advance toward Manassas, a naval action took place in Hampton Roads, off Fortress Monroe, which was a perfectly new experience in marine warfare, and it attracted great at-

THE "MERRIMAC" SINKING THE "CUMBERLAND."

tention, not only here, but throughout the world. It revolutionized the mode of fighting at sea, and rendered the ships, the armaments, and the tactics of Trafalgar as obsolete as those of Actium. Since then, all maritime nations have been compelled to arm their ships with iron plates of enormous thickness, to invent artillery of ever-increasing size and power, and to depend more on revolving turrets than on the old-fashioned tiers of guns. There has been no great naval war since 1862, and we are still ignorant of the ultimate effects likely to ensue from these new methods of warfare. But the combat of the *Merrimac* and the *Monitor* drew a deep line between the past and the future; and the naval heroes of days to come will have to fight under conditions the nature of which has not yet been fully tested.

The Union fleet stationed in Hampton Roads consisted of five vessels, under the command of Captain Marston, of the *Roanoke;* and it would be a great gain to the Southern cause if these could be destroyed or taken. The Confederates had raised and refitted the frigate *Merrimac*, which had been sunk, as we have seen, on the evacuation of the Navy Yard at Norfolk. This vessel had been converted into a shot-proof steam-battery. Its proportions had been cut down, and its sides plated with iron, which had been subjected to various experiments, calculated to show the resisting power of the armor, and the best methods of managing such a ship when in actual conflict with an enemy. A ram had also been added to its appointments, and the *Merrimac* was now in a condition to inflict the maximum of injury on her opponents, while receiving the minimum of injury herself. Under her new designation of the *Virginia*, the *Merrimac* bore ten guns—eight at the sides, one at the bow, and one at the stern; and she was placed under the command of Captain Buchanan, an officer who, previously to the Civil War, had been in charge of the Washington Navy Yard. Towards noon on March 8, the vessel was seen approaching the fleet in Hampton Roads, coming from the direction of Norfolk. The Union ships were immediately prepared for action, and the *Cumberland* was laid across the channel, so that her broadside could be brought to bear on the *Merrimac*. The latter, owing to her heavy structure, which assimilated her appearance to that of a sunken house, with the chimney just appearing above the water, could not move with much rapidity; but this was not the object for which she was designed. At the distance of about a mile, the pivot-guns of the *Cumberland* opened on her, but without the slightest effect. Not deigning to reply to the attack, she continued on her course, receiving a broadside from another ship, as well as from the *Cumberland*, but giving no sign that she was at all injured by this powerful cannonade. She now fired in return, and again received several broadsides, with the same result as before. The pilot of the *Cumberland*, in a statement which he afterwards made, spoke of the balls bouncing from her sides, as if the vessel had been made of India-rubber. A shot from one of her guns killed five marines on board the *Cumberland*, and that vessel, being unable to escape, was soon crushed by the iron horn of the *Merrimac*, which knocked a hole in her side near the water-line, as large as the mouth of a hogshead, and drove the unfortunate ship back upon her anchors with great force. Although the water came rushing into the hold with the utmost violence, the *Cumberland* replied with spirit, and the action continued for half an hour. The broadsides of the *Merrimac* were doing fearful execution on the deck of the Union ship, which caught fire in the forward part. The flames were soon extinguished, but the water proved a more formidable enemy. Nothing could keep it from pouring in at the horrible gash which the ram had torn in the side of the *Cumberland*, and, although the guns were still served with persistency, notwithstanding that the dead and dying lay about in large numbers, the bow kept sinking deeper and deeper into the sea, and it was plain that the injured ship must speedily succumb to the superior power of her foe. She went down with the flag still flying; and even after her hull had grounded on the sands, 54 feet below the surface of the water, the pennant was yet seen fluttering from the topmast above the waves. None of the men were captured, but many perished as the vessel sank. Of the 400 on board, nearly half were killed during the fight, or drowned as the waters closed above the wreck. Some of the crew swam ashore, and others were rescued by small boats; but the list of dead was lamentable. The only consolation to the people of the Union was to be found in the splendid gallantry which had been exhibited, and the noble sense of duty which kept the flag flying to the last.

The *Merrimac* now attacked the *Congress* at a distance of 240 yards, and getting astern, raked her fore and aft with shells, while one of the steamers attending on the ironclad kept up a fire on the starboard quarter. All this while, the *Merrimac* ranged slowly backwards and forwards, firing broadside after broadside, to which the *Congress* replied with resolution, but with scarcely any effect on the mailed vessel by which she was attacked. After 100 men had been killed, and the ship had taken fire in several places, and with no relief possible, the Union flag was hauled down, and the stubborn contest ended. The remaining officers, and a portion of the crew, escaped on shore; the others were taken off by a Confederate gunboat; and during the night the vanquished ship was burned to the water's edge, and sank. The *Congress* had been even less able to resist her

A BLOCKADE RUNNER.

THE MONITOR.

ERICSSON.

121

opponent than the *Cumberland*. Her only means of defence were two guns at the stern, and these were soon disabled. The *Merrimac* was accompanied by five armed steamers, which took part in the action, and placed the Union ships at a still greater disadvantage. To make matters worse, the steamship *Minnesota*, which had left Fortress Monroe shortly after the appearance of the *Merrimac*, got aground, and was unable to render any assistance. The frigate *St. Lawrence*, which followed her, was equally unfortunate; and the *Roanoke*, which also made an attempt to reach the spot, was obliged to return, owing to the shallowness of the water.

On the evening of the same day, the *Merrimac*, accompanied by two other vessels, proceeded towards the *Minnesota*, which lay some three miles below Newport News, quite unable to stir, having grounded while the tide was running ebb. The commander of the ironclad, wishing to capture the grounded vessel without inflicting any serious injury, made no attempt to run her down, but, standing off about a mile, threw shot and shell into her. The *Minnesota* replied with so much animation that one of the steamers attending the *Merrimac* caught fire, and was towed off by her companion. At nightfall, the *Minnesota* still remained untaken, and the *Merrimac* steamed in behind Sewall's Point. The effect of the day's operations was alarming to the Unionists in the neighborhood of Hampton Roads. They anticipated that the terrible stranger would again appear on the following morning, and resume its work of destruction, to which, it seemed, no effective resistance could be offered. It was only too probable that the *Minnesota* would be taken; that all the other ships would be sunk or driven off; that the stores and warehouses on the beach would be fired; and that the troops would be compelled to seek refuge in the fortress. A great surprise, however, was in preparation, both for the Union men and for the *Merrimac*. An ironclad, called the *Monitor*, had just been completed at New York, and was taken in tow by a steam-tug on the 6th of March. Her destination was Hampton Roads, and it was intended that she should be used against the Confederate ironclad, of which the Government had received some information. The *Monitor* was a small vessel, more like a raft than a ship-of-war; she was derisively called "A Yankee cheese box;" but her construction admirably fitted her for the kind of naval encounters which now seemed likely to be general. She was built in two parts, forming an upper and a lower vessel. The length of the upper vessel, which was shot-proof above the watermark, was 172 feet; that of the lower vessel, 124 feet. Of these two vessels, the depth of the former was five feet, and of the latter six feet six inches; with a breadth, in the one case, of 41 feet 4 inches, and, in the other, of 36 feet at the top, and 18 feet at the bottom. The sides of the upper vessel were constructed of 25-inch thickness of oak, coated with iron plates of 5-inch thickness. The turret, built of 8-inch plates of rolled iron, increased in thickness near the port holes to 11 inches. The deck, which was of 8-inch thickness of oak, was coated with 2-inch plates of wrought iron. The pilot-house was built of 9-inch plates of forged iron, but in the event it was found to be of insufficient strength. The vessel drew 10 feet of water; the height of her turret was 9 feet, the diameter 21 feet. She was armed with two Dahlgren guns, carrying shot or shell of from 162 to 168 pounds' weight. The deck was from two to three feet above water; the cabins, which were below the water, were lighted artificially day and night; and the commander's post was in the pilot-house, whence he directed the steering of the vessel and the movement of the turret. The architect of this remarkable ship was Captain Ericsson, and great reliance was placed on its power to meet any floating battery which the Confederates could bring into the water.

At ten o'clock on the night of March 8, shortly after the disappearance of the *Merrimac*, the *Monitor* entered Hampton Roads, and took up a station near the *Minnesota*. The crew of that vessel were greatly relieved in the appearance of this much-needed friend; but the powers of the *Monitor* had yet to be tried; and it was still uncertain whether she would be able to cope with the Confederate ironclad. Her appearance was so unwonted that it was impossible for ordinary seamen to form any precise idea as to her powers. Her deck was unprotected by any bulwarks, and stood not more than two feet above the water. The heavy turret and the dwarfish pilot-house were strange features in a sea-going vessel; indeed, the structure of the *Monitor* was so novel that, before she was launched, doubts were entertained as to whether she would float at all. Nevertheless there she was in Hampton Roads; and, although she had encountered a heavy gale on her passage, and had suffered not a little from the effects of the storm, she had proved herself seaworthy. Whatever the result of the morrow's action, she would undoubtedly fight; and the surprise in preparation for the *Merrimac* had a character that was truly dramatic.

During the night the *Monitor* lay between the *Minnesota* and Fortress Monroe; so that when the Confederate vessel approached in the early morning, the presence of the new-comer was entirely concealed. The *Merrimac* had been a good deal damaged in the action of the previous day. In men she had indeed lost only two killed and eight wounded, though among the latter was her commander, Captain Buchanan; but the vessel itself was much the worse for the encounter. Two of the guns were disabled; the anchor and the flag-staff were

NAVAL ENGAGEMENT BETWEEN THE "MERRIMAC" AND "MONITOR."

shot away; the smokestack and steam-pipes were riddled; the prow was twisted; the armor was battered, and the ram was wrenched. The officers, nevertheless, felt perfect confidence in the ability of their vessel to dispose of all the Union ships which they expected to fight. At six o'clock on the morning of the 9th, the ironclad was observed rounding the point of land at the mouth of the Elizabeth River, accompanied by two of her satellites. It must have been with some astonishment that the crew of the *Merrimac*, shortly afterwards, saw emerging from the further side of the *Minnesota* a small dark vessel, with an ironclad turret which rose almost sheer out of the water. The two floating batteries approached one another, and the *Monitor* was the first to open fire, which she did at the distance of a hundred yards. Her antagonist at once replied, and a vigorous interchange of shots went on, at first with rapidity, but afterwards with slowness and caution. The distance between the two combatants varied from fifty to two hundred yards, and it was found that the *Monitor* could move with greater speed than her opponent, and was more easily turned. The *Merrimac* soon discovered that she had her match in the strange-looking craft which had so suddenly started out of the waves. She had begun by attacking the *Minnesota;* but it was now evident that she had quite enough to do in holding her own against the *Monitor*. For a little while the *Merrimac* ran aground, but, on getting afloat again, steamed up the harbor towards Elizabeth River, followed closely by the *Monitor*. Her shot produced no effect, and the *Merrimac* now made an attempt to run down her formidable antagonist. Five times did these two ironclads come into collision; but the *Merrimac's* ram, already injured by the first day's action, was by this time entirely broken, and her engines were of insufficient strength to propel her with the necessary speed. Each time that the vessels struck one another, one of the guns of the *Monitor* was discharged directly against the plated sides of the *Merrimac*, and the latter replied by bringing her guns to bear on the turret and pilot-house of her adversary.

The *Monitor* withdrew between one and two P. M., owing to her commander having been injured in the eyes by a shot which struck the pilot-house. The disappearance of the Union ironclad was viewed by the captain of the *Minnesota* with dismay; but he was shortly afterwards relieved by seeing the *Merrimac* and her companions steam up the river towards Norfolk. The great misfortune the *Monitor* experienced in the loss of her determined commander prevented her from pursuing, and forcing the battle to a surrender. No one had been killed on board either vessel. The *Merrimac* was a good deal damaged. During the fight, the working of the *Monitor* guns had been directed from the pilot-house by signals to the first lieutenant stationed in the turret; and the action proved that vessels of this character were capable of effective handling.

Concerning this eventful action, Swinton remarks: "Had the *Merrimac* continued the triumphant career which she began, it is difficult to compute her possible devastation. Beginning with the *Minnesota*, which she would quickly overcome, she would have burst through the Union fleet in Hampton Roads like an avenging fury, destroying everything in her course, and scattering all she did not destroy. The wooden fleet would have been powerless against this one mailed monster, as the story of the first day's battle tells." There certainly was a Providence in the timely arrival of this David before the modern naval Goliath.

CHAPTER IV.

THE PENINSULA CAMPAIGN, FROM YORKTOWN TO GETTYSBURG (1862–1863).

INSPIRED by the better condition of their armies, the Northern people, in the early days of 1862, became eagerly desirous for another advance on the Potomac. The Confederate position was unquestionably strong; the troops who had conquered at Bull Run and Ball's Bluff seemed capable of conquering again; and the country undoubtedly presented many difficulties to an invading force. McClellan had spent eight months organizing and disciplining his army; and the people wearied of his cautious tactics, and murmured at his "masterly inactivity."

In order to give a clear account of the campaigns about Washington and Richmond, down to the battle of Gettysburg, we shall present all these operations as one continuous narrative.

McClellan's plan was to march against Richmond from the lower part of Chesapeake Bay, by way of Urbana, on the Rappahannock. The town was not far from Richmond, and could be approached by vessels of heavy draught. Its occupation would compel the enemy to abandon his positions near Manasses, so as to cover Richmond and Norfolk. The President did not approve of this scheme; he thought it would be safer to march around Alexandria, or the entrenchments at

BATTLE OF WINCHESTER, MARCH 23, 1862.

Bull Run. He, therefore, ordered a general movement, on February 22, 1862, of the land and naval forces against the enemy's positions on the Potomac. But the early weeks of the year slipped by without anything decisive being done.

On March 10, General Joseph E. Johnston withdrew from his lines near Manasses, and took up a new position better adapted to support the defences on the Yorktown peninsula. Washington being full of spies, Johnston had been informed of the contemplated movement. Great disappointment was felt in the North that it was no longer possible to avenge the defeat of Bull Run on the very ground where it had been suffered.

At length the main body of the Union army crossed the Potomac into Virginia. Now came tremendous downfalls of rain which rendered the fords on the large rivers impassable, the destruction of the bridges interposed another obstacle to any advance, and it was speedily seen that the route by the sea was the only route open. The army was countermarched; and owing to the insufficiency of transports a fortnight elapsed before the 85,000 men could be conveyed to Fortress Monroe.

WINCHESTER.—General Banks was to open communications with the Valley of the Shenandoah, where the Confederates were still in force. He occupied Winchester, on March 12, and General Shields advanced to Strasburg, where a strong body of Confederates were posted under "Stonewall" Jackson. Here, on the 23d, Shields was attacked by Jackson, and he retreated to Winchester. The Confederates were driven back, but the battle was obstinately contested.

A little before the advance towards Manasses, took place the naval action between the *Monitor* and the *Merrimac*. McClellan felt free to change his base of operations when the ability of the *Monitor* to encounter the *Merrimac* became known to him. On April 1, he reached Fortress Monroe, and then learned that the naval fleet could render but little assistance. The *Merrimac* still kept the forces in terror, and the James River was practically closed by its lurking presence. It was too late to draw back, and 56,000 men, and 100 guns, forming the first detachment, began their march to Yorktown.

YORKTOWN (May 4, 1862).—General Magruder, who opposed McClellan, had defended the Yorktown Peninsula by a line of entrenchments, extending 13 miles. Yorktown was very slightly fortified, but the York River was dominated by powerful water batteries, and by various works on Gloucester Point. Magruder had but 11,000 men; of these 6000 were at Yorktown, and 5000 were strung along this long line of defence.

McClellan had 90,000 infantry, 10,000 cavalry, 330 field-guns, and a siege train of 103 guns. It seems remarkable that he should not have struck a telling blow at an adversary so slenderly supported, and owing his safety to the line of works by which he was covered.

On May 16, General Smith forced a passage across Warwick Creek, and 18 pieces of artillery were brought to play on the Confederate trenches. These troops were attacked, and after a sharp combat, they were driven back with considerable loss. McClellan's hesitating nature again declared itself. He gave up the direct attack on the enemy's works, and undertook the slower operations of a siege.

At the beginning of May, it was generally believed in the Union ranks that all the batteries would open fire on the Confederate works in a very few days. This would probably have been the case but that the enemy, losing heart, determined to evacuate his positions. In the early morning of May 4, it was discovered that the Confederate Army had retired, and McClellan ordered a vigorous pursuit. The Union forces had anticipated a signal victory at Yorktown, and this sudden disappearance of the foe was a great and bitter disappointment. The capture of the place was a gain of a certain kind, but it was not the brilliant success desired and expected by the country. The Southerners had accomplished their object. They had delayed the approach to Richmond; had given the authorities time for increasing the defences of the city; and brought the hot season nearer. The tedious work of crushing out the Confederacy at its capital had to be begun afresh. The pursuit of the Confederates was conducted by a strong force of infantry, cavalry, and artillery, under General Stoneman. It was hoped to cut off a portion of the rear-guard; but the hope proved delusive. The retreaters were conducting their movement in good order.

Stoneman's advance-guard at length caught up with the Confederate rear-guard, close to Fort Magruder. The fort opened fire, and a gallant attempt was made by the Union forces to take the position; but it was impossible for a mere force of cavalry to take a fortified post, and Stoneman was obliged to retire. The infantry did not arrive till after the skirmish had terminated, and the conflict could not be renewed. During the night rain fell to such an extent that in the morning the roads were converted into channels of mud, which rendered necessary the laying down of planks. The delay thus created was very prejudicial to the Union forces and equally advantageous to the Confederates. The latter had now reached the narrowest part of the peninsula between the James and York Rivers, and had there fortified themselves in the city of Williamsburg; which it was now proposed to attack.

WILLIAMSBURG.—On the morning of the 5th, General Hooker's division attacked the Confederates' forces with infantry and artillery. The forts opened fire, and the

GENERAL GEORGE B. McCLELLAN.

advancing columns were driven back after nine hours of hard fighting. They retired to the woods and held their ground till other divisions came up. Deluging rains descended on the men hurrying to Hooker's relief. The sound of the cannon was heard in front, but the advancing divisions could not hasten their pace. On McClellan's arrival, new dispositions were ordered, which soon produced their effect. The enemy was attacked at the point of the bayonet, and driven back. In two hours the battle was over. The Confederates evacuated Williamsburg during the night, and McClellan's army entered unopposed.

The Southern troops were now on their way to Richmond, and the Union forces were not in a condition to pursue at once. Some desultory fighting occurred, but the Confederates reached Richmond, with their baggage, and their supply train. They found it necessary to evacuate Norfolk. Some of the stores were saved; the rest, together with several steamers and other vessels, were destroyed; and the Confederate force marched for Richmond on May 10. Norfolk was at once occupied by General Wool. Both shores of the James River were now occupied by the Union troops, and Commodore Tatnall, who now commanded the *Merrimac*, believing he could not save the vessel, ordered her to be run ashore, set fire to, and blown up. Delivered from their enemy, the Union gunboats pushed on to within twelve miles of Richmond, but on May 15 were worsted in an encounter with some Confederate batteries at Drury's Bluff. In the meanwhile McClellan's forces were moving on Richmond by the line of the Pamunkey, and on the 21st the advance-guard had reached the River Chickahominy. The Confederate capital was now near at hand, but the most difficult and dangerous part of the expedition remained to be accomplished.

SHENANDOAH VALLEY.—About the middle of April Banks had advanced along the Shenandoah River, and established himself at Newmarket. To his right was Fremont (at Franklin); to his left McDowell, who had occupied Fredericksburg, after its surrender. Stonewall Jackson commanded the Confederate forces in the Valley. He had fewer men at his disposal, but his thorough knowledge of the country, combined with his military tact, gave him great advantage over his Union opponents.

Banks incautiously advanced up the Valley, and Jackson retreating, drew Banks after him. Banks saw that Jackson was in a dangerous position. He was placed between the regiments of Banks, moving from the east, and the advance-guard of Fremont's army, under Milroy, coming from the west. By rapid marches he got away from Banks, and hastened to the relief of a Confederate detachment menaced by Milroy's division. Having inflicted a crushing defeat on that body, he turned back with masterly suddenness on Banks. A detachment of 1200 men, under Colonel Kenly, were overpowered and nearly all killed, wounded or captured. Banks, fearing to be cut off, retreated to Winchester. An encounter with the Confederates on the 25th, outside the town, ended in the defeat of the Union troops, who were driven as far as Martinsburg; whence they continued their course to the Potomac. Since the beginning of the retreat they had marched 53 miles (35 miles of which were performed in one day). Jackson was not strong enough to pursue, and did not venture upon crossing the Potomac.

The fears prevailing at Washington calmed down after a few days, when it was found nothing more was attempted; and reinforcements were sent to Banks at Harper's Ferry. He, with Fremont (at Franklin), and McDowell (at Fredericksburg), were ordered to capture

Jackson. His position was now extremely dangerous; but by the excellence of his arrangements, and the coolness and audacity of himself and his men, he escaped. He rapidly retreated, burning the bridges as he passed.

GENERAL THOMAS J. JACKSON ("STONEWALL").

Fremont stopped him at Cross Keys (June 8). The losses on both sides were heavy, but Jackson had the best of the action, and the Union troops were not in a position to prevent Jackson falling upon Shields, who struck at him at Port Republic the next day, but was driven back, and Jackson made good his escape from the Valley, having burned the bridges behind him.

With 15,000 men Jackson occupied the attention of three generals and 60,000 men, prevented McDowell's junction with McClellan, alarmed Washington, and saved Richmond.

FAIR OAKS (May 31, 1862).—Jackson's success in the Valley embarrassed McClellan's operations in his advance on Richmond. It deprived him of the assistance of McDowell's corps, and introduced an element of uncertainty into the whole campaign. Lincoln insisted on the immediate attack of Richmond. McClellan, therefore, ordered a reconnoissance in force to be pushed forward in the direction of Hanover Court House. On May 27, General Porter marched at the head of the Fifth Corps. The Confederates were attacked, and retreated, followed by the Union cavalry and a portion of the infantry. The bridges over the Pamunkey were burned, and the adjacent railway was destroyed, after an action, in which 700 of the Confederates were brought in prisoners. The main body of McClellan's army was thus enabled to advance, and at the close of May the several corps were stationed on a curved line not far from Richmond. Two of these corps had been pushed beyond the Chickahominy River, and were exposed to a dangerous attack in the absence of their comrades, from whom they were separated by the stream at their back. Johnston had under his orders an army consisting of four divisions, commanded by Generals Longstreet, Smith, D. H. Hill and Huger, all of whom had formerly served in the U. S. Army. It was determined to attack the left wing of the Union forces on the morning of May 31; but the rains made the roads so heavy and difficult that one division of the Southern army was unable to reach the post to which it had been assigned, and was therefore prevented from taking part in the action. Longstreet nevertheless ordered Hill's division to commence the attack at 2 P. M. Casey's division of the Union Army bore the brunt of the assault. Several of the troops fell back, and the camp was captured, together with the hospital and baggage-wagons. A stand was subsequently made, and Casey sent word that he was being hard pressed, and needed reinforcements. Some time elapsed before Sumner could effect the passage of the the stream; but he at length did so by means of two hastily-constructed bridges. The battle in the meanwhile had become hot, and the right of the Union left wing was driven back with great loss. Johnston personally directed the attack until, wounded by the splinter of a shell, he fell from his horse, and broke two of his ribs, when the command devolved on General Smith. Sumner's arrival did little to change the relative positions of the combatants. The Unionists continued to fall back; the Confederates continued to advance; and it was only night which put an end to the combat.

The two armies bivouacked that night on the field for which they had so furiously contended, and the Confederates were reinforced by Huger's division, which had overcome the difficulties of the muddy and forest-cumbered roads. The engagement was renewed early next morning. It was now the Unionists that attacked, and the Confederates, finding themselves opposed by large bodies of fresh troops, fought with considerable languor and hesitation, and, after a struggle of five hours' duration, were repulsed along the whole line. The Union troops again stood on the ground they had occupied before the first day's operations. McClellan arrived towards the close of the battle. There was little for him to do; but much for him to see, and that of the most distressing nature.

The Confederates had suffered equally with their adversaries, and endured the mortification of losing the battle. Their retreat was facilitated by the forests which covered the face of the country; and even had the land been more open, it is probable that little would have been done in the way of pursuit, owing to the exhausted state of the conquerors. The Union troops lay down on the ground which they had won. The contest had been of a very sanguinary nature. During the two days' fighting the North lost 7000 men; the South also suffered terribly; yet this obstinately contested battle was attended by no definite or decisive result.

Both armies entrenched themselves in the positions they had assumed at the close of the battle, which had been designated from two localities on the field, that of Fair Oaks, or Seven Pines. McClellan applied to Washington for reinforcements; but the necessity of checking Jackson in the Valley prevented the President from sending any fresh troops to the neighborhood of Richmond.

Johnston's injuries were so severe as to compel his retirement till he had recovered from their effects. The chief command now devolved on Lee, an officer of high reputation and known ability.

THE SEVEN-DAYS BATTLES.—Lee, who had taken the command, was anxious to assume the offensive. About the middle of June the Army of the Potomac were startled by a sudden exploit of the Confederates under General J. E. Stuart. McClellan had not expected any attack on his rear. The watchful Confederates knew where he was weakest, and Stuart, after leaving Richmond, on June 13, moved along the line of rail communicating with Fredericksburg. Having penetrated as far as Kelby's Station, the forces turned eastward, and bivouacked in the vicinity of Hanover Court House, 22 miles north of Richmond. The expedition was conducted with entire secrecy. The thickness of the forest favored their designs, and at daybreak on the 14th the troops marched on Hanover Court House, where they drove in a small force of cavalry, and afterwards defeated another and a large body of mounted troops. The camp was burned, and then Stuart determined to get into the rear of the Union army, by making a circuitous march. In another direction, the main body of the Confederate cavalry captured a large train of forty wagons, took several prisoners, burned a railway bridge, and then, about midnight, made for the Chickahominy on their homeward march. It was necessary to construct an extemporary bridge over that river; but, notwithstanding all obstacles, Richmond was safely gained in about two days after the expedition had set forth. The incursion had inflicted a certain loss on the Union army, and at the same time increased the self-reliance of the Confederate cavalry; and all had been obtained with the loss of only one man.

Jackson now excited uneasiness. His position and designs were shrouded in mystery, but it seemed probable that he was concentrating a force at Gordonsville, on the railway leading to Richmond, and that he was preparing to attack the Union rear on June 28. McClellan determined to anticipate any such movement by advancing along the Williamsburg road in the vicinity of Seven Pines. This was done on the 25th, by which time the bridges over the Chickahominy were completed, and the lines of entrenchment finished. After a very arduous engagement, the Union forces at the close of the day found themselves half a mile in advance of the positions they had quitted in the morning. It was determined to make the grand attack on the enemy's lines next day; but that night McClellan received a confirmation of the rumors respecting Jackson. He wrote to the Secretary of War, stating that the rebel force was believed to be 200,000 in number, including

Jackson and Beauregard; and that he would have to contend against vastly superior odds, if those reports were true. So apprehensive did McClellan feel for the safety of his position, that, on June 26, he abandoned his base of operations on the Pamunkey for one on the James River. Jackson was marching through the country lying between the Chickahominy and the Pamunkey, while other divisions had crossed the former of those rivers, and were proceeding down the stream on the left or north-eastern bank—that is, on the side farthest from Richmond. Hill, in command of one of these divisions, attacked the village of Mechanicsville, and, taking possession of it, posted himself on the road to the Confederate capital. In conjunction with General Branch, he then assaulted the Union lines at Beaver Dam Creek. Descending the right bank of that creek, which runs into the Chickahominy, the two commanders confronted the ranks of their enemies, who were stationed on the opposite side. The attacking forces endeavored to cross, but were driven back by the terrific fire opened on them from the breastworks crowning the left bank. Foiled in this attempt, they occupied a position on the right bank, and at nine o'clock at night the combat terminated without any definite results. Lee, who commanded in person intended to cut off that portion of the Union army which was encamped on the left bank of the Chickahominy; but he failed in his design. Still McClellan felt insecure, and during the night withdrew his troops to a position some two miles lower down the Chickahominy. He was mistaken in assuming that he had 200,000 men in his front. The Confederate forces were not more than half that strength; and, as McClellan himself had command of about 95,000 troops, his inferiority to the enemy was but slight.

On the night of June 26, General McCall, on the extreme right of the Union position, was ordered to fall back on the bridges across the Chickahominy near Gaines' Mill, to join Porter's corps, and to make a stand in that locality, in order to give the army time to carry out its change of position. Porter was not to cross the bridges until evening, and was then to destroy them. Early on the 27th, the Confederate division under Hill, which had been held in check the previous day, opened a heavy fire of artillery on the front ranks of McCall, who retreated farther down the stream. Other Confederate troops now crossed the Chickahominy near Mechanicsville, and shortly afterwards the whole of the Southern line, except the right wing, under General Magruder, was ordered to advance.

Porter's retreating corps were presently assaulted, but they stood firm, and, after a fierce and doubtful encounter, the Confederates gave way in considerable disorder. Being reinforced and formed anew, they again advanced to the attack, but as yet with no better success than before. Towards nightfall, they brought up large bodies of reserves, and the Union left, where the men had been fighting all day, and were exhausted, receded with precipitation. The alarm soon extended to the centre of the Union lines, which also fell back in confusion, until supported by fresh brigades under Generals Meagher and French. The presence of these troops, and the opening of a battery which had been placed in position, checked the pursuit of the enemy, and darkness soon afterwards closed over the scene.

During the night, the train of 5000 wagons, the siege-train, 2500 oxen and other material were in motion for the James River. The bridges over the Chickahominy were then destroyed, and Keyes' corps took possession of the road across the White Oak Swamp, and of the principal lines of communication by which the Union army could be annoyed by the enemy. The wounded were abandoned where they lay, and many perished in the woods and swamps. The Confederates flattered themselves that McClellan would be cut off from all power of retreat, and that the capture or destruction of the entire Union army was certain. They were disapointed on finding that the immense stores accumulated at the White House had been partly removed and partly destroyed by McClellan's instructions, and that the several divisions had crossed the river. No further steps could be taken on the 28th, owing to the necessity of burying the dead, attending to the wounded, and allowing an interval of repose to the others; but it was hoped to pursue the retreating adversary on the following day. The two armies were now divided by the line of the Chickahominy. The greater number of the Confederates were on the left bank, and the whole of McClellan's army had been united on the right bank. It was the afternoon of the 28th before Lee understood that his opponent was on his road to the James River, to form a junction with the fleet. It was believed, however, that this design could be frustrated, and measures were taken for intercepting the Union army, and cutting off its communications with the river. The morning of the 29th was spent by McClellan's troops in destroying all that could not be carried away. The corps of Sumner and Franklin were left at Fair Oaks, with instructions to protect the baggage and supply-trains on their way to the James River; and McClellan pursued his course with the main body of the army. He was in a position of much gravity; but, strange to say, the Confederates at Richmond were equally exposed to a reverse. After the action of the 27th, the Union troops were much nearer to the Southern capital than the chief divisions of the Confederates. The latter were posted on the farther side of the Chickahominy; the Union troops had been compelled to cross the stream, and were now on the side where Richmond itself is situated. The corps of Sumner and Franklin, acting as a rear-guard, were attacked, on the 30th, by Jackson, but maintained their ground, and prevented the further advance of the enemy. Later in the day a battle was fought with the main body of the Confederates, who were attempting to advance so as to cut off the Union retreat. They were led by Longstreet, Hill, and Huger, and a conflict of the most furious and desperate nature took place between the opposing armies. Hill charged the Union masses several times; and it seemed as if the Northern troops would have driven their opponents back upon Richmond, and have entered that city at the head of their victorious legions. 'The cry of "On to Richmond!" was raised by them, and the imminent danger of losing their metropolis excited the Confederates to the pitch of madness. The contending ranks were mixed together in a dark, bloody and tumultuous affray. Fighting hand to hand, in the rage of mortal hate, they neither asked nor gave quarter, but seemed bent on mutual extermination, if that were a thing possible. On no previous occasion had the two sides fought with such unmitigated ferocity. The hot and murderous encounter swayed to and fro with varying success; the ground was strewn with dead; and the horrible conflict did not terminate even with the approach of night. When at length the combatants ceased from sheer exhaustion, no substantial advantage had been obtained by either. The Confederates were checked, but not repulsed; the Unionists held their ground, but were not delivered from the threatened peril. On the 30th, the long lines of baggage-wagons reached the height called Malvern Hill; and here they were in a position of some strength, and in communication with their transports and supplies.

BATTLE OF MALVERN HILL (JULY 1, 1862).

All the Union divisions were united at Malvern Hill during the night, and the worst dangers had now been overcome. The Confederates were still close at hand; but the position occupied by the Northern troops was favorable to defence, and in any case the river was available for retreat.

The several corps had their backs to the river, and the left flank, held by Porter, was strengthened as much as possible, since it was in that direction that the enemy would be most likely to attack, supposing him to resolve on any further movement. That such was his intention became manifest as the day proceeded. Some skirmishing took place before noon, but nothing like a a general action occurred until three, when the Confederate artillery opened on Kearney's division of Heintzelman's corps, and on other portions of the army stationed towards the right of the line. The Confederates advanced at the charge, but were driven back by the steady fire which was poured into their columns. The attempt to carry the position was frequently renewed, and the Confederates reformed their shattered ranks in the shelter of the surrounding woods. In this encounter, the troops engaged on the Southern side were from Magruder's corps, which on the previous night had supported the divisions of Longstreet, Hill, and Huger, in their desperate attack on Heintzelman's forces. Toward the evening of July 1, Magruder's regiments were reinforced by those of Jackson, who arrived from the White Oak Swamp, but too late to render any important service. When darkness put an end to the strife, the Union forces were still in undisturbed possession of the ground and the Confederates had been worsted, with a serious loss in dead and wounded. The latter, finding that the adversary was now beyond their power, withdrew to Richmond and the Army of the Potomac took up a position at Harrison's Landing.

which had been selected by the engineers and naval officers as the most favorable spot for defence and for receiving supplies. By the night of July 3 all McClellan's divisions were in safety, and the general believed he had acquired a base of operations from which another advance on Richmond might in time be made.

The movements executed by McClellan from June 25 to July 1, had cost him dear, and left him in a worse position than before. He estimated his losses at 15,249 men, and 25 guns; Lee, in a proclamation from Richmond, issued on July 9, said that the immediate fruits of the Confederate triumph were—"the relief of Richmond from a state of siege; the rout of the great army that so long menaced its safety; many thousand prisoners, including officers of high rank; the capture and destruction of stores of the value of millions; and the acquisition of thousands of arms, and fifty-one pieces of superior artillery." It is probable that the truth lay somewhere between the two statements, but in any case it is clear that McClellan had reaped nothing but disaster. Still, it must be recollected that his opponents were unfortunate as well as himself. The Confederates had lost 20,000 men, and although the enemy had withdrawn farther from the threatened capital, he was not vanquished, nor completely driven away, and it seemed probable that the operations of the last few months would be renewed, with a more resolute determination than before.

CEDAR MOUNTAIN.—Secretary Stanton visited McClellan to learn whether there was any possibility of an advance on Richmond in the position which the Army of the Potomac then held. McClellan demanded 50,000 additional troops for any ulterior operations. These could not be sent without leaving Washington and Baltimore defenceless. McClellan was then ordered to unite with General Pope, and to act under his command.

Pope's main divisions were at Culpepper, about 70 miles from both Washington and Richmond; and at Fredericksburg, which was connected with Washington by steamboat and railway. He had about 38,000 men, and one part of his design was to cover Washington, while at the same time he diverted a portion of the Confederacy then threatening McClellan.

Early in August, the Union out-pickets reported that the enemy was advancing towards Culpepper Court House. On the 8th, Jackson crossed the Rapidan, and took up a position near the main road from Gordonsville to Culpepper. Fighting did not occur until next day, when an obstinately-contested action took place in the vicinity of a hill called Cedar Mountain. The battle commenced at five P. M., and continued until late in the evening, by which time the Union troops had been driven back about a mile. The action might, perhaps, have been resumed next morning but for a disastrous incident which occurred late at night. The light of a bright moon showed the Confederate artillerymen that their adversaries, as they bivouacked on the ground, were within range of their guns. They at once opened fire, and a panic spread through a portion of the Union army. Some of the Confederate cavalry then charged the weary and dispirited troops, and Pope himself, with the officers of his staff, narrowly escaped capture. The loss on both sides was very serious, especially on that of the Unionists; but, the latter having been reinforced, Jackson retreated during the night of the 11th, and, recrossing the Rapidan, got safely off. The Government was so much alarmed at this exploit of Jackson, that McClellan was ordered to detach the divisions under Burnside (who had recently been recalled from North Carolina), and send them to Aquia Creek. At the same time, McClellan himself was to retreat to Yorktown and Fortress Monroe with a view to ulterior movements. The stores, baggage, and sick, belonging to the sometime Army of the Potomac, were shipped on board the transports at Harrison's Landing, and from the 17th to the 20th of August the army marched by way of Williamsburg to Yorktown and Newport News. The defences at Yorktown were strengthened, and the campaign in the Peninsula was now at an end, after a series of operations extending over four months, involving an immense expenditure of life, yet productive of no results commensurate with the efforts that had been made.

Great activity and boldness were evinced by the Southern troops, and on August 22 Stuart marched into the rear of the Union troops, seized a good deal of the headquarters' baggage (including letters and plans of the commander), and got safely off. It was now determined to execute a flank march round the right wing of Pope's army. The corps under Jackson was concentrated at Jefferson, opposite the Sulphur Springs, and on August 21 set out for THOROUGHFARE GAP. The men were badly clothed, and so ill-provided with food that they were compelled to feed on grain which they plucked in the open fields, and on the offerings of the peasantry. But they had confidence in themselves and in their commander, and thus inspirited they made their way through the mountain-pass which conducted them to the rear of their opponents. Pope had by this time been joined by most of the divisions under McClellan, and the combined army was both numerically strong and well appointed. But the soldiers were not pleased with their chief, and were wanting in the military qualities of subordination and self-reliance. These facts will explain the disasters which ensued.

Jackson was favored with his usual success in the the daring enterprise on which he had entered. Thoroughfare Gap was so entirely free of Union soldiers that his troops encountered no opposition in passing through it, and on the evening of the 26th they struck the line of rail in Pope's rear at Bristow Station. The great depot at Manassas Junction was captured and set on fire, and the Union commanders seem to have been bewildered as to the exact locality of their opponents, and the precise combinations they ought to make in order to repel so threatening a movement. Taking advantage of this perplexity on the part of the Northern chiefs, the Southerners continued to advance, and to get still farther in Pope's rear. Some of them pushed forward to the old battle-ground of Bull Run, while others proceeded to Centreville. Jackson's corps was now actually between the Union army and Washington. A large amount of stores had been destroyed; the telegraph wires had been severed, and the rails torn up; so that Pope's forces were at once discomfited and cut off from succor. When, however, they had recovered from their astonishment, they took measures for attacking the enemy, and, if possible, crushing him in his exposed position. Hooker's division had an encounter with Jackson's rear-guard, at Bristow Station, on the evening of the 27th. Pope marched along the Orange and Alexandria Railway, while McDowell, at the head of another large force, moved from Warrenton, with the intention of interposing between Jackson and his line of retreat by Thoroughfare Gap. Jackson was certainly in danger of being annihilated It is true that the remainder of Lee's army was marching to his assistance; but it was still in the defiles of the Blue Ridge Mountains, and might not arrive in time. The efforts of the Union forces were thwarted by the want of concentrated supervision, by the scattered positions of the several corps, and by the confused and contradictory orders sent out from headquarters.

Jackson appeared still confident of success. He now

reversed his course, and moved south, to meet the Union troops who were following on his track. On the 28th, General Kearney attacked the rear of Jackson's corps, and, occupying Centreville, reopened the communication with Alexandria, which the Southerners had momentarily closed. Towards the end of the day, a portion of Sigel's corps had an engagement with the Confederates, which resulted in the latter gaining possession of a ridge of hills near Sudley Springs, on the north-eastern bank of Bull Run. By the morning of the 29th, a large part of Jackson's corps had reached the other side of the stream, and he took up a position similar to that of McDowell when, in the same locality, he advanced against the rebels on July 21, 1861. The left of the Confederate line was now stationed near Centreville, on the ridge of hills which had been seized the previous night; the right and centre were on the opposite bank of the little river, and stretched along the Manassas Gap Railway towards the main road from Warrenton. The several divisions, consequently, faced towards the south-east, and from that direction were attacked during the day by the Union troops, who had united their forces on the old battle-ground of a year before. Pope reached the field about noon, after the action had been going on for some time; but he doubted the propriety of ordering an advance along the whole line, as many of his troops had suffered severely from the fire of their antagonists. He was expecting the arrival of McDowell and Porter; but Jackson himself was reinforced by the appearance, towards sunset, of the leading division of Longstreet's corps, which, after overcoming the resistance offered to its progress through the defile of Thoroughfare Gap, joined the regiments that had been contending since morning on the banks of Bull Run. Previous to this welcome advent, the Confederates, though inflicting serious loss on their opponents, had been compelled to give ground slightly; and Pope telegraphed a victory to Washington. In the afternoon he had been reinforced by McDowell; but Porter's corps did not arrive during the 29th. Its commander was afterwards tried for disobedience of orders, and dismissed the service; and certainly he appears to have done nothing towards helping the operations of the day. When darkness put an end to the combat, no decisive result had been achieved. The advantage, on the whole, was with the Union forces, for the Southerners had receded, but the Northern troops had been very sharply received, and were out of spirits with respect to their commanders. The Confederates were full of confidence, and eager for renewed action on the morrow.

Early next morning the remaining divisions of Longstreet's corps, which had been arriving all through the night, had joined the corps under Jackson, and the Confederate army was now very strong. Longstreet took the right of the line, and the united forces covered a distance of five miles. Porter's corps was in position on this second day, and indeed commenced the battle by attacking some of the forces under Longstreet. A general action followed, and continued for several hours, with terrible slaughter on both sides; and, toward evening, Lee, who was now commanding in person, ordered an advance. The Union troops who had already begun to lose form under the devastating fire of some batteries of artillery posted in commanding positions, were driven back in confusion, and, under cover of darkness, crossed Bull Run, and took refuge behind the field-works at Centreville, where they were supported by the corps under Sumner and Franklin, which had arrived from Alexandria and the lines round Washington. The losses of the two previous days had been immense, and they were not due solely to death and injury in the field. Skulking had gone on to an extraordinary extent, and in many instances these fugitives could not be recovered. Banks, who had lingered behind at Bristow Station, in order to guard the railway, now hastily marched to join his comrades, having previously destroyed large quantities of stores and railway stock. When all Pope's divisions were concentrated behind the entrenchments at Centreville, the army felt tolerably secure against further mischances, though its confidence soon proved to be misplaced. Lee hesitated about attacking the enemy in front, now that he occupied so strong a position; but a demonstration against the right flank was made on September 1, and Pope, finding the Confederates on the road to Fairfax Court House, and actually threatening Washington, begun to retreat with precipitation. Night closed in on the disheartened and scared ranks of the Union army; a violent thunderstorm broke over them; and the rear was harassed by frequent attacks. On the morning of the 2d, the whole of the Union legions (including the divisions at Fredericksburg and Aquia Creek) entered the fortifications immediately protecting Washington, where they were a year before.

One thing was clear—that Pope must be removed from the position to which he had been appointed under a total misapprehension of his abilities. McClellan was reinstated in his command and assigned to the protection of Washington. For this purpose no better man could have been selected. His genius lay much more in defence than in attack. Where an enemy was to be assaulted or out-manœuvred, a certain timidity always restrained him, so that his opportunities slipped by again and again. But he was an admirable organizer, a strict disciplinarian, a watchful observer of what was going on in his front. He had saved Washington before, and might save it again by his prudence and caution. In conferring on McClellan the control of the Washington Army the President did not restore him to the position he had held from the beginning of November, 1861, to the early part of March, 1862. Halleck still remained at the head of the military forces, and McClellan came under his directions.

Pope was sent off to Minnesota to look after the predatory Indians.

THE INVASION OF MARYLAND.—Flushed with success, Lee now crossed the Potomac, and entered Maryland, hoping to secure volunteers and incite an insurrection. Jackson's corps entered Frederick City, on September 6, while Lee continued his march into Maryland. Jackson advanced up the northern bank of the river, and recrossing into Virginia he occupied Martinsburg, where he seized a large quantity of stores. Harper's Ferry was invested by Jackson, and on both sides of the Potomac squadrons of cavalry guarded the direct road to Pennsylvania. So far Lee had been entirely successful.

McClellan was ordered to pursue the invaders. He had nearly 100,000 men under him, beside the garrisons at Harper's Ferry and Washington. To meet this immense army, the Confederates had about 75,000 men. Lee was put to great difficulty in avoiding the consequence of his spirited and daring movements. He abandoned the line of the Monocacy, sent a portion of Longstreet's forces to Boonesboro', north-west of Frederick; and directed Hill to guard the passes of South Mountain, and to cover the siege of Harper's Ferry.

Lee's order to Hill fell into McClellan's hands. From this it appeared that Lee's aim was to obtain possession of the ferry, where a garrison of 11,000 men were under the command of Colonel Miles. The position was strongly entrenched on heights overlooking the ferry, and commanding the main road from the Shenandoah Valley to Frederick and Baltimore. Three distinct portions of Lee's army made a vehement attack on Miles on the 13th. Powerful batteries were erected, and on the morning of the 15th a cross fire of terrible intensity was poured into the Union entrenchments. Miles felt obliged to surrender. A small body of cavalry escaped into Pennsylvania; but the rest were made prisoners of war, and 73 pieces of artillery, 13,000 small arms, and other stores fell into the hands of the victors.

McClellan's troops were moving to the relief of Harper's Ferry; but they had obstacles to overcome. The passage of South Mountain was stoutly disputed by the Confederates. McClellan's subordinates showed extreme dilatoriness in bringing up their respective divisions, and the afternoon had arrived before the main body could come into action. Ultimately, however, the Confederates were driven back. They were reinforced by Longstreet, and the contest was resumed with much energy. At nightfall no great advantage had been gained on either side, but the Confederates had succeeded in delaying the progress of the Union troops.

Lee was in a dilemma, although he had sustained no decided reverse. Different portions of his force were separated from each other, not only by the Potomac, but by McClellan's army, which was moving forward in a north-westerly direction by roads leading from the two passes through which the troops had forced their way. But there was no time to be lost. On withdrawing from South Mountain, Lee took up a position on a a range of hills extending in a semi-circle from the lower part of Antietam Creek to an angle of the Potomac, a little nearer to the north-west. Lee was now established on the western side of Antietam Creek, the lower part of which, near its junction with the Potomac, protected the right of his line. He had his back to a bend of the Potomac, with his face turned to the north-east; and the centre of his line was at Sharpsburg. The

Antietam is crossed by four bridges, and at that part of its course is too deep to be forded by troops. Jackson was summoned from Harper's Ferry. Lee's object was to concentrate nearly all his forces on the hills about Antietam Creek, as he knew he would soon be attacked by a superior force. Jackson's troops were so much exhausted by their previous exertions that many of them straggled and fell out, and only a portion of their number reached Lee on the 16th. Fortunately for the Southerners, the Union troops also were slow in their proceedings. Their movements were extremely sluggish, and McClellan waited for the arrival of *all* his divisions on the eastern side of the creek before he ventured on offering battle. As they came up he massed them on both sides of the road leading to Sharpsburg. Three of the bridges across the creek were in front of him; but they were covered by Lee's batteries. McClellan planted his own batteries, and fighting began on the 17th.

In the early morning the Union batteries on the left bank opened fire on the opposing lines drawn up beyond the bridges. Thus aided, three divisions crossed the stream, and facing to the west, began a vigorous attack on the left of the Confederate line, that being the weakest point. Excepting as regarded position, McClellan was the better off. He had nearly 95,000 men at his disposal. Lee, owing to the non-arrival of a large part of his army, had no more than 35,000 at the beginning of the engagement. That small force, however, was animated by the courage of desperation. Hooker's three divisions established themselves upon the other side of the creek, and erected field-batteries in a belt of wood which at that part covered the land. A sanguinary conflict ensued; but the Confederates held their ground for some hours, though more than half the brigades forming the first line were either killed or wounded, together with nearly every regimental commander. At length they were borne down, and the Union troops pressed forward, cleared the woods of their opponents, and took possession of Dunker Church, situated to the north of Sharpsburg. Beyond this point the Confederates made a fresh stand, and changed their defence into an attack, causing the Union line in some places to break and recede. Reinforcements to Lee's army arriving, the attack was renewed with confidence and energy, and nearly all the lost ground was in time regained.

Hooker's corps was completely routed. Portions of Sumner's corps were also considerably shaken; but the artillery in the first line of woods now came once more into play, and the Confederate pursuit was checked. Fresh Union divisions were hurried up to retrieve the fortunes of the day; but they did little to alter the general posture of affairs. During the action on the left, McClellan visited the field in person, and felt uneasy as to the result of the several operations. The attack made by his right had to a great extent failed, and he feared the enemy would attack his center, and break his whole line of battle into fragments.

On the Union left, Burnside's corps at an early hour of the day had been given the very difficult task of carrying the lower bridge over the Antietam. The approaches were swept away by the enemy's batteries, and it was only after a severe struggle that the opposite bank of the creek was gained. The heights were not in Burnside's possession until the afternoon; but by that time the Confederates had been driven back. After a while they rallied, and bringing up fresh troops, recommenced the combat. Burnside's advance had carried him almost to Sharpsburg, near the center of the Confederate line; but the Southerners on the arrival of their reinforcements, opened new batteries on the hills, and drove back Burnside from the position he had carried, so that it was all he could do to hold the bridge. McClellan ordered Burnside to hold the bridge at all risks, but did nothing to help him by sending up fresh troops. Porter's reserves were posted between the two wings; but McClellan feared to employ them, lest the Confederates should break through his center in their absence. Burnside maintained his ground, and when night came on, both wings of the attacking force were still on that side of the stream, though in positions not so far advanced as those occupied earlier in the day. The troops bivouacked on the ground that night and McClellan telegraphed to Washington that he had gained a victory. McClellan had been in a specially good position for overwhelming his antagonists. When the action began his numbers were more than two to one; and even after the arrival of the Confederate reinforcements, Lee had not nearly so many men as his opponent. Moreover, McClellan had by a rare stroke of luck acquired a knowledge beforehand of Lee's designs, and of the disposition of his several corps; and the component parts of the Confederate army had for a time been separated by the advancing forces of the North. Yet, owing to that extraordinary hesitation which neutralized all McClellan's better qualities, every opportunity had been thrown away, and the general result was little short of failure. There had been no attack along the whole line, and the right and left wings had been checked in detail by operations which the Confederates had had time to transfer from one part of the field to another, as occasion required.

The losses of the day were severe. On the Union side, the killed and wounded amounted to about 12,500, and among them were many general and superior officers. The Confederates had to mourn the loss of 9000 men, together with some of their divisional com-

BATTLE OF ANTIETAM—TAKING THE BRIDGE.

manders; and for all this expenditure of life neither side could show any result of equal value. The following day was passed in inactivity, for both armies were too much exhausted to renew the battle. The Southerners were sadly weakened by the fighting, and it appears that their total strength was now reduced to less than 60,000 men. Disorganization existed on both sides.

The invasion of Northern territory, although daringly conceived and ably conducted, had entailed considerable losses on Lee's army, and had brought home to the Confederates the unwelcome knowledge that the rebellion had no chance of spreading north of the Potomac.

McCLELLAN'S REMOVAL. On November 7, 1862, McClellan was ordered to surrender the command of his army to General Burnside, and to report at Trenton, New Jersey (his home). Halleck alleged that he had needlessly delayed his movements; that he was constantly complaining of want of supplies, clothing, and horses; and that there had been no such want as to prevent his compliance with the order of October 6, to cross the Potomac at once, and give battle to the enemy, or drive him south. Burnside was a personal friend of McClellan, and possessed his confidence. He had on two or three occasions exhibited a fair amount of skill as a general, and had, before, been requested to take the position of McClellan, but refused, and now accepted the command only on the peremptory order of the War Department.

The position of the Union army rendered Lee anxious for the safety of Richmond. He feared that his communications with that city might be severed, and he had an extensive tract of country to watch with a comparatively small force. While he was considering what he should do, Burnside was reorganizing his army with a view to active measures. He now arranged it in three grand divisions, under the orders of Sumner, Hooker, and Franklin; and a body of reserves was formed, under the command of General Sigel. It was decided to make a demonstration on the Rappahannock, to march rapidly down the north-eastern bank of that river, to cross by means of pontoons at Fredericksburg, and to advance on Richmond by Hanover Court House. Accordingly, a few days later, Sumner was ordered to march on Fredericksburg, followed by Franklin and Hooker. The right rear of the army was to be protected by the cavalry under General Pleasanton, while Sigel was to guard the Upper Potomac, and to occupy the direct route between Gordonsville and Washington. The success of the plan depended on the rapidity with which it was carried out; but there proved to be delays that were not anticipated. Burnside calculated on Jackson being still west of the Blue Ridge, and on Lee having no knowledge of the scheme by which he was to be out-manœuvred. In

AMBROSE E. BURNSIDE.

these respects he was mistaken; and the consequence was another miscarriage, in addition to those which had gone before.

FREDERICKSBURG.—Lee had received information of Burnside's projects, and a portion of his army had consequently moved on a parallel line to that of the Union forces. The movements of his detachments were executed with greater quickness than those of Sumner and his colleagues, and the Confederate batteries were already posted at Fredericksburg, on the southern side of the Rappahannock, when, on November 20, Sumner's troops arrived at Falmouth, on the northern side. It was evident, therefore, that Fredericksburg could not be occupied without an engagement, and that the undisputed advance on Richmond, which it had been hoped to accomplish, was no longer possible. Still, something might have been done had Burnside been able to cross the river at once; but the necessary pontoons had not arrived, and he was obliged to wait. The delay was much to the advantage of the Confederates, for it gave time to Jackson to join the other forces, so that by the 25th the whole Confederate Army was in position on the heights overlooking Fredericksburg. It was the policy of the Southerners to await attack; it was equally Burnside's policy to eject them from their posts by a vigorous assault. But for the present no movement was possible. Three weeks passed in this state of compulsory inaction. Burnside at length felt compelled by the stress of popular opinion to do something. He determined to cross the river as soon as he could complete his pontoon bridges. The passage was to be effected at two points—immediately opposite Fredericksburg, and a mile and a half lower down the stream. Burnside had now no fewer than 150,000 men; his line extended over four miles on the northern side of the river; his guns, which were extremely numerous, commanded the town of Fredericksburg, and the opposite bank of the Rappahannock; and he was therefore able to make a powerful demonstration, with fair probabilities of success. Lee's forces did not amount to more than 80,000 men: but they held a strong position on a semicircle of hills sweeping round from the river to the vicinity of Newport. Lee also was well provided with artillery, which he massed towards his center. To the right of his line he had the little river Massaponax; other small rivers ran through the hills on which his divisions had been drawn up; and in every respect his position was one which a resolute army would be likely to maintain.

During the night of December 10, the Union pontoons were carried down to the river, and the artillery was so placed as to be capable of being brought to bear immediately on the town. Next morning the men commenced building four extemporary bridges. For some hours the work of construction was not perceived by the Confederates on the opposite bank, but when it was discovered a heavy fire of musketry opened from various positions on the shore, and from the houses in the town. The Union troops were for a time driven away, but, having been rallied, they again proceeded with their task. Once more they were compelled to abandon the attempt, and orders were then given to the artillery to open fire on the city. This dispersed the Confederate sharpshooters, and did great damage to the city itself. The operation of throwing over the pontoon bridges was once more resumed, and although the Confederates for a time interrupted the progress of the work, they were unable to prevent its completion in the course of a day. Before dusk, Sumner's division had got over, together with a section of Hooker's. The transit was resumed early on the 12th, without further molestation; and

Burnside massed his corps near the river, in readiness for an advance when the proper moment had arrived.

Very little of importance took place that day; but the battle known as that of Fredericksburg began at an early hour on December 13, 1862. Franklin misunderstood Burnside's orders, and, instead of making a vigorous attack on the Confederate right, did nothing more than execute a feint, though he had two army corps under his command, and might therefore have struck a telling blow against the adversary. Burnside had hoped to cut the Confederate army into two portions, and, having taken the heights beyond Fredericksburg, to destroy the right wing of his enemy; but he had entirely miscalculated the knowledge possessed by Lee of the manner in which he was to be assailed. Lee declined to weaken his line, so as to repel a false attack which Burnside had ordered to be made some miles below Fredericksburg. Had he fallen into the trap thus laid for him, it is possible that he might have been beaten in detail; but he kept his troops well together. On the left of the Union line an attempt was made to drive the Confederates across the Massaponax, by turning their position; but, although the Southern troops were forced back nearly a mile, no decided advantage was gained. Franklin misapprehended his orders, and failed to bring up all his divisions, and to press the attack with vigor. On the right of the line, the fighting was desperate the whole day. The Confederates were posted among the woods and hills at the back of Fredericksburg, and two Union divisions were ordered to expel them at the point of the bayonet. In the face of a tremendous artillery fire, the assault was renewed again and again; but as often as the endeavor was made, the regiments were shattered and driven back in extreme confusion. Sumner ordered up his artillery in support of the attacking force, and the contest continued until dark, without the

FREDERICKSBURG.

Union troops winning a single yard, or their opponets being dispossessed of the positions they had assumed in the morning. During this terrible combat, which strewed the plain with dead and wounded, Lee personally superintended the operations of his men. Towards the close of the attempt to carry this strong position— made all the stronger by a stone wall behind which the Confederates were entrenched—Burnside sent instructions to Hooker, who with a larger part of his division was still on the other side of the river, to hasten his men over the bridges, so that he might support Sumner and his lieutenants. Hooker proceeded to the scene of action, but soon afterwards sent word to his superior that the heights were impregnable. Burnside insisted on the movement being carried out, and Hooker then sent forward one of his divisions, with orders to assault the position. Nothing, however, could be done. The men staggered back before the terrible fire of their opponents, and, leaving a third of their number on the ground, sought shelter in the rear. At half-past five in the evening, the musketry fire ceased; that of the artillery continued until long after dark.

Next day was Sunday, and both armies remained comparatively quiet. It was a day of great misery and depression. The shattered houses of Fredericksburg were crowded with the dead and dying, and there were numerous stragglers, who would have crossed the bridges to the northern side of the river, had they not been driven back by the guards posted there. In many instances the men refused to be led forward again, so that Burnside felt that he was in no position to renew the struggle. Personally, he was desirous of once more advancing against the enemy; but his lieutenants saw that in the existing temper of the troops such a movement could entail none but the most fatal consequences. To many it was a subject of surprise that

Lee did not assume the offensive on the 14th, and by a determined onslaught drive his enemy into the river. It appeared that Lee expected to be himself attacked; at any rate, he made no preparations for an advance, but on the contrary threw up fresh works of defence. His army was inferior to that of Burnside, and the batteries on the opposite side of the Rappahannock were sufficiently powerful to suggest caution. Probably for these reasons, combined with ignorance of the real condition of the Union troops, the Confederates remained inactive and so allowed the Northerners to repair the disaster they had suffered. There was, in truth, only one way of repairing it, and that was by a retreat across the river. Influenced by the advice of his generals, Burnside determined to withdraw from the perilous position in which he found himself. The greater number of the wounded were removed on the 15th, and during the ensuing night the army evacuated Fredericksburg, and retired to its former lines. Lee was astonished, on the 16th, at beholding nothing before him but a deserted land, a ruined town, a winding river, and a line of batteries frowning from the opposite shore.

The Union loss was certainly great. It probably amounted, in killed, wounded, and missing, to 13,771 men. The "missing" are said to have been 2078. The Southerners, having been sheltered by their works, lost comparatively few men; the total is stated at 1800. The affair altogether was most disastrous to the Union cause; but Burnside took upon himself the entire responsibility of the movement. He attributed his reverses to the fog on the morning of the 11th, and to the unexpected and unavoidable delay in building the pontoon bridges, which gave the enemy 24 hours to concentrate his forces in a strong position. "As it was," he said, in his report to Halleck, "we came very near success. Failing in accomplishing the main object, we remained in order of battle two days—long enough to decide that the enemy would not come out of his strongholds to fight us with his infantry." Burnside was perhaps hardly to be blamed for the misfortune by which he had been overtaken. His plan of operations had a reasonable chance of success, and it failed partly because the Confederates were in a stronger position than had been supposed, and partly because the Union troops were not so well handled by the subordinate generals as had been hoped. Nevertheless, the ruin of Burnside's scheme proved the ruin of Burnside himself. He had now entirely lost his hold on the officers and men under his command. Desertions were increasing to an alarming extent, and he found himself confronting a powerful enemy with a weapon which was almost broken in his hand. The army before Fredericksburg accordingly remained inactive for several weeks.

CHANCELLORSVILLE (May 2, 3, 1863).—Burnside, after his defeat at Fredericksburg, was succeeded by General Hooker, on January 26, 1863. Winter passed away without any actions of importance. Nothing on a large scale could be begun because the roads at this season are flooded with rains so as to make the movement of large bodies of men almost impossible. From the commencement of hostilities till the beginning of 1863 there had been about 2000 battles and skirmishes. The expenditure of men and money had been appalling, and the end seemed still distant. The Confederate Army was at its strongest about the beginning of 1863; its numbers soon afterwards diminished to a considerable extent, owing to the expiration of the term of enlistment of several of the men. In the spring of that year, the numerical superiority of the Northerners was marked.

Longstreet and his corps had been sent off to Tennessee to assist General Bragg. This left Lee with but 60,000 men to oppose the Potomac army of over 100,000 men, and offered a favorable opportunity for an attack.

In this condition of affairs, it became known that Hooker was contemplating a renewed attack on Richmond. The Confederate capital was at the same time being threatened by General Foster, operating from North Carolina, by General Peck from South-eastern Virginia, and by General Key from the vicinity of the Pamunkey. Lee was therefore compelled to divide his forces among several localities, and the numbers at his disposal were small in comparison with those of his opponent. Hooker determined to make his attack in two places. To cross the Rappahannock and Rapidan some distance west of Fredericksburg, and so fall on the left wing of the Confederates, while at the same time his own left wing should occupy the heights above the same city, and seize the Richmond Railway. The cavalry was to co-operate with these movements by getting round the Confederate position, cutting off the retreat of Lee's army on Richmond, destroying the railways and burning the bridges over the North and South Anna Rivers. Crossing the Rapidan on the 30th, the Union troops entered an uncultivated and almost deserted country called the Wilderness. Here they camped near Chancellorsville, and were presently joined by two more corps. Sedgwick made a simultaneous movement across the Rappahannock below Fredericksburg, and Lee was thus perplexed as to the precise direction in which he was to be attacked.

In a little while it became evident that the brunt of the battle would be at Chancellorsville, and, on the night of April 30, Lee massed the greater number of his divisions on the roads leading from Fredericksburg to that town. A detachment under Early was left to guard the lower position, and Lee threw up some earthworks on the roads which would be traversed by the enemy. The Union cavalry were already in possession of the Richmond Railway, a portion of which had been destroyed; so that, in the event of the Confederates being vanquished, their retreat would be seriously endangered. The position was undoubtedly very perilous, and some of the Confederate officers looked upon it with gloomy forebodings. Lee himself, however, was cheerful and self-possessed.

Hooker directed an advance to be made from the vicinity of Chancellorsville towards Fredericksburg. Immediately after, on ascertaining that Lee was marching against him with his whole army, he drew back on a line of earthworks and felled trees which he had hastily constructed in the forest, and which he strengthened during the evening and night. His front was towards the east, and Fredericksburg was the objective point at which he aimed. He desired to choose his own ground for fighting, and force his opponent into accepting it; but Lee was too wary to be thus entrapped. Hooker was endeavoring to outflank the Confederate; the latter determined that he should himself be outflanked. Lee therefore sent the corps under Jackson round the right rear of the Northern army, while with but two divisions he kept the army engaged in front. The chances were very much against the Southerners; but the desperate nature of their situation required a bold and daring policy. Nothing could be better suited to secret operations than the character of the land where the contending armies were now watching one another. The whole of the country is covered with dense forests, and in the midst of these tangled thickets the Union pioneers had thrown up very strong entrenchments at right angles to the turnpike and plank-roads which connect Chancellorsville with Fredericksburg. Drawn up within the line of their entrenchments, with their artillery massed on some high ground a little in the rear, the Northerners presented a formidable appearance, and it was at once evident to Lee that any attempt to carry the position from the front must be attended by a fearful loss of life, and would probably end in failure.

Fighting occurred on May 1, though not to any serious extent. It was necessary to the success of Lee's plans that he should conceal the flank movement of Jackson, and he therefore made a series of feigned attacks on his front. Hooker was thus led to suppose that the Confederates were in full strength immediately before his position, and, conceiving it advisable that he should be supported by nearly the whole of his forces, he ordered Reynolds' division to cross the Rappahannock, and join the main army about Chancellorsville. While this movement was being carried out, Jackson was commencing his flank march. He started on the night of May 1, taking with him three divisions, commanded by Hill, Coulson, and Rhodes. The thickness

GENERAL JOSEPH HOOKER.

of the forest was favorable to his design, and by the afternoon of the 2d, he had gained the road from Orange to Fredericksburg, south of the Rapidan. Having deployed his columns, he suddenly poured down like a torrent on the rear of Hooker's position, where he unexpectedly appeared about five o'clock in the evening. The first part of Hooker's army to feel the brunt of Jackson's attack was Howard's corps, which was bivouacking in the forest with so complete an unconsciousness of danger that in this direction no defensive works had been thrown up. The Confederates burst upon their antagonists with a tremendous yell, and the Union divisions on the right fell back in panic. Nearly the whole of the 11th corps was routed, and driven in towards Chancellorsville. Some gallant attempts were made to rally the fugitives, and Hooker himself did his utmost to inspire confidence in the troops. At the same moment a vigorous atack in front was being made by Lee, and a feeling of terror spread through the masses of the Union army. There was one exception to this rule of fear and disorganization. The reserves, under General Sickles, exhibited the qualities of good soldiers. Sickles himself, his staff, and a body of cavalry under Pleasanton, took post near a stone wall directly in the line of retreat, and placing themselves boldly in a gap of that wall, through which alone the road could be pursued, succeeded in rallying some of the artillery, though the infantry, overcoming all obstructions, managed to continue their discreditable flight. Howard, who was in command of the corps that had been first surprised, strove hard to rally the flying troops. Hooker himself spared no pains, and freely exposed his life where his presence appeared specially needed; for, whatever his deficiencies as a commander, he undoubtedly possessed great courage. Towards nightfall, something like order was restored to the shattered divisions. The Union guns were turned on the advancing enemy, and the pursuit was checked; but the Northern army was now in a contracted position between Chancellorsville and the fork of the two rivers, and it became doubtful whether Hooker's plans were not damaged beyond the hope of recovery.

The Confederates had so far attained a marked success; but they also suffered a great personal misfortune in the death of General Jackson. In the evening after his successful onslaught, while riding back to camp from a reconnoissance of the front, Jackson was fired upon by his own men, who mistook his escort for Union calvary. This heroic officer died on May 10, bequeathing to his country generally, a reputation for prowess, gallantry, and military genius which the Western Continent has never surpassed.

The battle, cut short by darkness on the night of the 2d, was resumed next morning (Sunday). To drive the Union forces back towards the rivers, and thus sweep them out of the advantageous ground which they held, was the difficult task now undertaken by the Confederate commander. The three divisions of Jackson's corps had been placed under Stuart's command, and these veteran troops began the renewed attack. They were received with so hot a fire from the Union entrenchments that the advancing ranks wavered and hung back, but, on being rallied and inspirited by General Rhodes, again pushed forward with energy, and drove their opponents towards Chancellorsville. At another part of the field, the strongly fortified position held by Slocum was attacked with equal spirit. The outer defences was carried after a fierce struggle, and the Union forces were compelled to take refuge behind a second line of breastworks, in the rear of Chancellorsville. Some time before noon, the Northern troops had been compelled to recede about a mile towards the river, and Hooker, beaten out of his first entrenchments, was obliged to create a second line with as much expedition as he could.

Satisfied with what he had accomplished, Lee directed his attention toward the neighborhood of Fredericksburg, where events of importance were proceeding.

It has already been related that when the Union troops began their movement south of the Rappahannock, Sedgwick's division crossed below Fredericksburg, in order to divert a portion of the Confederate army. After parting with several of his troops to reinforce Hooker, he was still left with about 25,000 men. He soon ascertained that Lee's division had vacated the whole of their works, except Marye's Heights, and had gone to encounter the Union ranks at Chancellorsville. The Southern garrison on the heights was a very small one, as Sedgwick knew from balloon reconnoissances. Yet, though his numbers were superior, he took no action at the very time when action would probably have ensured success. Although his position was assumed on April 28, he did not attempt to aid his Chief until the evening of May 2. Throughout the whole of the 1st and 2d, had he marched upon the rear of Lee, who had only half as many troops as his opponent, it is not unlikely that he would have given a totally different character to that memorable affair. When at length he moved, his advance was slow, and unnecessarily cautious. Not more than four miles of ground divided him from the two regiments drawn up behind a wall on Marye's Heights; but it was not until midday of the 3d, that he came within sight of his enemy. The elevated ground was then surrounded, the works were carried with a loss of about 1,000 killed and wounded, and at six o'clock in the evening Sedgwick sent forward a column four miles on the road towards Chancellorsville. Lee, on hearing of the capture of

Marye's Heights, despatched McLaws to check any further advance of the Union detachment, which he did by a rough breastwork. An attempt to carry the posi-

GENERAL J. E. B. STUART.

tion resulted in the loss of numerous troops. Nothing more was done at that time, and Sedgwick's division spent the night loosely scattered about the road leading from Marye's Heights to Salem Church. The battle was renewed next morning; but Sedgwick's troops fought with so much languor that the Confederates, on the arrival of reinforcements under Early, had but little trouble in defeating them. They were speedily outflanked by the Confederates, who re-took Marye's Heights, and captured a Union convoy. Fearing that his communications with Fredericksburg would be cut off, Sedgwick hastily withdrew, leaving behind him numerous supply-wagons, mules, and horses. The retreat was no better than a disorderly flight, and after dark the Union detachment recrossed the river on pontoon-bridges, their movement accelerated by a renewed attack of the Confederates, which spread confusion and dismay through several regiments. A diversion which might have been attended by the happiest results, had it been vigorously and boldly pushed, had ended in nothing but disaster, rout, and loss.

Lee lost no time in pursuing the advantages he had already gained. Having disposed of Sedgwick, whose advance had for some time threatened his rear, he once more turned on the main body of the Union forces cramped within their narrow lines in the neighborhood of Chancellorsville. But a change in the weather occurred on the 5th. A deluge of rain caused the waters of the Rapidan and Rappahannock to rise so as to threaten the bridges at the United States Ford, by which alone the Union army could retreat. To withdraw from their desperate position was now the only course open to them. Hooker consulted with his chief subordinates, and determined upon relinquishing his enterprise.

Preparations for the retreat began immediately after dusk, and at daybreak on the 6th, the whole army stood in safety on the left bank of the Rappahannock, and commenced marching back to its former camps at Falmouth.

CHANCELLORSVILLE.

Again had the Union troops been defeated in their endeavors to march on Richmond; again had there

GENERAL ROBERT E. LEE.

been an enormous expenditure of life without any corresponding advantage. The number of killed and wounded in that week of fighting has been variously stated; but Hooker admitted a loss of nearly 11,000 men. The prisoners were numerous: no fewer than 4600 were sent back from Richmond upon exchange, within a fortnight after the battle. In Sedgwick's force alone, 5000 men were returned as killed, wounded and missing. The Confederate loss was about 10,000; so that altogether nearly 30,000 men must have been removed from the ranks of the combatants. The disaster to the Union cause was so extreme that Lincoln and Halleck visited Hooker at his camp, to investigate the causes of so grave a misfortune. On their return to Washington, they announced that Hooker's demonstration was not a disaster, but simply a failure. This opinion did not find acceptance with the public. It was seen that Hooker had been completely beaten, and it was certain that his removal from command could not be long delayed. The spring campaign in Virginia was now at an end; for the Union ranks were weakened, not merely by the casualties of battle, but by the departure of many regiments whose terms of service had expired, and who showed no readiness to re-enlist.

The Southerners, induced by these successes, would have assumed the offensive, had their strength been equal to such a feat; but their numbers were comparatively small, and they feared at that time to risk a repetition of the ill luck which had attended their invasion of Maryland the year previous. Frequent cavalry skirmishes occurred in the open country, and in the passes of the Blue Ridge Mountains; but, though characterized by great gallantry on both sides, and by varying fortune, they produced no lasting or important effects.

The two Presidents now put into effect in their respective sections the laws for obtaining soldiers by enrolment and draft.

GETTYSBURG (July 1-3, 1863).—Lee now planned to conquer upon the soil of the loyal States. Swinton tells us that the official records show that "the Southern agents near the leading governments of the Old World were at this time able to announce that should Lee, after the astonishing successes he had achieved in Virginia, carry his army into the North, and there make a lodgment promising some degree of permanancy, the South could receive the long-coveted boon of foreign recognition."

Since the time when Lee had been forced to abandon Maryland, two great battles had been fought. At Fredericksburg, the Army of the Potomac, under an incompetent leader (Burnside), was hurled in reckless slaughter against a fortified position of impregnable strength, and after a fearful carnage, was repulsed, terribly shaken in *morale*. At Chancellorsville, Hooker, after a successful passage of the river, contrived by unskilful combination to be thoroughly beaten in detail by a greatly inferior force acting on the offensive, and was forced to recross the Rappahannock, leaving his reputation as a General behind him. In these two actions the Confederates killed nearly 30,000 men, and their experience in these battles inspired them with a sense of invincibility. The Union forces, distraught by repeated disaster and change of commander, had sunk in energy, and lapsed from their faith of victory.

These two causes conspiring together determined the Richmond authorities to assume the offensive, carry the war into the Northern States, and dictate terms of peace in Philadelphia or New York.

The Confederate forces now in Virginia amounted to 75,000 men—irrespective of Stuart's Cavalry. They were divided into three corps of equal size, and the ability of Lee, Longstreth, and Ewell was a guarantee that they would be handled in the most effective manner. Lee rapidly moved down the Shenandoah, crossing the Potomac, and advanced to Chambersburg.

Hooker, though he exhibited dashing qualities as a subordinate, was no match for these men. He requested to be relieved of the command, and was succeeded by General George G. Meade.

Towards the end of June Lee's headquarters were at Chambersburg, Pennsylvania. Ewell, who preceded him there, was then ordered to send Early's division to the eastern side of South Mountain, so as simultaneously to threaten Harrisburg and Baltimore. Other divisions were sent in various directions, charged with the task of burning bridges, and destroying railways and canals, so as to hinder the advance of the Union troops. Orders for a forward movement were issued by General Meade the day he assumed command (June 28). Maryland was entered on that day, and the garrison at Harper's Ferry was called in, under an incorrect impression, on Meade's part, that it was destitute of provisions. The Army of the Potomac was then concentrated in and around the city of Frederick, Maryland. On June 29, Lee's forces moved in an easterly direction towards Gettysburg. With the exception of two corps, Meade's army was moved northward at the same time; but on the morning of the 30th Meade changed his line of march, and directed the whole of his corps towards Gettysburg. Thus the two hostile armies were moving in parallel lines on the same place. Gettysburg was indeed a position of importance to both; for it is a central point to which many roads converge. Lee was ill-supplied with information as to his adversary's movements. The cavalry had not yet rejoined him, and it was only by a difficult march round the right flank of the Union forces, and therefore between them and Washington, that Stuart was able, on July 2, to recombine his detachment with the main body of the Confederate army. On the two previous days, Lee had scarcely any means of ascertaining what Meade was

GENERAL GEORGE G. MEADE.

doing; so that in marching on Gettysburg he was ignorant of the fact that the Union commander was marching there too.

At this moment, the position of the Southern Confederacy was one of extreme peril. Nearly all the defenders of Richmond had been sent to join Lee in his invasion of the North; and the naked condition of the Confederate capital, and of the country surrounding it, became known to the Federal Government.

Meade's army was within a few miles of Gettysburg on June 30. A little to the north, but moving in the same direction, was Lee's army. Meade ascertained the proximity of his adversaries in the course of that day, and, pushing forward with celerity, entered Gettysburg on the morning of July 1. In the meanwhile the Confederates continued their advance, and at ten A. M. one of their divisions became engaged with Reynold's corps on the western side of the town, a little beyond a line of hills called Oak Ridge. Reynolds rode forward to superintend his troops in person, but was immediately killed by a rifle-bullet. The command of the corps then devolved on General Doubleday, who was enabled to bring three divisions into action; yet the Confederates were not checked. The scene of the fighting was a small open valley, consisting of ploughed fields bounded by thickly-wooded uplands. The encounter was prolonged and desperate, and the Southerners themselves admitted that the Union troops fought well. Before his death, Reynolds had sent orders to the 11th corps, under Howard, to come to his support as quickly as possible. This body was to the south of Gettysburg, and it was some time before it could turn towards the north-west, cross the Oak Ridge, and deploy into the little valley. Its arrival was eagerly desired by the overmatched Union forces in the latter position; but it was not until about one P. M. that Howard, riding in advance of his troops, reached the field of action. He took command of the entire force, and his men, coming up shortly afterwards, occupied a position to the right of the 1st corps. Notwithstanding this accession of strength on the Northern side, the Southern troops continued to gain ground. The 11th Union corps, consisting principally of Germans, was driven back in broken heaps, though not without a very

GENERAL W. S. HANCOCK.

creditable attempt to withstand the enemy. The discomfiture of this body spread dismay through the rest, and a retreat towards Gettysburg soon afterwards set in.

By this time General Hancock had been sent forward by Meade to take the principal command, and, with the assistance of Howard, he formed the broken corps afresh on the summit of the rising ground. The Southern Generals, Hill and Ewell, were at first disposed to resume the attack at once, but as the evening drew near, and the exact strength of the opposing forces was not known, it was considered advisable to abstain from further action for the present. The Confederates therefore occupied the town, and prepared for renewed action on the following day. In the course of the night Meade arrived, and posted his troops in a semi-circular line, of which the convex center was towards Gettysburg. The hill formed part of a curving ridge, which in some portions was rocky and thickly wooded; and Meade's left flank, lying to the south-west of Cemetery Hill, rested upon an almost perpendicular peak, covered with forest trees, called the Round Top. To the west and north of this ridge was a narrow valley, between one and two miles in width, beyond which the heights known as Oak Ridge ran nearly parallel with the first line of hills. On the morning of July 2 the Confederate line of battle was formed on the slopes of the further ridge, its right facing the Round Top, its left overlapping Gettysburg, and turning somewhat to the south. Believing that the whole Confederate army was in his front, Meade had on the previous evening hastened up all his outlying corps; and his entire force was on the ground by seven A. M. on the 2d, with the exception of the 6th corps, which did not arrive until 2 P. M. The Confederates had concentrated their divisions by about the same time, and it was seen on both sides that an action of a desperate character would presently ensue. The Union troops held a strong position, the advantages of which they augmented by throwing up breastworks and other defences. Lee questioned the prudence of attacking an enemy so formidable in numbers, and so well entrenched on commanding hills. But these considerations were overruled by the suggestion that to retreat without a further engagement might have been attended by consequences abso-

GENERAL LONGSTREET.

lutely fatal. A battle thus became unavoidable; and Lee determined to fight, though it would appear that he and Longstreet were both apprehensive of the result, and doubtful as to the propriety of an offensive movement.

The key of the Union position was Cemetery Hill, which was regarded as the center of the line, though it lay much more to the right than to the left. Here Meade established his headquarters; and at about a quarter past four in the afternoon, the Confederate batteries opened fire. Under cover of their guns, the Confederates then advanced simultaneously against the extremities of the opposing line, and the Union left, commanded by Sickles, was vehemently assaulted by Longstreet in person. Sickles was an amateur soldier, but his courage, as he had shown at the battle of Chancellorsville, was all that could be desired; and he clung to his position with grim tenacity. After awhile, however, he was badly wounded, and carried from the field; his men were driven back with terrible loss from the advanced position which he had taken up; and the Southerners pushed on towards the eastern ridge. Meade now strengthened his left by the 5th corps under Slocum, and the Union guns did murderous execution among the Confederates, who lost some of their best officers. Longstreet headed the attack with remarkable gallantry; fresh troops arrived in support of those whom he already commanded; and at one time the summit of the ridge was nearly gained. But the Union forces were being continually reinforced, and the Southern troops were finally compelled to retire towards the undulating ground, near Emmetsburg road, which Sickles had previously occupied, but from which he had been expelled. While the left was thus assailed, Ewell attacked Cemetery Hill, and demonstrations were also made against other portions of the Union line. These attempts, however, were not well supported, nor sustained with sufficient spirit; consequently, although some breastworks were temporarily carried, the general result of the day's operation was that the Confederates were driven back with enormous loss. But the loss was not wholly on one side: Meade's troops also had suffered very severely, and their commander was doubtful, when night closed in, whether his army could bear another attack. Orders were drawn up by the chief of the staff against the contingency of a retreat; but, on considering all the circumstances of his position— the valor which his men had shown, and the formidable nature of the rugged hills on which he was entrenched —Meade determined to remain, and once more offer battle on the following day.

The struggle began again on the morning of the 3d; this time on the left of the Confederate line. The assault was conducted with so much vigor that for awhile Meade was apprehensive lest his right flank should be turned; but, after a desperate effort, the Confederate left was hurled back, and the fighting was then transferred to the center and the Union left. Great delay, however, ensued in carrying out these later movements, and the time was turned to good account by the Union troops in adding to their outworks, and strengthening the batteries which were to sweep the intervening valley. At half-past twelve a furious cannonade was opened from more than 100 guns forming the batteries of Longstreet and Hill, as well as from Ewell's artillery, stationed in the neighborhood of Gettysburg, and directed against the slopes of Cemetery Hill. They were replied to with equal vehemence, and for two hours the narrow valley blazed and roared with this infernal interchange of fire and death, which tore great limbs from the trees, splintered the rocks, and scattered destruction far and wide. Then the Confederate brigades descended the hill on which they had been posted, and moved against the Union line. The slaughter was excessive, for the men were within full range of the Union guns —guns of enormous size and power. Nevertheless, they pressed forward with devoted gallantry, and

Pickett's Virginians even planted their colors within the hostile works. But the less experienced troops were in time staggered by the obstacles before them, and, after wavering in their march, halted, and then fell back in confusion. Pickett's regiments, composed of men who were justly regarded as among the best troops in the army, were exposed, by the retreat of their comrades, to the utmost fury of the adversary. Attacked both in front and flank, these courageous men were swept off the works they had captured, and at length, though unwillingly, forced to retreat. In that desperate struggle every brigadier of the Virginian division was killed or wounded, and, out of 24 regimental officers, only two escaped unhurt. Leaving an enormous proportion of their number dead or wounded on the ground, the Virginians retired to the slopes from which they had started, and Longstreet, apprehending an immediate advance by the Union forces, made hasty preparations for defending his position. Lee himself rode amongst the shattered ranks, reassuring the soldiers by his calm and sympathetic manner. The several detachments were formed again, under cover of the woods, and the men were ordered to lie on the ground until the moment when they should be attacked. But no attack came. The Union troops were exhausted, and had spent nearly all their ammunition. The third day's battle, therefore, came to a close about six o'clock in the evening. Detached engagements of a desultory nature took place in other parts of the line, but were attended with no important effect. The attack had not been well planned, and Longstreet afterwards admitted that the Confederates had made a mistake in not concentrating their army more, and in attacking with 15,000 men, instead of 30,000. The Southerners had found the position of their opponents too strong to be carried, and it was obvious that any further attempt would lead only to the worst results.

On the other hand, Meade saw that it would be highly imprudent on his part to follow up his success by any attack upon the enemy. He admitted having lost during the campaign upwards of 23,000 men in killed, wounded, and missing. Meade therefore remained quietly within his lines, probably expecting the speedy retreat of his adversary. Lee had in truth determined to abandon a country in which little could be gained, and everything might be lost; but it was not necessary to act with precipitation, and the greater part of the 4th was devoted to burying the dead, and sending the wounded to the rear.

GENERAL GEORGE E. PICKETT.

At night, the several corps began their retreat, and by the morning of the 5th the whole force was out of view. Sedgwick, with the Sixth corps, was sent in pursuit, and came up with the Confederate rear-guard on the evening of the 6th. The position, however, could not have been attacked without great risk, and the main body of the Union army marched on Middletown in a direction parallel with that of the Southerners. Part of the Confederate train moved by the road through Fairfield, and the rest by way of Cashtown, guarded by Imboden. The great number of the wagons exposed them, while passing through the mountains, to the attacks of the Union cavalry; yet they succeeded in reaching Williamsport without serious loss. At that place they were attacked on the 6th, but the assault was repelled by Imboden, and detachments of Meade's cavalry were subsequently defeated by Stuart, and pursued for several miles in the direction of Boonesborough. The Union army crossed the South Mountain on the 9th, and Meade then established his headquarters at Antietam Bridge.

The discomfited army, with its immense train of wagons and ambulances, halted at Williamsport and threw up entrenchments and batteries to guard the position. The Union troops lay in force barely two miles off, but did not venture to attack. Meade, acting on the advice of his generals, decided to await reinforcements. Late on July 13, the movement into Virginia commenced. The Union cavalry made a spirited dash at the Confederate rear-guard, which was covering the approaches to the bridge; but the assailants were driven back with considerable loss, and by one P. M. the whole of Lee's army was again in the Old Dominion.

Thus ended the second invasion of Maryland and Pennsylvania. It had entailed a loss of at least 50,000 men, if both armies are taken into the account; and it had been unproductive of the slightest good to the Confederate cause, while it made still more apparent the ever-increasing power of the Union Government, and its ability to encounter the Southerners wherever they dared to show their flag. The effect of this battle was to put an end to the idea of a Northern invasion.

BATTLE OF GETTYSBURG (JULY 1–3, 1863).

CHAPTER V.

VICKSBURG AND THE OPERATIONS IN THE WEST (1863).

THE reduction of Vicksburg was determined upon, and no pains were spared to bring about the result. Grant resolved on cutting off all communication with the east by turning the defences on the Mississippi and the Yazoo. His headquarters were at Milliken's Bend, on the western shore of the Mississippi—the shore opposite to that on which Vicksburg stands; and on March 29 McClernand was sent to occupy New Carthage, some miles to the south. These operations were assisted by the advance of Banks from New Orleans, so as to threaten Port Hudson in combination with the fleet. The movements of Banks and of the ships were impeded by the burning of bridges and the placing of obstructions in the river. Banks passed into a region west of the Mississippi called Bayou Teche. Constantly driving the enemy before him, he advanced, on April 20, to Opelousas, a town lying about 180 miles to the northwest of New Orleans; after which he established himself for a few weeks at Simmsport. The Red River, another tributary of the great stream, which it enters between Port Hudson and Natchez, was blockaded by Farragut after he had succeeded in passing the river-batteries with two of his vessels. Porter, who was still above Vicksburg, made frequent attempts to join his comrade, but for a long time without success. On the night of April 16, however, the feat was accomplished by an act of great boldness and resolution.

During that day eight gunboats, three transports and several barges laden with supplies, tried to descend the Mississippi after dark. The movement was watched in breathless silence by the Union troops stationed about the town, and the passage of the huge, dim, almost shapeless vessels through the wide obscurity was most impressive in its stealthy mystery and lurking possibilities of harm. Silently and darkly they passed on, and drew near to Vicksburg. Nearly an hour elapsed without anything being heard; then, two bright, sharp lines of flame pierced the darkness, and in another moment the whole length of the heights was ablaze. The forts had opened fire on the vessels; the vessels were not long in replying to the forts. It was a part of Porter's plan that his fleet of gunboats, when in front of the batteries, should engage them with their broadside guns, and then endeavor to descend the stream under cover of the smoke. The batteries, however, had been the first to fire. Presently all down the river the bristling guns of the Confederates poured forth flame, and smoke, and storm of deadly missiles; and the roar and rush of sound added another terror to the fierce encounter. The passage of the fleet was visible in gliding fire, as point after point was reached, and battery after battery replied to the moving gunboats.

After the cannonade had gone on for some time, a gleam of light, different from that of the guns, spread upward into the heavens immediately above the city. This grew and intensified every moment, passing from pallor to redness, and at last glaring upon the night with such fulness and power that the Union on-lookers exclaimed, "Vicksburg is on fire!" But the light proceeded from a beacon-pile, which had been kindled in order to illuminate both reaches of the river (at that point curving with a rapid bend), and thus to enable the gunners to aim with greater accuracy at the Union vessels. The flame burned steadily and keenly, without any smoke, and served its purpose well; but it also helped the gunboats to reach the batteries with more certainty than they could have done in the dark. The vessels were still pursuing their way down the river, but the artillery duel continued with the utmost fury. It was a duel in which the boats necessarily had the worst of it. The *Forest Queen*, one of the transports, received a shot in the hull and another through the steam-drum, which at once disabled her. In consequence of this accident the *Henry Clay*, another transport, which came next, was stopped, to prevent her running into her unfortunate comrade. The result was disastrous. The crew of the second vessel became alarmed by the stoppage, which left them exposed to the unmitigated force of the Confederate fire; and in a little while they launched the yawl, sprang into it, and made for the shore. Shortly afterwards the *Henry Clay* caught fire, owing to the explosion of a shell amid the cotton with which the engines were protected, and, giving out great volumes of smoke and flame, floated down the stream until it disappeared below Warrenton. The *Forest Queen* was taken in tow by a gunboat, and escaped without further injury; while the third transport, the *Silver Wave*, ran past without being touched. Before the approach of dawn, the whole of the gunboats had got beyond the uttermost batteries without any material damage. On the *Benton*, Porter's flagship, one man was killed, and two were wounded, by the bursting of a shell; but this was the utmost injury to life. The great exploit had been accomplished, and Porter was now safe in the waters below Vicksburg.

Grant was so well satisfied with what had taken place that he ordered six more transports to be pre-

IRONCLAD GUNBOATS PASSING BEFORE VICKSBURG.

pared to run the batteries in the same manner. These were to carry supplies for the army, which it was hoped would soon be engaged in an attack on the southern side of Vicksburg, and ultimately to convey the army itself across the river. These six vessels, towing 12 barges, set out on the night of April 22, and all but one succeeded in getting past the batteries, though six of the barges were either sunk or injured. By this time, Grant had arrived with two army corps, at New Carthage, where Porter's gunboats were stationed. He had been compelled to follow a very circuitous route, and to make his way through a country rendered peculiarly difficult by marshes and streams; but the obstacles were all overcome after much delay, and he was in a favorable locality for ulterior operations. A few days later he moved his forces still farther south to a place called Hard Times, lying on the Louisiana shore of the Mississippi, and thus took up a position just opposite Grand Gulf, which is situated a little below the mouth of the Big Black River. It was essential to Grant's plans that Grand Gulf (which was strongly fortified) should be quickly taken; and he had repeatedly instructed McClernand, when at New Carthage, to make the attempt. McClernand always hesitated, making perpetual excuses for his delay; and Grant, seeing that the opportunity was slipping away, went to the front himself and took immediate command. His vigilance during the whole of these operations was very remarkable.

On April 29 Grant embarked a portion of his army on board the transports and moved to the front of Grand Gulf. His scheme was that the gunboats under Porter should silence the fortifications, and that the troops should then land, under cover of the gunboats, and carry the place by storm. The attack from the river began early in the morning, and lasted nearly six hours, at the end of which time Porter had silenced the lower batteries. The upper battery, however, being high, strongly built, and mounted with guns of a very heavy calibre, was able to maintain its fire. Grant, finding that the enemy's works could not be entirely neutralized, and fearing to risk the lives of his men in an attempt to storm them, determined to land lower down the stream, and take the position in reverse. The army was disembarked, and ordered to march down the western side of the Mississippi, and be ready for crossing opposite Bruinsburg. The transports were to run past the batteries at Grand Gulf, and to take up positions such as would enable them to ferry the troops across. As soon as it was dark, the gunboats again engaged the batteries, and all the transports got by without much injury. Next morning, the soldiers embarked, and the 13th corps landed on the eastern bank of the river, and was pushed forward towards Port Gibson, situated near the Bayou Pierre, and connected with Grand Gulf by a railway. These troops were followed by others; but no action took place that day.

The position of Pemberton, who commanded at Vicksburg, was becoming grave. He telegraphed for instructions to Johnston, and was ordered to attack Grant at once. Johnston was not able to send any reinforcements, being himself closely pressed by Rosecrans in Tennessee. Pemberton was therefore obliged to do the best he could with the troops at his disposal, and he directed General Bowen, commanding at Grand Gulf, to cross the Bayou Pierre, and oppose the march of the Union troops to Port Gibson. At two on the morning of May 1, Bowen's division was encountered four miles south of the latter place. A hotly-contested action followed, and at the close of the day the Confederates were driven towards Port Gibson. The country was so cut up by ravines, swamps, canebrakes, and jungles, that very little generalship could be exhibited on either side; but the hand-to-hand fighting was furious, and strewed the dismal, solitary ways with the bodies of the fallen. Grant was in personal command shortly after the action began. Fresh divisions continued to arrive throughout the combat, and they were able to advance in force on the morning of the 2d, when it was found that the Southerners had retreated across the two forks of the Bayou Pierre, on the road to Grand Gulf, and had burned the bridges behind them. So hurried was Bowen that, in retreating, he abandoned his hospitals and many of his wounded. A brigade of Logan's division was sent forward on the 2d, to occupy the attention of the Confederates while a floating bridge was being thrown across the south fork of the bayou at Port Gibson; and, on the bridge being completed, McPherson's corps got over, and pushed on to the north fork, eight miles off. Here, the bridge at the Grindstone Ford was found still burning; but the fire was extinguished, and the bridge repaired in the night. Early next morning the troops passed over, and the Southerners were pursued to Hankinson's Ferry, on the Big Black River. Skirmishing continued during the whole day, and many prisoners were brought in; but the fighting in itself was not important. Nevertheless, the Union successes were such as to make their adversaries doubt the possibility of defending Grand Gulf. They accordingly evacuated the position, and Porter, on making a demonstration during the 3d, discovered that he had no enemy to encounter.

Grant rode into the town and found Porter's naval force in possession. The place was one of great strength, and was in course of being made still stronger. The Confederates, however, considered it advisable to concentrate their forces at Vicksburg; but before leaving Grand Gulf they blew up their magazines, and buried or spiked their cannon. Pemberton said that Grant's movements were so rapid, and his facilities for transportation so great, that his own actions had been seriously embarrassed in consequence. He had been unable to withdraw his heavy guns, and thirteen pieces fell into the hands of the conquerors. The Union base of operations was now transferred to Grand Gulf. For three days, Grant had not been in bed, nor had his clothes off; but his energy continued unabated, and he wrote to his subordinate commanders at distant points, giving them minute instructions as to what they should do. To Sherman he stated that the road to Vicksburg was open, and that that fortified position would shortly fall into his hands.

When the major part of the Union army moved from Milliken's Bend, Sherman was ordered to make a demonstration against Haines's Bluff, in order to prevent reinforcements leaving Vicksburg for Grand Gulf. Sherman crossed the Mississippi, landed his forces on the left bank of the Yazoo, and, with the aid of the gunboats, made an attack on the position on May 6. It was no part of his design to take the bluff, and on the 7th the expedition returned. The Confederates had been prevented from sending reinforcements to the south, and the divisions under Sherman now prepared for joining Grant, who intended to collect his forces at Grand Gulf, and to concentrate at that spot a large supply of provisions and ordnance stores before moving against Vicksburg. An army-corps was then to be detached, to co-operate with Banks against Port Hudson, and ultimately a recombination of the forces was to be effected; but as Banks could not return to Bâton Rouge, from his position west of the Mississippi, before the 10th, Grant was compelled to abandon this portion of his scheme. Delay might have wholly ruined his chances of success. Troops were to be sent to Jackson by Beauregard; and it was therefore essential that

Grant should act with promptitude, so as to strike while the adversary was at his weakest. He determined to anticipate the arrival of the Confederates at Jackson by attacking that town himself. The campaign was being managed by a master, and all the collateral arrangements conspired to a happy issue. A cavalry expedition in the rear of Vicksburg, pursued during the month of April by Colonel B. H. Grierson, was of great service in destroying the enemy's lines of communication, and preventing the early concentration of reinforcements at the chief Confederate position. Grierson was in command of the first cavalry brigade of Grant's army, and the descent into Mississippi was an idea originating with himself. At the head of three regiments, he left La Grange, close to the southern frontiers of Tennessee, on April 17, and crossing the Tallahatchie, moved southward until he struck the Macon and Corinth Railway. He tore up the rails, cut the telegraph-wires, burned the stores, and sent out detachments in various directions. When these had executed their several purposes, all tending to the distraction of the enemy, and to the harassing of his lines of communication, the force was once more concentrated, and resumed its principal march. Grierson now turned towards the south-west, seized the bridge over the Pearl River, and burned a number of locomotives on the Jackson and New Orleans Railway. He next moved along the line of that rail in a southerly direction, crossing many streams, and making his way with difficulty through swamps and marshes. On May 2, he entered Baton Rouge, then in possession of the Union troops, who were astonished at the feat that had been performed by those jaded and wayworn men. The whole of this great ride had been accomplished in not much more than a fortnight, and in the course of that brief interval several towns had been attacked, many spirited skirmishes had been fought, numerous prisoners had been seized, and Confederate supplies to a large amount had been destroyed.

Sherman's corps having arrived at Hankinson's Ferry by the 7th, an advance was ordered by Grant. The united army moved up the eastern bank of the Big Black River; McClernand's corps on the right, McPherson's on the left, and Sherman's in the rear. All the ferries were closely guarded against surprise until the troops had got well on their road. McClernand marched on Raymond, a small town 18 miles south-west of Jackson, and connected by a branch line with the Jackson and Vicksburg Railway. Here his progress was disputed by two Confederate brigades, with whom a brisk engagement took place on the 12th. The action resulted in the defeat of the Southern troops, and the Union forces entered the town. On the same day, McPherson's and Sherman's corps encountered the enemy near Fourteen Mile Creek, across which they succeeded in forcing a passage. Grant now received information that Johnston had arrived at Jackson, at the head of a force with which he hoped to relieve Vicksburg. Grant determined to make sure of the former place, and to leave no enemy in his rear. On the 13th, McPherson was ordered to move on Clinton. Occupying the town, he destroyed the railways and telegraphic wires. McPherson and Sherman advanced towards Jackson on the 14th, and an action took place in front of that town. The Confederates occupied a strong position on the crest of a hill, but, after a fierce encounter, were driven back towards the city, which they shortly afterwards evacuated. Jackson was then entered by McPherson, who found the place deserted and the stores on fire. Johnston had not been in sufficient force to defend the position, and he, therefore, retired to the north.

Shortly after arriving at Jackson, Grant learned, from

intercepted despatches, that Johnston had ordered Pemberton to march out from Vicksburg, and attack the Union rear. Grant resolved to meet any such attack by advancing towards the enemy, and intercepting him on the line of the Vicksburg and Jackson Railway; but, for the present, Sherman was left at Jackson, to destroy the railway, bridges, factories, workshops, and arsenals, the obliteration of which was considered necessary, as Grant had no intention of holding the place, and feared it might become a base of operations for Johnston while he himself was besieging Vicksburg. The orders were carried out with unfaltering severity on the 15th, and very little was left of the town after the torch was once applied.

By this time, Pemberton had crossed the Big Black River; and Grant ordered Sherman to evacuate Jackson, and join the rest of the forces. Pemberton was at the head of nearly 18,000 men, whom he posted on the south-west bank of Baker's Creek, across the Vicksburg and Jackson Railway. On the morning of the 16th, Grant's army was a good deal scattered. Three divisions were on the line of the railway; four were advancing on the road from Raymond; one was still farther to the left on the Big Black River, and two were under Sherman in the neighborhood of Jackson. The Confederates held a good position among woody hills, and Grant had come upon them sooner than he expected. Seeing the gravity of the situation, he sent orders to the three divisions approaching from Raymond to quicken their march as much as possible. The action, however (which has received the title of the battle of Champion's Hill), had proceeded some time before these reinforcements could reach the ground. The division of General Hovey, which had begun the battle by attacking the center of Pemberton's line, was repulsed with some loss, but was again sent forward by

Grant, on his being told by Logan, commanding on the right, that, if the Confederates could be again attacked in front, he could act with advantage against their left flank. The renewed advance was attended by temporary success, but after a while Hovey's division was once more driven back and thrown into disorder. The divisions from Raymond, however, had now arrived, and the whole line swept onward against the Confederates. The southern forces were completely shattered; panic set in among their ranks, and a precipitate flight ensued. Their defeat had been rendered still more extreme by Logan's operations against the left and rear, which distracted their attention and divided their strength. Thus assailed in three directions at once, the Southern line was broken into fragments; the regiments became mingled in tumultuous rout and for a time all military order was at an end. Some degree of discipline was afterwards restored by the exertions of the principal officers; but the fortunes of the day could not be retrieved. The greater portion of the army retired towards the Big Black River; but one division was cut off from the rest, and compelled, with the loss of its artillery, to withdraw in a different direction.

On finding the Confederates in full retreat, Grant ordered Carr to pursue them with the utmost speed to Big Black River, and to cross that stream if he could. The movement continued until after dark, and stores to a large amount were captured; but the retreating columns were not overtaken. The bridge across the river was strongly guarded by the Southerners, who presented so formidable a front of artillery and infantry that the Union forces considered it prudent not to push their advantage any farther for the present. The pursuit was renewed early next morning when the enemy was found strongly posted on both sides of the

Big Black River, at a point where the bluffs on the west side extend to the water's edge. On the east side the land was open and cultivated, surrounded by a bayou of stagnant water, and protected by a line of rifle-pits, to which the bayou served as a species of external ditch. This difficult position was at once attacked by the Union troops, who afterwards discovered that by moving under cover of the river-bank they could gain a position from which the enemy might be successfully assaulted. The attempt was made; the ditch was passed, and in a few minutes the entire garrison laid down their arms, and surrendered 17 pieces of artillery with which the works had been defended. On the 18th, Sherman crossed the river, and after a brief rest, began his march on Vicksburg by the road from Bridgeport. When within three miles of the great object of attack, he turned to the right, in order to obtain possession of Walnut Hills and the Yazoo River. This accomplished he occupied a strong position to the north of Vicksburg, and the other corps, on arriving, placed themselves so as nearly to surround the town and its fortifications. In the meanwhile, Porter, from his station in the Mississippi, had been anxiously looking out for the approach of Grant's army. About noon on the 18th, firing was heard by him in the rear of Vicksburg. The cannonading continued for some time, and by the aid of a telescope he discovered a company of artillery advancing, taking position, and driving the Confederates before them. Sherman's division had got to the left of Snyder's Bluff, and the Southerners at that place had been cut off from joining the forces in the city. Porter accordingly sent a number of gunboats up the Yazoo, to open communications with Grant and Sherman. The vessels and the troops arrived at Haines's Bluff about the same time, and found that the works had been evacuated, and the place abandoned. The garrison had withdrawn within the lines of Vicksburg. Porter described the works at Haines's Bluff as very formidable. Such a network of forts, he declared, he had never seen before, and the guns were supplied with ammunition enough to last a long siege. Fearing that the position might again fall into the enemy's hands, he burned the gun-carriages, blew up the magazine, and destroyed the works generally.

After receiving intelligence of the defeat at Baker's Creek, Johnston had ordered Pemberton, in the event of his being unable to hold Haines's Bluff, to evacuate Vicksburg, and to form a junction with his own army, which was stationed at Canton, some way to the north of Jackson. These orders it was now impossible to execute, because of the positions assumed by the Union army. Pemberton was in fact completely shut up in Vicksburg, and the position was rendered desperate by his having only sixty days' provisions with which to feed his troops and the inhabitants of the town. Johnston made endeavors to bring together a sufficient force to relieve his comrade, and to break up the Union investment; but this was no easy task, for the Confederates in that part of the country were nearly exhausted, and the Union forces were strong, not only in numbers, but in the consciousness of success. Pemberton's men, however, did not yet despair. The works were strengthened wherever they seemed weak, and the fortifications were manned by soldiers who were at least determined that any further triumph should be dearly purchased. Fearing that he might be attacked in his rear by Johnston, Grant resolved to assault the position at once. At two A. M. on May 19, the 15th army-corps advanced to the attack, followed by the 13th and 17th corps. The ground over which these troops had to move presented many obstacles not easy to overcome.

The clay soil had been rendered muddy by the overflowing of streams, and was covered with a dense forest. Rugged chasms frequently intervened, and a large amount of timber had been felled by the Confederates to obstruct the progress of any attacking force. The difficulties of the way prevented the assaulting parties from reaching the trenches in good military form. A body of infantry, however, got up to the external works, and planted the national colors upon the slope; but immediately afterwards the commander, Captain Washington, was mortally wounded, and 77 out of 250 men were either wounded or killed. The troops maintained their position during the whole day, keeping up a sharp fire on the defenders of Vicksburg, who replied with equal spirit; but the attempt was not successful, and after nightfall a retreat was ordered.

The enterprise was renewed on the 22d. This time the attack was to extend along the whole line, and all the commanders of corps set their watches by Grant's, so that the movement should be absolutely simultaneous. At ten A. M. the three army-corps then in front of the Confederate works commenced the assault. Again was no small degree of gallantry exhibited; again were Union flags planted on the outer slopes of the bastions; again did the troops remain in their exposed positions till nightfall; but the attack was no more successful than that which had gone before. The best soldiers in the Union army flung themselves repeatedly against the Confederate works, and were as often driven back with grievous loss. For a moment they gained a footing in the rifle-pits, but were swept out of them by the fierce recoil of the Southerners. Their fire was rapid and deadly throughout, and the assailants suffered a loss of 2,500 men before they retreated to their lines.

During the attack, Porter had engaged the defences on

the river, and had thrown shells into the town from his mortar-boats. The river-forts, however, replied with so much effect that Porter received more damage than he inflicted. Several of his vessels were struck below the water-line, and the whole fleet dropped down the river, and got beyond the range of fire. Although the attempt to carry the defences had been unsuccessful, the people of Vicksburg had all that day endured the utmost anxiety and alarm. They had excavated caves in the hill on which the city stands, and here they hid themselves during the height of the bombardment, expecting every moment that the enemy would burst his way into the heart of the town. By the close of the day, their apprehensions were for a time relieved; but next morning the bombardment recommenced, and for six weeks a devastating storm of shot and shell was hurled into the place. Still, the casualties were not numerous, and people in time grew familiar with the appearance of the bursting shells, and regarded them with more of curiosity than fear. After the 26th the firing on the town continued day and night, and it was estimated at Vicksburg that 6,000 mortar-shells were thrown into the town every 24 hours, and 4,000 on the line in the rear of the city. The month of June was rainy, and the civilians were compelled by the influx of water to abandon the caves in which they had for some weeks shrouded themselves. In addition to their other sufferings, the prospect of famine now became imminent. For five days after the commencement of the siege, the troops had been allowed full rations; but the daily amount of food for each man was reduced. By the middle of June, Grant's army had been reinforced, and this enabled him to make his investment more complete, and at the same time to appoint a large reserve for watching the movements of Johnston. Haines's Bluff was now fortified on the land side, and preparations were made for resisting any detachment which might come to the relief of Vicksburg. Sherman was placed in command of all the troops designated to look after Johnston, who on June 25 crossed the Big Black River with a portion of his force. Grant's army was by this time strongly entrenched, and Johnston hesitated to attack it. The siege continued in regular form. Parallels and approaches were constructed, and mines were sunk; every day the deadly coil of the attacking force grew closer and more strict in its embrace; and at length the Union works were pushed so near the walls that the sharpshooters on the opposing sides were within 20 yards of one another, and the contending batteries not more than 300 yards apart.

Some feeble and desultory attempts to reach Vicksburg were made by the Confederates in various outlying localities; but Grant's stubborn grip was not to be shaken off. A heavy mine was fired by the Union troops on June 25. This mine, which was excavated in the cliff on which one of the forts had been erected, extended 35 feet from the point of starting; and 1500 pounds of powder were deposited in three branch mines, together with 700 in the center one. Fuses were arranged so as to explode them all simultaneously, and troops were held in readiness for ulterior operations. A severe artillery fire having been opened along the line, so as to distract the attention of the besieged, the mine was fired, and the ground was rent as if by an earthquake. A red glare burst forth, and a few rebel soldiers were hurled into the air; but the Southerners had detected the making of the mine, and had withdrawn most of their troops beyond the reach of harm. The cavity thus produced was large enough to hold two regiments; and before the smoke had cleared away, a column of Union infantry, which had laid concealed in a hollow near the fort, rushed forward into the breach with loud and repeated cheers. These devoted men were met by a number of Southerners of equal gallantry, and a desperate fight took place within the crater which the explosion had torn in the earth. Hand grenades were used by both sets of combatants, and the gunners in the rear joined in this infernal conflict, even at the risk of killing their own men. With quiet determination, the Confederates erected a new line of breastworks inside the gap, so that the Union troops were unable to force their way into the town. Nevertheless, they did not give up the favorable position they had won, and, on the night succeeding the explosion, fresh troops relieved their predecessors in the difficult and perilous task of holding the chasm. The sanguinary struggle was prolonged during the whole of that night; for, although the Southerners had retired out of view, they continued, from a distance, to throw grenades into the attacking force. The crater was called by the soldiers "the death-hole;" yet the Union men desperately clung to the ground, and the next day constructed a line of rifle-pits across the aperture. A covered gallery was also commenced, from which further mines could be made to open out, and one of these was sprung on July 1, causing the demolition of an entire redan.

The condition of the city and of its inhabitants was fast becoming desperate. Provisions were extremely scarce; the flesh of mules and dogs was eaten by all classes, for meat of any other kind was hardly to be obtained. Bean-meal was made into bread, and cornmeal served in place of coffee. The soldiers were almost worn out by constant duty in the trenches; the weather was hot and oppressive, and the numerous unburied corpses infected the air with horror. Scarcely a building in the town had escaped the Union shells; even the hospitals were occasionally struck, though of course not intentionally. Fodder was exhausted, and the horses were reduced to subsist wholly on corn-tops. Pemberton was able to communicate now and then with Johnston, and repeatedly implored relief; but Johnston's forces were not strong enough to encounter the serried ranks of Grant, and every day brought nearer the inevitable catastrophe. Grant felt assured that the fall of Vicksburg was certain, and it had become evident to the Confederates themselves that this was the case. Sherman was informed that another assault on Vicksburg would be made at daybreak on July 6, but the necessity for any such attempt was removed by the action of the besieged themselves.

Early on the morning of July 3, a flag of truce was seen on the crest of a hill outside the town. A messenger was sent to bring in the bearers of the flag. They carried a despatch from Pemberton to Grant, in which proposals were made for an armistice, with a view to arranging terms for the capitulation of Vicksburg. Pemberton said he made this proposition to save further effusion of blood, which must otherwise be shed to a frightful extent, but added that he felt himself fully able to maintain his position for a period still indefinite. Grant declined to appoint commissioners, because he would consider no other terms than an unconditional surrender of the city and garrison. An interview subsequently took place between Grant and Pemberton. The scene was an orchard, midway between the contending forces. Grant said he would put his propositions into writing, and after some interchange of notes, it was agreed that the garrison should be paroled, and allowed to return to their homes, not to serve again until properly exchanged, and that the town, stores, arms and trophies should become the prize of the victors. The negotiations were concluded on the 4th of July—the great historical day now rendered more illustrious by the surrender of a fortified city for the possession of which both sections had for two years fought with equal valor, devotion and military skill. Grant had receded from his demand of unconditional capitulation; but in his report he said that this alteration saved the Government the trouble of sending the garrison all the way to the North, while it left the

INTERVIEW BETWEEN GRANT AND PEMBERTON.

Union troops free to operate against Johnston. At 10 o'clock on the 4th, the Confederates marched out, and stacked arms in front of their works; after which the city was occupied by three divisions of the Union troops. At night, fireworks were let off; but this was done in celebration, not of the victory, but of Independence Day. By the surrender of Vicksburg, the Confederates lost the services of nearly 27,000 men, including three major-generals and nine brigadiers, with upwards of ninety pieces of artillery, and about 40,000 small-arms. During the whole of the campaign, Grant had captured 37,000 prisoners, including 15 general officers; and arms and munitions of war for 60,000 men had fallen into his hands. Equally important was the command which the Union forces had in this way obtained over the great Mississippi River, which enabled them to divide the Confederate States into two distinct portions—that to the east and that to the west of the stream—and to render it very difficult for either to give assistance to the other. The fall of Vicksburg was lamented all over the South as a weighty misfortune; and certain it was that the Confederate cause was materially weakened by Grant's splendid success.

After the capture of this great stronghold, Grant reported that his troops were so much fatigued as to require several weeks' rest before undertaking another campaign. Those who were the least exhausted he sent out on various expeditions; but the greater number remained at Vicksburg, the defences of which they strengthened against any movement which the Confederates might undertake. Sherman went in pursuit of Johnston, who was menacing the rear of the Union army; and his operations were so vigorously carried out that Johnston evacuated Jackson on the night of July 16, and retreated towards the east. Grant had become the hero of the day. He had proved himself the best general that the North had yet produced, and the President wrote to him:—"I do not remember that you and I ever met personally. I write this now as a grateful acknowledgment for the almost inestimable service you have done the country." Grant afterwards left Vicksburg to assume the command east of the Mississippi, and McPherson then moved with a part of his force to Canton, where he scattered the

Confederate cavalry, destroyed a large amount of material, and broke up all the roads by which the enemy might annoy the Northern forces.

The tide of success was now running completely in favor of the Northern men, and the capture of Port Hudson on the Mississippi was an event second in importance only to that of Vicksburg. Banks quitted Simmsport about the middle of May, and, having crossed to the eastern side of the Mississippi, advanced towards the object of his attack on the 22d. On the 25th, the defenders of Port Hudson, who were commanded by General Gardner, were driven from the outer works, and a powerful assault was made on the 27th. Banks had a large army with which to conduct his attack, and was assisted by a fleet of gunboats, which bombarded the defences from the river. Gardner could not place more than 6,000 men within his entrenchments, and the works, which had been hastily constructed, were furnished with but feeble artillery. Nevertheless, a successful resistance was offered to the attacking force; but the Union troops were in a position of such immense superiority that the capitulation of the city was only an affair of time.

The assault of May 27 having failed, Banks commenced the siege in regular form. Gardner was summoned to surrender on June 13, but replied by a refusal. Next day, another assault was delivered. Several storming parties were led against the works, and a few men even got within them; but the supporting column did not arrive in time, and the assailants, falling back, lay down for hours in the cotton-furrows, as their only protection against the hail of bullets which came rushing out of the forts. Banks now resumed his siege operations, and the trenches were pushed forward still nearer to the walls. The garrison were getting short of provisions, and the probability of any succor arriving grew less with each succeeding day. When at length it came to Gardner's knowledge that Vicksburg had surrendered, he saw that further resistance would be altogether vain. The place was surrendered on July 9, and the Confederates were treated with kindness and consideration by their conquerors. *Full possession of the Mississippi was now restored to the Union forces*, who held possession of that magnificent stream from its source in Minnesota, down to its outfall in the Gulf of Mexico. The great bulk of the Confederacy was split in two, and through the rift the enormous forces of the Union could pass to and fro, dealing their bolts of death far to the right hand and to the left—to the west and to the east.

To pursue their advantages in Tennessee was now one of the chief objects of the Union commanders. After the battle of Murfreesboro', at the beginning of the year, Rosecrans refrained for several months from any important operations. Detachments from his main body had several encounters with the enemy; but for the most part the Union Army of the West maintained an observant attitude. Early in June Rosecrans was requested to take measures for driving Bragg into Georgia, and thus securing Eastern Tennessee. It was believed that Bragg's ranks had been greatly weakened by the despatch of reinforcements to Johnston, in the neighborhood of Vicksburg; and it was therefore thought that the time was singularly propitious for an advance. Rosecrans himself did not share this view. He represented that his army was not then prepared for a forward movement, and that his subordinates doubted the advisability of active operations until the fate of Vicksburg had been determined. Notwithstanding these opinions, Halleck considered that something should be done, and expressed the dissatisfaction of the President with the inactivity that had so long prevailed. Influenced by Halleck's representations, Rosecrans, on June 24, commenced a series of movements from Murfreesboro', for the purpose of forcing Bragg to retreat from his position on the Duck River. In this design he was successful. Some scattered actions occurred on various parts of the line, and Bragg, finding himself in danger of being outflanked by his adversary's occupation of some of the mountain passes, retired to Chattanooga, on the south side of the Tennessee River, not far from the borders of Georgia and Alabama, though nearer to the former than the latter. The town was a place of some importance as a seat of industry, and as a meeting-point of several lines of rail; and here Bragg determined to make a stand. He fortified his position, and constructed defensive works at the crossing of the river. His retreat had been much vexed by the Union cavalry, and his operations were hampered by the desertion of several of his men belonging to Tennessee, who, now that their State was about to be abandoned, considered, according to the true Southern view of Confederate claims, that they had done everything which could in reason be demanded of them. But as soon as he had entrenched himself at Chattanooga, Bragg felt tolerably secure against attack.

That Rosecrans might have every assistance in his movement against Bragg, Burnside was directed to march from the Ohio into Eastern Tennessee. Great slowness, however, continued to mark the proceedings of the Union troops, owing partly to the prevalence of heavy rains. On July 4 Bragg withdrew to Chattanooga; it was not until August 16 that Rosecrans commenced his advance on that town, and that Burnside left Camp Nelson, in Kentucky, for the scene of his ulterior operations. The progress of Burnside was scarcely disputed by the Confederates, who retired before him, and united their small scattered forces with those of Bragg.

General Buckner was among the Confederate officers who retreated towards Chattanooga; but two of his brigades were cut off from the main body. One of these held Cumberland Gap, and Jefferson Davis was greatly incensed at the readiness with which, on September 9, the position was yielded to two Union detachments, without a shot being fired in its defence. Cumberland Gap commands one of the principal roads from Kentucky into Tennessee, and its surrender exposed Eastern Tennessee and Southwestern Virginia to hostile invasion, besides breaking the line of communication between the Confederate seat of government and the region where Bragg was desperately contending against superior odds. In his march through Eastern Tennessee, Burnside was received with enthusiasm, and the populace displayed their attachment to the old Union and the old flag. The inhabitants of that mountainous land had never been well-affected to the Confederacy, and Burnside was hailed as a deliverer wherever his forces penetrated.

The delay in Burnside's march, caused by his turning aside to reduce the Confederate position in Cumberland Gap, prevented his joining Rosecrans as early as was desirable. In the meanwhile Bragg was receiving reinforcements from the Army of the Mississippi, from Lee's Virginian Army, and from other sources, and was ultimately enabled to present a much more formidable front to his adversaries than would have been possible a short time before. The army under Rosecrans reached the northern bank of the Tennessee River, opposite Chattanooga, on August 20, and preparations for passing the stream were completed by September 4, when a large part of the army crossed over to the southern shore, and threatened the communications of Bragg with the country in his rear. The position became untenable, and on the 7th it was abandoned. Chattanooga was then occupied by a Union corps, and Bragg retreated to Lafayette, in Georgia. Here he concentrated his divisions, and matured his plans for resisting the enemy. The forces of Rosecrans were now divided into three columns, widely separated from one another by the defiles of a mountainous region, extending in a south-westerly direction from the southern side of the Tennessee River towards Alabama. Rosecrans supposed the enemy to be weaker than he really was, and that he might safely advance in loose order against a flying foe. Bragg considered that he could attack these scattered bodies in detail, and thus secure a series of victories, such as would have been utterly beyond his reach had the several corps been united. But he was met by an unexpected degree of opposition in one of his subordinates. General D. B. Hill objected to making a forward movement against General Thomas, who was encamped at the foot of Lookout Mountain, to the left of the Union advance; and the duty was consequently assigned to Buckner, in combination with General Hindman. The movement resulted in failure. Owing to the dilatory proceedings of Hindman, Thomas had time to withdraw among the mountain-passes, and

GENERAL BRAXTON BRAGG.

by about the middle of the month the two other corps, under McCook and Crittenden, effected a junction with the one which had been so seriously menaced. Simultaneously with the attack upon Thomas, Polk was to fall on Crittenden's corps, forming the center of the three advancing bodies; but he was as unsuccessful as Hindman and Buckner, and on September 18, the whole of the Union army stood on the western bank of Chickamauga Creek. Not far to the east were the Confederates, and it was obvious to both sides that a general action must presently ensue.

By this time, Longstreet, with the divisions of Hood and McLaws, had been despatched by Lee to the support of Bragg, and the advanced brigades of the reinforcement had already arrived. Rosecrans felt that his line was weak towards the left, and he feared lest he should be cut off from Chattanooga. He therefore, on the evening of the 18th, moved some of his divisions from the right to the opposite extremity, and next morning the two armies were fronting one another in a narrow valley formed by two lines of hills called Mission Ridge and Pigeon Mount—the former to the west, the latter to the east. Between the two uplands flowed Chickamauga Creek, which the Confederates had by this time crossed, so as to seek their enemy. The ground was uneven, and covered with oak-woods; it therefore presented many opportunities for effective manœuvering. The line of battle, roughly speaking, ran north and south; the Union Forces facing towards the east, the Confederates towards the west. Bragg was desirous of executing the very movement which Rosecrans dreaded. He would gladly have interposed between his adversary and Chattanooga; but Rosecrans thwarted any attempt of this nature by the change which he effected in his front. On the morning of the 19th, Rosecrans brought on an engagement by moving forward a brigade of Thomas's corps, which attacked the Confederate right wing. The fighting soon became general; a sanguinary and hotly-contested action strewed the field with dead and wounded; and for awhile the Confederates seemed to be carrying all before them. When night put an end to the battle, however, the Southerners had been checked. Still, they were in advance of the morning's positions, and had gained possession of the road to Chattanooga, besides having driven the Union forces about a mile west of Chickamauga Creek, almost to the foot of Mission Ridge.

Longstreet, the most eminent and capable of Lee's lieutenants, arrived at Bragg's headquarters near midnight on the

GENERAL LEONIDAS POLK.

19th, together with an additional division, and was placed in command of the left wing. At the same same time, a fresh disposition of the forces was carried out by Bragg's directions, and it was ordered that the action should recommence at daybreak on the 20th. The night was an anxious one. Rosecrans was uneasy about his communications with Chattanooga, and, on the representations of Thomas, who commanded in that direction, again transferred some of his troops from the right to the left. While this dangerous movement was in course of execution, the Confederates began their attack. It was now ten o'clock in the day, for owing to some error or negligence, the Southern troops had not opened fire at the early hour originally contemplated. The delay had enabled the Union troops to throw up breastworks, and to strengthen them by repeated additions. Against these entrenchments the right wing of Bragg's army repeatedly hurled itself, but without any permanent gain. On the left of the line, however, Longstreet met with almost uniform success. His men rushed forward with fierce impetuosity, and interposed themselves between the two wings of the Union army, where the removal of the center, to strengthen the left, had created a wide gap. Operating in both directions at once, the Confederates, headed by Longstreet in person, struck confusion into the Union line. Several of the divisions were thrown into extreme disorder, and Rosecrans rode off to Chattanooga, to secure his supply-train, and his pontoon-bridges over the Tennessee River. At this critical moment, Hood, one of the bravest of the Southern Generals, fell severely wounded, and the Confederate advance was momentarily delayed while another commander was being put in his place. The Union forces now rallied; reinforcements were concentrated at the weak points; and a fresh stand was made on the lower slopes of Mission Ridge. The day, however, was beyond retrieval. Advancing once more with fresh vigor, the right wing of the Confederates, under Polk, carried the opposing breastworks; the left wing, after a brief repulse, also moved forward; and the whole army retreated, but for the most part in such good order that Bragg thought it prudent to refrain from pursuit. Longstreet was desirous of following on the track, but his chief countermanded the orders he had given with that view. That the Union forces had

BATTLE OF CHICKAMAUGA, SEPTEMBER 19–20, 1863.

not been utterly routed, was due to the firmness with which Thomas clung to his position on the left, and to the promptitude with which Granger, on hearing heavy firing in the distance, sent up the reserves from Rossville. Longstreet was the chief hero on the Confederate side. In neither army did the principal commander greatly distinguish himself.

The sacrifices on both sides had been very severe. It has been estimated that the Confederates lost 12,000 men, and the Unions loss was 16,000. Bragg confessed that two-fifths of his army had been taken from him; and on that side alone three Brigadier-Generals had been killed. The Union forces, however, were the greatest sufferers. Thirty-six of their guns were captured, and large quantities of small-arms were left behind upon the field. Rosecrans was considered to have exhibited so little generalship that he was shortly afterwards succeeded by Thomas, while McCook, Crittenden, Negley, and Van Cleve, were suspended from their commands, that inquiry might be made into their conduct. Of the Confederate superior officers, the only one removed from the scene of the recent operations was Polk, who was thought to have acted with hesitation in the battle of the 20th. Much blame was thrown by the Southern public on Bragg himself, for not having completed a victory which had been so well begun; but Davis refused to recognize these complaints. Even in removing Polk, he paid a high compliment to that officer for his past services, and promised him a speedy appointment to some new command.

On quitting the banks of the Chickamauga, the Union corps retreated to Chattanooga, where they speedily entrenched themselves. On September 23, Bragg appeared before the Union lines, and, finding them too strong to be taken by assault, determined to invest the position. Attempts were made to cut off all the sources on which the Northerners depended for their daily needs; but these endeavors were defeated by the activity of the Union cavalry, though the supply of food still remained a matter of great difficulty. The position of the army at Chattanooga threatened disastrous results, if it could not be relieved; and Halleck and the authorities at Washington saw in Grant the man most likely to cope with existing troubles. He was accordingly appointed to the command of the West, and large bodies of troops were set in motion to provide him with the necessary means for acting decisively. The 11th and 12th corps, under Hooker, were transferred from the Army of the Potomac to that of Tennessee. These two corps consisted of 23,000 men, who, together with their artillery, baggage, and animals, moved from the Rapidan, in Virginia, to Stevenson, in Alabama—a distance of 1,192 miles—in seven days, during which they crossed the Ohio twice. With the advance of autumn, several columns were converging on Chattanooga, to the relief of the Union forces; and Bragg's forces, though continuing to watch the imprisoned enemy, could do little else. Burnside's operations in Eastern Tennessee had prevented his joining Rosecrans in time to avert the catastrophe of Chickamauga; and he was now withheld from marching to the succor of his comrades at Chattanooga by the operations of a Confederate detachment. Yet Bragg either could not or would not make a direct attack on the Union position; and, while every day brought rescue nearer to the Union forces, it rendered still more problematical the chances of ultimate success on the part of their adversaries. Among those who were hurrying towards the invested city was Sherman, who started from Vicksburg, and advanced towards Athens, in Alabama, near the borders of Tennessee. He was now appointed to succeed Grant in the Tennessee Department, and, while at Iuka, Mississippi, on his route to Athens, was directed to march on to Bridgeport, a small town situated on the north side of the Tennessee River, 24 miles to the west of Chattanooga. Thomas was by this time in the principal command at the beleaguered place; and he was endeavoring to open a road along the southern bank of the Tennessee, so as to establish a connection between Hooker's force, which at the close of October had arrived at Bridgeport, and the main army. The base of the Union army was at Bridgeport and Stevenson (both in Alabama), and the regiments were supplied from depots at Nashville (in Tennessee and Kentucky) by a single line of rail. The southern side of the Tennessee River was in possession of the enemy, with the exception of Chattanooga and the surrounding lines; and the road on the north side was rendered impassable by the Confederate sharpshooters, who fired across the stream. The Union forces were consequently obliged to bring all their supplies in a circuitous way from a distance of nearly 60 miles; and it was therefore of the highest importance to open the river, and secure a shorter communication with the military base.

Hooker's arrival at Bridgeport relieved the troops at Chattanooga from any further anxiety about their supplies; and, as we have seen, Sherman was on his way to the same point. Thomas now directed his principal engineer officer, General W. F. Smith, to seize the mouth of Lookout Valley, and the neighboring heights, on the southern side of the river (the side on which Chattanooga itself is situated), while Hooker crossed from Bridgeport, on the opposite bank. On the night of October 27 Smith descended the river in boats to Brown's Ferry, accompanied by infantry and engineers. Landing at the mouth of the valley early next morning, with but slight opposition from the enemy, he made good his position in the contemplated spot, and immediately proceeded to construct a pontoon bridge, which, though 900 feet in length, was put together in five hours. During the day (the 28th) Hooker crossed the river at Bridgeport, and marched eastward, so as to join the force already in possession of the entrance to Lookout Valley. This movement was known to the Confederates. Bragg and Longstreet observed its progress from the brow of Lookout Mountain, but at the moment refrained from attacking, lest a general action should be brought on with inconvenient precipitancy. On the night of the 28th, Longstreet assailed a detachment of Hooker's Corps, which was separated from the rest on the western side of Lookout Creek; but the attempt was unsuccessful, and the Confederates then abandoned the position to their opponents, and retired across the creek, leaving behind them a large number of dead and wounded.

Bragg now determined to detach Longstreet against Burnside, who was occupying Knoxville and Kingston, in Eastern Tennessee. This, however, had the effect of weakening the Confederates before Chattanooga to so serious an extent that their position became extremely hazardous. Grant, who had arrived at Chattanooga on the night of October 20, repeatedly and urgently telegraphed to Burnside to hold Knoxville at all costs, while he himself operated against Bragg. The railway from Bridgeport to Brown's Ferry was speedily repaired by the Union troops, who being now in possession of both shores of the river, were in a far better position, in every respect, than those of the South, and Bragg, whose abilities were not of a shining order, had to deal with an adversary of very superior powers. Bragg's arrangements were indeed marked by extraordinary carelessness. His divisions were widely scattered, while the Union troops were adding to their numbers and concentrating their forces at the most available points. Sherman reached Chattanooga on November 15, and was speedily instructed by Grant as to the part he was to assume in the attack which it was resolved to make with as little delay as possible. A division of his troops was to be marched to Trenton (west of Lookout Mountain), so as to threaten the enemy's left flank; and under cover of this movement the main body was to cross General W. F. Smith's pontoon-bridge at Brown's Ferry, and enter a concealed camp on the north side of the Tennessee River. Ultimately the troops were to be re-conveyed to the southern side of that stream, near the mouth of Chickamauga Creek, and to take up a position on the left of Grant's line of battle, while Hooker and Thomas operated in other directions against the Confederate masses. The arrangements were of a complicated character, and were designed to deceive and surprise the enemy. Over the frail causeway of the Brown's Ferry bridge, which had already been damaged by the rising waters of the river, and by rafts which the Confederates had sent floating down the current, the men and horses of Sherman's corps advanced on the 23d from the southern to the northern shore, under heavy torrents of rain. When all but one division had got across, the bridge broke up; but, in the main, the first part of the operation had been accomplished. On the same day, Grant ordered Thomas to push forward a reconnoissance from the lines of Chattanooga. The result of this movement was that with but little fighting the Union troops captured some rifle-pits, and occupied a small hill between Chattanooga and Mission Ridge. Just before this event, Bragg had set in motion additional reinforcements for Longstreet; but they were recalled, on its becoming evident that the Union forces were about to undertake operations of a very menacing character.

THE UNION LINES AT CHATTANOOGA.

The arrival of Sherman's corps had raised Grant's army to nearly 90,000 men, while Bragg had only about half that number with which to defend his lines. Bragg felt the weakness of his position and the insufficiency of his resources. Perceiving how seriously his right was threatened, he drew off a whole division from his left on Lookout Mountain, while still retaining that position with a most inadequate force. On the morning of the 24th, his army was thinly distributed along an irregular line of 12 miles, reaching from the western slopes of Lookout Mountain to a point near the outfall of Chickamauga Creek into the river with which it blends. The fighting on that day was not considerable; yet the combined operations of the Union forces were such as to make Bragg still more sensible of the peril in which he stood. He evacuated Lookout Mountain after dark, relinquished the Valley of Chattanooga, and re-formed his line of battle along Mission Ridge; his front directed nearly to the west, his right covering Chickamauga Station, and his left overlooking the little town of Rossville. The morning of the 25th was foggy; but when the mists cleared off, the Confederates, from their high ground, beheld the dark masses of Sherman's corps (which had recrossed the Tennessee on the previous day) advancing towards the extreme right, in the vicinity of Chickamauga Station. Against this attacking force a heavy fire of artillery was opened; but the Union forces swept on, and presently attained the base of the ridge. Then the cannonade slackened, and the sharp rattle of musketry broke forth. Sherman's division was endeavoring to scale the steep and difficult ground occupied by the Confederate right wing, commanded by General Hardee. The attack was pressed with the utmost gallantry, and maintained for a full hour; but the breastworks which the Southerners had erected were manned by stubborn troops, the incessant flash of whose rifles carried death into the Union ranks at every discharge.

Sherman's men at last reeled back to the rear; but Grant ordered the attack renewed. Again did those devoted soldiers move up to the assault. The ground in many parts was slippery with blood, and, rising sharply towards the barricades, presented difficulties of no ordinary kind; yet the breastworks were once more reached, in the face of a terrific fire, both of artillery and musketry. A desperate combat took place in front of the batteries; but again the heroic masses of Sherman's corps were hurled back into the valley. Grant now directed a general movement on the left centre of the Confederates. Here also the opposition was most determined, and resulted in fearful carnage; but the weak point in the Confederate line had at length been struck.

GENERAL HARDEE.

A whole brigade of Hindman's division gave way; the Union troops leaped into the trenches, and scattered their antagonists right and left; and the routed line fell back towards Ringold, to the southeast of the Confederate position. Thousands of prisoners were taken, and munitions of war to a large amount fell into the conquerors' hands. Hooker started in pursuit, and on the 26th the Confederates retired from Ringold, after an unsuccessful attempt to hold that place. They then took up a position on a line of hills called Taylor's Ridge, where they presented so menacing a front to their opponents that on the 27th Grant determined that the pursuit should not be pushed any farther, but that Hooker should remain at Ringold, while Sherman, at the head of a strong force, marched against Longstreet. By this time, Cleveland, lying to the east of Chattanooga, had been occupied by a portion of Sherman's command, and the railway between that place and Dalton had been effectually destroyed, so as to prevent the possibility of a flank movement against the column advancing upon Knoxville. Bragg had completely lost the confidence of the Southern people. Though personally supported by Davis, he was removed from his command, and the direction of the Georgian forces was for a time conferred on Hardee, whose stubborn courage and good generalship on the 25th had won the admiration of all.

It is now time to consider what was passing at Knoxville. That town is situated on the East Tennessee and Georgia Railway, south of Clinch River, and north-east of Chattanooga. The point is one of great strategical importance, since it commands the whole valley of the Upper Tennessee; and on this account Grant had ordered Burnside to do his utmost for the retention of his post, threatened by the advance of Longstreet from the army before Chattanooga. Burnside was in command of two corps; but they were not very strong in numbers, and the several divisions were distributed at considerable distances from one another, and from the center at Knoxville. A sudden attack on these scattered forces seemed not unlikely to be attended by success. Longstreet left the neighborhood of Chattanooga early in November. He took with him about 12,000 men, who were to be reinforced by the two divisions which he expected to find at Sweetwater, near Loudon; but, on arriving at that place, he discovered that the forces stationed there had been ordered to join Bragg on the banks of the Tennessee, and that some had already started. He was therefore obliged to rest contented with the regiments he already had in hand, strengthened by about 5,000 cavalry under General Wheeler. It had been part of his engagement with Bragg that he was to be furnished with supplies; but no supplies were forthcoming, and he was compelled to halt for some days at Sweetwater, while he sent out foraging parties to collect corn, thresh it, and bring it into a proper condition for being made into bread. Not only were his men ill-supplied with food; they were also destitute of tents, and poorly furnished with clothes. Longstreet, however, had the confidence of his troops as much as Lee himself. He had been associated with many victories, and entire reliance was placed on his ability to overcome the most adverse circumstances with which he was likely to be encountered. He accordingly marched forward towards Knoxville, strong in the devotion of his men; and, having crossed the Little Tennessee, came into collision with two divisions of Burnside's forces on November 16. The attack was vigorously conducted, but the Union troops held their antagonists in check sufficiently to effect their retreat within the fortifications of Knoxville. Those fortifications extended from hill to hill round the town; and within the works were collected nearly 15,000 infantry and artillery, together with a proportion of cavalry; Knoxville was invested by Longstreet on the 17th and 18th, and on the second of those days an assault was undertaken against one of the principal outworks, which was carried after a very obstinate resistance.

Although one of the outworks was now in possession of the Confederates, Longstreet doubted his ability to carry the whole of the fortifications by assault. It was equally impossible to reduce the place by a regular siege, for which it was not at all likely that time would be allowed by the vastly superior forces under Grant. There was consequently nothing to be done but to cut off the supplies, and thus reduce the town by famine. This, however, was in itself a work of time, and after the total defeat of Bragg it became evident that the plan was no longer practicable. A large body of Union troops would soon be marching to the relief of Knoxville, and Longstreet feared to be caught between two fires. He therefore fell back on his first idea of an assault. The attack was to be made on the morning of the 29th, and Fort Sanders, or College Hill, was the point selected for the difficult and perilous attempt. The necessary preparations were completed on the night of the 28th; and early next morning the storming-parties were sent forward. The Union batteries having been silenced, these brave men moved across the open ground, and gained the edge of the ditch; but it was then seen that there were no scaling-ladders, and, while the assailants were pausing in hesitation as to what they should do, the Union troops poured so deadly a fire into their ranks that the column was broken and disorganized. Some of the men clambered up the side of the works on to the parapet, but were immediately shot down or captured. The ditch was choked with dead and wounded; and when a number of hand-grenades were thrown into the staggering mass, its cohesion was entirely destroyed, and nothing remained but to retreat.

Though greatly disappointed by the result of this attempt, Longstreet still maintained his positions round the town, the garrison and inhabitants of which began to suffer from shortness of provisions. Sherman, however, was now on his road to Knoxville, and it was known to the army, from the reports of prisoners, that Bragg had been defeated before Chattanooga, and that succor could not be long in arriving. Marching with rapidity, and only pausing to repair broken bridges or construct new ones across the rivers by which the country was intersected, Sherman reached the vicinity of Knoxville on December 5. Longstreet, though lately reinforced, knew that he was not strong enough to resist the united armies of Burnside and Sherman; and when the latter arrived upon the spot, he found that his adversary had already departed. He had quitted his lines on the previous night, and had moved in a north-easterly direction to the borders of Virginia. Sherman met Burnside outside the fortifications, and proposed to him to pursue Longstreet with a force sufficient to ensure the withdrawal of the Confederates from Eastern Tennessee; but the offer was refused by Burnside, who is said to have exhibited some jealousy of his distinguished colleague. He declared that Granger's corps, in addition to his own, would be sufficient to guarantee Knoxville against further attack, and that the pursuit could be undertaken by his cavalry. Very little, however, was done to harass Longstreet's rear. Sherman returned to Chattanooga, and shortly afterwards Burnside, whose health was failing him, solicited recall, and was superseded by General Forster, from the Department of North Carolina.

The fame of Sherman was now almost equal to that of Grant. He was at the time in his 44th year, and during the early period of the Civil War had been regarded as a man of inferior abilities. The test of actual service, however, had shown that he was possessed, not merely of the very ordinary gift of courage, but of real military genius, of tireless energy and quick discernment. Sherman's troops were proud of their General; their General was equally proud of them. Referring to the recent course of events in one of his official despatches, he said:—" In reviewing the facts, I must do justice to the command for the patience, cheerfulness and courage which officers and men have displayed throughout—in battle, on the march and in camp. For long periods, without regular rations or supplies of any kind, they have marched through mud and over rocks, sometimes barefooted, without a murmur, without a moment's rest. After a march of 400 miles, without stopping for three successive nights, we crossed the Tennessee, and then turned more than 100 miles north, and compelled Longstreet to raise the siege of Knoxville, which gave so much anxiety to the whole country." In Sherman and his troops were to be found all the elements of success, and a series of triumphs attended their operations wherever they carried the flag of the Republic. Nearly three years of civil war had taught both the North and the South to be soldiers in every sense of the word. They were no longer the amateurs who had been helplessly driven to the slaughter in the dark and evil days of 1861. They had acquired the professional feeling and the professional habits of veterans, to whom war is not an affair of declamation in the first instance, and of panic in the second, but a stern and terrible duty, to be faced with courage and borne with resolution. In the earlier part of the struggle, the fighting-men of the South, from their greater familiarity with arms and active exercises, had shown more military virtue than their brethren of the North; but the scale was now inclining in favor of the other side. Freedom had its heroes, as well as slavery; and not merely its heroes, but its men of genius and success. In Grant and Sherman alone, the Union found a guarantee that in the end its cause would certainly prevail.

The campaign in Tennessee was over for the present. The State had been snatched from the grasp of the Confederacy, and the forces of the Union were in a favorable position for acting against Virginia and the Carolinas.

CHAPTER VI.

CHARLESTON AND FORT SUMTER.

The flag of the Palmetto State audaciously waving from Fort Sumter in Charleston Harbor had long been looked upon as a sort of standing rebuke to the impotent power of the North. It appeared impracticable to attempt the recovery of the fort; so it was determined to destroy the present usefulness of the harbor, and thus prevent the egress of privateers to prey on Northern merchantmen, and the ingress of the swift-sailing British blockade-runners.

Accordingly, it was proposed to fill the channel by blocking it up with huge masses of stone. Charleston had been the cradle of the rebellion, and some degree of punishment for the immense wrong it had committed, and the misery it had spread far and wide in the prosecution of its wicked ambition, should be meted out, and it would have been nothing more than just. The plan met with approval, and 45 old whaling vessels and mercantile ships were purchased and filled with stones. These assembled at Port Royal, and, on December 17, under convoy of ships-of-war, sailed for the harbor of Charleston. The vessels to be sunk, together with their contents, were ships and barks of a burden between 200 and 500 tons, too old to be any longer employed in long sea-voyages, but very well adapted to the project in hand. They were for the most part double-deckers, and, having been stripped of their copper and other fittings, were loaded with stones as deeply as was considered safe. Each vessel was manned by about fourteen men, and precise instructions were given as to how they should proceed. Measures of a similar nature had already been taken on the coast of North Carolina, where Ocracoke Inlet, Pamlico Sound, had been to some extent blocked by sunken vessels, as a means of preventing the entrance of blockade-runners. The old boats were so sunk as not entirely to block up the outlets to the current, lest the stream, running with great force out of the harbor, should make for itself a fresh passage, equal to that which had been closed. On December 19, the fleet assembled off Charleston Bar, when the position where each ship was to be sunk was exactly marked. The act of sinking the vessels was believed to have been thoroughly effected; but the calculation proved erroneous. The strength of the current soon swept away the obstructions in its channel and the harbor was once more free.

The defences of Charleston had been greatly strengthened, and early in 1863 General Beauregard was placed in command of the department. Charleston had been watched by a large fleet of ironclads; but these had been scattered one dark night towards the end of January, 1863, by a bold attack conducted by Captain Ingraham, in command of two rams which had been built and equipped on the spot. One of the Union ironclads had been compelled to surrender and the Confederates claimed that they had raised the blockade. Such was the state of affairs when a fresh expedition was directed against the city under the command of Admiral Dupont.

In the course of March, the greater part of the fleet was transferred from Port Royal to a point about midway between that locality and Charleston Harbor, and about 100 vessels were collected at the mouth of the North Edisto River. The fleet sailed for Charleston Bar on April 6. The bar was crossed by the ironclads in the course of the day; and a position was taken up in the main channel along the coast of Morris Island.

On the 7th, a line of battle was formed, in which the

SOUTH CAROLINA FLAG.

ironclads were to take the principal part. The wooden vessels remained outside the bar. Attached to the leading ironclad, the *Weehawken*, was a raft, designed to explode torpedoes and remove obstructions.

The attacking force was allowed to pass the outer batteries; but as the *Weehawken* was about to enter the inner harbor, a gun was fired from Fort Moultrie, followed by all the batteries on Sullivan's Island and Morris Island, and by those of Fort Sumter. On reaching the entrance of the channel between Sumter and Sullivan's Island, the leading ship got entangled in a hawser stretched across the waterway, to which were suspended nets and various contrivances for preventing the action of the screws. The ironclads opened fire on the forts; but a good deal of confusion ensued in the movements of the heavy-armored ships. The *Weehawken* endeavored to steer into a more favorable position, and the whole squadron got mixed up in a way that was utterly destructive of order.

By four in the afternoon, the ironclads were ranged opposite the north-east front of Sumter, at distances varying from 550 to 800 yards, where they were exposed to the concentrated fire of 300 guns, possessing extraordinary range and power. Setting aside the *Weehawken*, which was incapable of rendering assistance, owing to the obstructions with which it was entangled, the number of the ironclads was but eight, carrying not more than 16 guns in all. It is stated that, at the hottest part of the fire, 160 shots were counted in a minute, and officers described the projectiles as sometimes striking their vessels as rapidly as the ticking of a watch. The narrowness of the channel, the dense clouds of smoke proceeding from the guns, and the necessity of avoiding collisions with one another, with the various floating obstructions, and with the submerged batteries, proved sources of great embarrassment to the commanders of the attacking fleet. Nevertheless, the action was maintained with much spirit, and Commander Rhind ran his vessel, the *Keokuk*, within a short distance of Fort Sumter, where she was so hotly received that at the end of half an hour she was forced to retire, lest she should be utterly destroyed. She had been struck 90 times in the hull and turrets, and 19

FORT MOULTRIE, CHARLESTON, WITH FORT SUMTER IN THE DISTANCE.

shots had pierced her sides, either at or below the waterline. It was only with much difficulty that she could be brought to anchor beyond the range of fire, and next morning she sank. The other vessels were injured in various degrees, though not so severely as the *Keokuk*. It was evident that the guns in the forts and batteries were stronger than those which were brought to bear in reply, and that the armor-plated sides of the ironclads were not of sufficient thickness to withstand the tremendous weight of metal that was hurled against them. Moreover, the land forces were too few in number to render any assistance. Dupont therefore gave orders for the attack to cease. Several men had been killed and wounded on board the fleet, while only two deaths had occurred in the forts. The east wall of Fort Sumter had been somewhat broken by the Union guns; but the damage was slight, and this was all that could be set against the enormous amount of injury that had been received by the vessels. A large proportion of these had been either wholly or one-half disabled in less than an hour's engagement, and the admiral felt convinced that persistence in the attack would have resulted in the loss of nearly all his ships. With the exception of the *New Ironsides*, which anchored outside Charleston Bar, the whole fleet returned to Port Royal on April 12. Next day Lincoln telegraphed to Dupont that he was to hold his position inside Charleston Bar, or, in the event of his having left it, was at once to return. He was not to allow the enemy to erect new batteries or defences on Morris Island, and, if he had begun to do so, he was to drive him forth. He replied by expressing his willingness to obey all orders with fidelity, while at the same time pointing out that the course imposed on him would be attended with great risks. He was superseded in July by Admiral Dahlgren, and arrangements were made for combined operations against Charleston by land and sea.

A third attack was now begun on Charleston, that city having already successfully resisted two powerful assaults. It was settled that a military force should seize Morris Island, and bombard Fort Sumter. The troops were to be aided by a strong fleet under Dahlgren; and it was hoped that the monitors and ironclads would be able to enter the harbor, to pass the batteries, and to reach the city. An army was collected on Folly Island, to the south of Morris Island, and early in July batteries were erected among the woods. Under cover of these guns, a brigade of 2000 men, commanded by General Strong, prepared to assail the position which it was first desired to occupy. The southern end of Morris Island was defended by 700 Carolinian infantry, two companies of artillery, and some other forces, under the direction of General Ripley, who acted under Beauregard. Strong's attack, which took place on July 10, was successfully conducted, and the Southerners were driven back to Fort Wagner, situated near the farther end of the island. The fort was strongly constructed, and armed with 20 guns of various calibre, nearly all covering the only approach to the walls, which was along a barren and shifting beach, extremely narrow, and subject to frequent overflow. Being in communication with Charleston, the armament and garrison of this work could be easily maintained at its highest standard, and any attacking force was within reach, not merely of the guns in Wagner itself, but of those in Fort Sumter, and of the adjacent batteries. After forcing the Confederates to take shelter within their lines, the Union forces refrained from commencing an immediate assault upon the works, owing to the exhaustion which they had already suffered from the heat of the day. During the night, two fresh regiments of Confederates were sent to Fort Wagner, to reinforce the garrison; but at daybreak on the 11th, an assault was made by Strong's troops, who, proceeding along the narrow neck of land between the sea on the right hand and a marsh on the left, advanced in good order to the outer defences. A Connecticut regiment, which occupied the front position, crossed the *glacis*, and leaped into the ditch; but all attempts to climb the parapet were defeated by the terrific fire of the Confederates. At length the storming party was compelled to retreat, losing many gallant men in struggling back to their lines, as well as in the attack itself. Gillmore determined to proceed against the fort by the erection of opposing batteries, which were aided by the fire of the monitors. The garrison suffered greatly from the artillery of their foes, and from the suffocating heat engendered in the bomb-proof galleries by the July sun, and the continual discharges of the cannon. The troops, however, could be frequently relieved, and occasional sallies varied the monotony of passive defence.

A terrible bombardment was opened on July 18. The Confederate guns replied feebly, and the garrison in Fort Wagner saw that they would shortly have to defend the walls against a renewed assault. Their anticipations were realized that very evening. In the midst of a thunderstorm, the Union columns were formed upon the beach. The head of the first brigade consisted of a negro regiment, and the whole body, consisting of blacks and whites, pushed steadily on, under a concentrated fire from Forts Wagner, Gregg, and Sumter, and from the batteries on James and Sullivan's Islands. The attempt to mount the walls was fiercely resisted by the Southerners, who poured into the Union ranks a stinging fire of musketry aided, whenever the antagonists came to close quarters, by the action of the bayonet and the sword. The dead

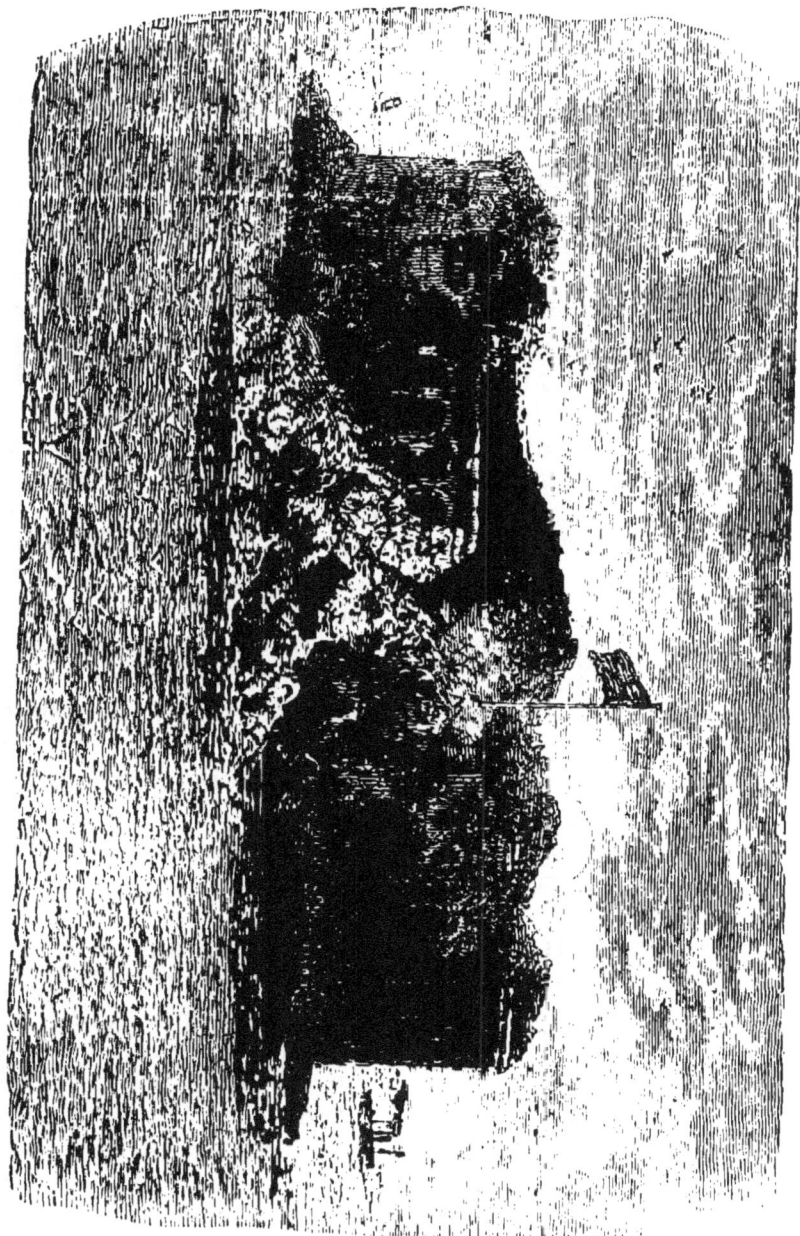

FORT SUMTER IN RUINS.

and dying dropped from the ladders into the mud and ooze of the ditch, and the first brigade was repelled by the vigor and determination of the defenders. This, however, did not deter the second brigade from advancing to the assistance of the first. A lodgment was effected in one of the angles of the fort, and a fierce encounter was kept up in that confined space for about an hour; but the assailants were at length driven out, and forced to retire. General Strong had by this time been wounded, and nearly all the superior officers had fallen. Owing to some error, the third brigade did not arrive to the support of the two first; and when the attacking forces had regained their own positions, it was found that their numbers had been fearfully reduced. The Confederates in the fort had lost 174 in killed, wounded, and missing; but the position was almost as strong as ever. General Taliaferro, who commanded the garrison, estimated that 9000 shot and shell had been hurled against the works; yet the walls were but slightly injured. The fort was constructed of compact sand, which dulled and turned aside the heaviest projectiles, while such damages as were inflicted could be easily repaired.

Parallels were now opened against the fort, and the Union forces proceeded with all the regular gradations of a siege. The ironclads in the surrounding waters frequently engaged Fort Wagner and Fort Sumter; but the garrison of the former were regularly reinforced and periodically relieved, and the batteries were strengthened by fresh guns, which were conveyed thither during the concluding part of July, and in the early days of August. The breaching batteries of the Union forces were opened on August 17. They were directed, however, not against Wagner, but against Sumter, which was reached by firing over the intervening fort. The distance from the batteries to Sumter was not far short of three miles; but the ramparts crumbled before the awful concentration of power now brought to bear on them. Forts Wagner, Gregg, and Sumter were bombarded by the Union ironclads, and, replying with energy, added to the horrible roar which filled the air. The vessels were compelled to withdraw at noon, by which time the men were almost exhausted by heat and fatigue. They returned in the afternoon, but the defenders of Fort Wagner had in the meanwhile repaired the injuries which had been inflicted during the morning. The bombardment continued during the 18, 19, and 20th; and whenever the flag at Fort Sumter was shot away, it was immediately replaced, though he who bore it aloft stood in imminent danger of being slain in the act. By the 21st, the southern wall of Sumter was a mere pile of rubbish; on the north, the stones were crumbling into a mass of ruins; several guns had been dismounted, and others removed; but the garrison themselves had lost scarcely any of their number. Forts Wagner and Gregg had suffered very slightly, while the inner line of defences, extending across James Island in the direction of Sullivan's Island, had been greatly strengthened by the Southern forces.

Encouraged by the effect he had produced on Fort Sumter, Gillmore now demanded the surrender of that position, and of the works on Morris Island, on pain of the city of Charleston itself being bombarded if the requisition were refused. The letter was sent to Beauregard on the night of August 21; but he was away at the time on a reconnoissance, and, before an answer could be returned, the bombardment opened upon the city at one A. M. on the morning of the 22d. It necessarily produced consternation among the sleeping inhabitants, who, rushing confusedly into the streets, made for the open country. Beauregard sent a remonstrance with respect to this sudden attack upon the city. He remarked that among nations not barbarous the usages of war prescribe that, when a city is about to be attacked, timely notice shall be given, so that non-combatants may have an opportunity of withdrawing beyond its limits; that generally the time allowed is from one to three days, but that Gillmore had given only four hours' notice; and he characterized this mode of warfare as "atrocious, and unworthy of any soldier." Gillmore replied that he had been steadily advancing for a long time, and that an attack upon the city itself was to be expected, and should therefore have been guarded against by a timely removal of the women, children, and old people. He had reason to believe that many of these had in fact left the place long before; but, as several might still be there, he would give them until 11 P. M. on the 23d before he renewed the bombardment.

The bombardment recommenced at the expiration of the stated time, but did not long continue, owing to the speedy explosion of an immense Parrott gun, called by the soldiers "the Marsh Angel," which was employed in this particular work. In the meanwhile, the parallels were being steadily pushed forward towards Fort Wagner; the Confederate rifle-pits were carried at the point of the bayonet on the 26th, and a fifth parallel was then completed within 240 yards of the main work. Nevertheless the opposing fire from the Confederate forts and batteries continued as strong as ever, and the Dahlgren fleet being unable to pass the barriers defending the inner harbor, could do nothing to outflank the several positions which the army was endeavoring to take in front. The Union losses increased from day to day, and the men were discouraged at the seemingly endless nature of their task. The sappers could only work at night, and even then were often brought down by aid of the powerful moonlight. Yet

VIEW OF CHARLESTON HARBOR, SHOWING THE FORTS AND SUNKEN VESSELS.

247

Gillmore held firmly to his purpose, and now determined to open on Fort Wagner a bombardment more powerful than any which had gone before. This was to continue day and night without any cessation, and during the hours of darkness the gunners were to work by calcium lights, which had already been tried with good effect. The new bombardment commenced on September 5, and prevailed for 42 consecutive hours. The land batteries were assisted by one of the ironclads, which fired enormous shells from its eight broadside guns; and the garrison, compelled to keep watch against any assault that might be intended, lost many of their number in exposed positions. The work was, in fact, no longer tenable, therefore preparations were made for the withdrawal of the troops. It was resolved to abandon Fort Wagner, together with Fort Gregg, situated at Cumming's Point, which is the northern extremity of Morris Island. The evacuation commenced at nine on the evening of the 6th, when the guns were spiked, and fire was applied to the magazines. No explosion followed, as the matches failed to operate; and while the Union sappers were mounting the deserted parapet of Fort Wagner, the last of the Confederate garrison were quitting the island. Their retreat was scarcely interrupted by the enemy, and next morning the Union troops were compelled to repair the ramparts, to protect themselves against the batteries in Fort Moultrie and on James Island, which were immediately turned upon the positions just abandoned by the Southerners. It was believed by Dahlgren that Sumter must be surrendered now that Morris Island was in possession of his colleague. The fort was little better than a ruin; its artillery could no longer be worked, and the ground was held merely by a detachment of infantry, commanded by Major Elliott. To this officer Dahlgren sent a demand for the surrender of the fort.

Elliott replied that the admiral might have Sumter when he could take it. An attempt to obtain possession of the place was made by the ironclads, assisted by a military force, on September 9, but it was not successful. Some of the crews who had landed were received by so hot a fire that the survivors speedily surrendered, and the vessels thereupon retired. This put a termination, for the time being, to the Union successes before Charleston. The city and the remaining forts were occasionally bombarded; but it was not until the final days of the Civil War that this stronghold of rebellion submitted to the authority of the Union.

On the 14th of April—the fourth anniversary of the surrender of Fort Sumter, and the very day on which Lincoln was assassinated—the identical flag which had been lowered in 1861 was once more planted on the shattered walls of the great fortifications which protected the harbor of Charleston; and was planted there by its defender, General (formerly Major) Anderson.

CHAPTER VII.

Sherman's March to the Sea.

Sherman was entrusted with a series of operations, for the prosecution of which three large armies were committed to his charge. These were the Army of the Tennessee, under McPherson; the Army of the Cumberland, commanded by Thomas; and the Army of the Ohio, at the head of which was Schofield, who had recently succeeded to Forster. All were men of ability and experience, though Schofield was but 33 years old; and the supreme commander, Sherman himself, had given evidence of marked and brilliant powers as a military leader. The Confederate Generals were Hardee, Hood, and Polk, acting under the directions of Joseph E. Johnston. The three Confederate corps were inferior in numbers to to the Union troops; but their spirit was equal to that of the legions which were contending under Lee on the blood-stained fields of Virginia. The Northern plan of the campaign was sketched out by Grant, who visited Sherman at Nashville in the middle of March, when he was appointed to the control of the whole military power of the Union forces; and the conduct of the operations was confided with entire reliance to the known judgment and energy of Sherman.

The preparations for the campaign were necessarily very elaborate, and could not be perfected under several weeks. Supplies were sent from the depots at Nashville to Chattanooga; and these two cities were made the primary and secondary bases of the expeditionary force. For the economizing of food, it was ordered that no more rations should be issued to the people of Tennessee, who had for some time been partly supported by the Union authorities. Directions were also given for the entire devotion of the railways to the service of the army; and in the early part of May not far short of 100,000 men, with 254 guns, had been concentrated in and about Chattanooga. It was felt that to obtain possession of Georgia, or even of a portion of that State, would be a great advantage to the Government; for the mountainous district in the north-west abounds in iron-ore, which had been turned to great use by the Confederates. At Rome, and Atlanta, large iron-works had been opened, the capture of which by the Union troops, together with the cotton and woolen mills which were to be found at other places, would be a source of extreme embarrassment to the Southerners. Atlanta had become a chief center of railway communication and trade between the Western States and those on the Atlantic and the Gulf of Mexico. The machine-shops of the principal railways were stationed there, and the Confederate Government had set manufactories of arms, shot and shell, gun-carriages, cartridges, and military clothing. The place was therefore one of importance to the Southern Power; and, on its becoming known that Sherman was about to lead a powerful army in that direction, strenuous efforts were made for defending the approaches.

Abandoning his first idea of counteracting Sherman by invading Tennessee and Kentucky, Johnston now determined to dispute the road to Atlanta by making a stand on every hill and river in the intervening country which offered opportunities of temporary defence. He desired to avoid a general engagement, and to draw on his adversary until he should be able to take him at a disadvantage, far from his supplies and base of operations. The plan did not find favor with the Richmond Government nor with the Southern people generally, to whom it appeared a waste of strength to give up so many mountain-barriers without a more stubborn attempt to hold them than Johnston seemed disposed to make. These objections, however, had no effect in altering the views of the Confederate general, whose brilliant abilities and success in previous years had put him in a position to defy adverse criticism. On May 6th, his forces were drawn up on a range of hills traversed by a pass, known as the Buzzard's Roost, leading to Dalton and Resaca. The three Union armies were at different places in his front, and one of them—Schofield's—was in close proximity at the other end of the pass. Johnston's position was strongly fortified, and Sherman, fearing that he should not be able to take it simply by a direct attack, decided to send McPherson round by another pass, 18 miles to the south-west, and thus to threaten the left rear of his opponent with one portion of his army while with the rest he advanced against the centre. Tunnel Hill, directly in front of Buzzard's Roost, was occupied by Thomas, with but slight opposition, on the 7th of May, and two days later one of the lower ridges of the Confederate position was carried by a division of his army. An attempt even was made to seize the crest of that terrific natural rampart, and the troops advanced with such singular gallantry and devotion that for a moment the task seemed almost accomplished. But the fire of the Confederates was too fearful to be long endured, and, after a great sacrifice of life, the troops withdrew to less exposed quarters.

This was on May 9th. On the 8th, McPherson surprised a brigade of Confederate cavalry; and next day he approached Resaca. The place, however, was too well fortified to be open to attack; no convenient road existed for further progress of the troops; and McPherson, dreading a hostile demonstration on his left flank,

GENERAL JAMES B. MCPHERSON.

retired and took up a position where he was not likely to be assailed. That Johnston's position could be turned with a sufficiently strong force, was now evident: Sherman therefore resolved to make the movement at once with the greater part of his army. McPherson, preceded by Kilpatrick's cavalry, marched towards Resaca on the 13th. In an encounter with the enemy, Kilpatrick fell severely wounded; but the army pushed on, and ultimately drove the Confederates within their fortifications. Johnston left Dalton on the night of the 12th, and on the following day General Howard entered that town, and pressed the Confederates in their rear. With prudent foresight, Johnston had constructed a number of good roads from Dalton to Resaca, and by these he was enabled to transfer his army with despatch from the one town to the other. Sherman had overcome the first obstacle on his route to Atlanta; but he was now confronted by a strong line of entrenchments in a bend of the Oostenaula River, on which stream the town of Resaca is situated.

As soon as his whole army had arrived in front of the position, Sherman determined to attempt its reduction. Two divisions, one of infantry and one of cavalry, were ordered to cross the Oostenaula below Resaca, and to cut the railway between that town and Kingston, lying farther to the south; at the same time, the main army was to close in round the fortified lines. On the 14th, the Union forces threw up counter-works to those of the Southerners, and, under cover of these, directed several attacks against the Confederate positions on the neighboring hills. Severe and desperate fighting took place during that day and the next; but the Union forces were unable to carry the opposing lines in front. The operations against the flanks, however, had been more successful. McPherson, on the left, threatened to cut off his adversary from the bridges by which the Oostenaula was crossed, and the Union cavalry had penetrated to the railways in the rear. Johnston perceived that he must again retire, and on the night of the 15th crossed the stream at his back, and retreated to the Etowah River, forty miles south of Resaca. Sherman lost no time in pursuing. The division of Jefferson C. Davis, turning to the south-west, captured and occupied Rome, while the rest of the army followed on the track of the Confederates, who, crossing to the southern side of the Etowah, took up a position in the Allatoona Pass of the Etowah Mountains. Sherman had now conducted his soldiers a long way into the enemy's country. He was nearly a hundred miles from even his secondary base of operations, at Chattanooga; and in his rear he had a hostile population, and a mountainous and almost pathless region. His position, consequently, was in many respects a very perilous one, and Johnston reckoned on his antagonist's inability to maintain himself under such difficult circumstances. With less capacity in the chief commander, the expedition might indeed have entailed the most disastrous consequences. Sherman, however, maintained a watchful eye over all the arrangements of the campaign, and averted danger by anticipating it. The army marched in three columns; but the communications were well kept up, the flanks were watched by cavalry, and the several divisions were rapidly brought together whenever there was any reason to apprehend a concentration of the opposing forces. In this way an attempt on the part of Johnston, before crossing the Etowah, to crush the centre column of Sherman's army, was completely defeated, though not without a sharp engagement. Johnston was unable to beat his enemy in detail, and was glad to gain the shelter of another stream, where he could once more throw up defences against the constantly advancing foe. For some days the two armies continued watching one another. Sherman had ordered that his troops were to live on the country—a regulation which the evilly-disposed converted into a license for all kinds of plunder and devastation; yet for many of the supplies necessary to active operations the army was dependent on the railway, and the trains were frequently attacked by guerillas issuing from the thick forests that bordered the line. Had Johnston been sufficiently strong in numbers to detach a powerful force of cavalry for the complete and effectual destruction of the railroads, the situation of Sherman would have been grave.

Even as it was, the only safety for the invaders lay in a vigorous prosecution of their march. Crossing the Etowah at points near Kingston on the 23d, Sherman directed his course towards Dallas, and entered a wild and rugged country, where detached bodies of the Confederates were frequently encountered. Both armies entrenched themselves among the hills, and on the 28th Johnston attacked McPherson with sudden fury, but was repulsed with heavy loss. Sherman was again endeavoring to outflank his adversary, and in this he finally succeeded. Allatoona Pass was entered simultaneously from the east and west ends, and June 4, Johnston again fell back, leaving Sherman free to advance on Ackworth. At that town he received a welcome reinforcement, and by the 9th was once more in motion, after establishing in his rear a fortified position in the pass of Allatoona. Heavy fighting followed, and General Polk—a Bishop in the Episcopal Church of Louisiana, and for the last three years an officer of some ability and varied service—was killed by a round shot during a heavy cannonade on the 14th. Ultimately, Johnston was compelled to evacuate one part of his position, and to concentrate his army within shorter lines. A pause then followed for some days; but on the 22d Johnston attacked Hooker and Schofield, obtaining some temporary advantage, but in the end suffering a defeat. Sherman now abandoned his former tactics, and resolved to attack the center of his line with concentrated force. In this way he hoped to reach Marietta, lying to the rear of the Confederate position; but his motives were not merely strategical. He considered it right to prove his ability to make a direct attack, and feared that by a constant repetition of his first procedure he should lower the fighting ca-

GENERAL WILLIAM TECUMSEH SHERMAN.

pabilities of his troops, and induce in his adversary an opinion that he shrank from more onerous encounters. He therefore assaulted the left center of the Confederate army, and a sanguinary combat took place on the 27th. Sherman, however, had for once miscalculated his powers. He lost 3,000 men in an attempt to take the slope on which his enemy was posted, and in the end was compelled to withdraw. Nothing remained but to return to previous methods, and, by out-flanking the Confederates, to compel them once more to retire. A movement of the Union forces' right towards the Chattahoochee River so seriously threatened Johnston's communications with Atlanta that on the night of July 2 he evacuated Marietta, and assumed a new position five miles in its rear. Between the Union army and the works in front of Atlanta, there was now only this one line of defence; but Johnston made the most of it. Menaced, on the 4th, by another flanking movement on the part of his indefatigable foe, he carried the greater part of his army across the Chattahoochee, and strongly entrenched himself. Sherman did not care to risk a direct attack. He sent out parties of cavalry to destroy the flour-mills and cloth-factories in that part of Georgia, and then turned his attention to the enemy in front. By operating on various points at once, and thus distracting his adversary, he contrived, while seeming to proceed in the main against the left flank of Johnston, to obtain a command over the Chattahoochee in the vicinity of his right flank. In the prosecution of this difficult and somewhat dangerous manœuvre (which took place between the 5th and 9th of July), Sherman was obliged to shift large masses of his troops with the utmost rapidity from the extreme right to the extreme left of his own line. But the movement was attended by complete success, and, several pontoon-bridges have been thrown across the Chattahoochee, a portion of the Union army was speedily transferred from the western to the eastern bank of that river. This threatened to place Sherman once more in the rear of Johnston; and the latter, having lost the protection of the stream, was forced **to re-**

treat as quickly as he could, and to enter the defences in front of Atlanta.

Sherman now paused in his advance—partly to rest his men, partly in order that he might form depots for stores at Allatoona, Marietta, and other places, and partly that he might defend the railway by which he communicated with his base. His army was by this time much reduced in numbers, though admirable in discipline, and animated by the sense of triumph. The slaughter in the several battles had been great, and it had been necessary to leave detachments at various points, to protect the rear, and to keep open the railway line with Chattanooga. A reinforcement which Sherman had expected from Corinth, Miss., had been completely routed by Forrest, so that Sherman was compelled to look in other directions for the necessary augmentation of his corps. He accordingly sent a telegram to General Rousseau, commanding 2000 cavalry at Decatur, Ala., directing him to join the camp on the Chattahoochee, after having destroyed the railway which connected Alabama with Georgia. Before the arrival of this force on the 22d, Sherman had conducted the main body of his army to the farther side of the Chattahoochee, whither some of his divisions had preceded him a few days earlier. By the 17th the whole army had crossed, with the exception of Davis's division of the 14th corps, which was left to keep guard over the rear. The object was to march at once on Atlanta by turning sharply to the right; but the movement was fraught with peril, as the Confederate force was by no means small, and was now determined to make a desperate stand. Johnston felt that he had carried his policy of retreating to the very limits of prudence, and, urged by the clamors of the people, as well as by his own perception of what was necessary, had formed the resolution of giving battle to his adversaries before the fortifications of Atlanta. But this design he was not permitted to carry out. Bragg, the Commander-in-Chief of the Southern forces, had an interview with Johnston at Atlanta, and, not being satisfied with the conduct of that officer, or with his promises for the future, had recommended Jefferson Davis to place the direction of the Confederate Army of Tennessee, as it was called, in other hands. This was done, and on July 17, Johnston issued a farewell address to his troops. His successor was General Hood, an officer who enjoyed a high reputation for dashing courage, energy and spirit. Johnston had certainly failed in preventing Sherman's advance; but he had made him pay dearly for his success, and it may be doubted whether he could have checked the vast and highly-organized invasion of that commander, had he offered battle at every stage of his progress. The previous career of Johnston had shown that he was a general of very great ability, skilled in the most elaborate tactics of armies, and capable of winning victories when he met his enemy in an open field, and with anything like equality of conditions. But in the present campaign he was overmatched in numbers, and committed to the defence of a country which presented as many difficulties to the protector as to the assailant. It was not unnatural or surprising that the people of the Confederacy should have been angered at his frequent withdrawals from one position to another; but it is likely that a bolder policy would simply have resulted in more sanguinary losses, and no greater success.

The three armies of the Union commander converged towards Atlanta on July 20. By means of trestle-bridges, Thomas's army crossed the lower part of Peach-tree Creek, a small tributary of the Chattahoochee, on the same day; and a detachment of that army, while lying in a somewhat exposed position, was attacked by Hood. The ground was hotly disputed, but the Confederates were at length compelled to retire to their entrenchments. The remainder of the Union forces crossed Peach-tree Creek on the 21st, and Sherman was now immediately in front of the Confederate defences, which were drawn round the city at a distance of about three miles. The lines had been long prepared, but were not yet completed, for, when the Union troops approached, they found their adversaries engaged in connecting the redoubts with curtains, and in the construction of other works. McPherson had by this time obtained possession of a hill to the left of the line, from which he could overlook the city, and materially help in its reduction.

GENERAL J. B. HOOD.

Hood was disinclined to let him remain in that position, and about noon on the 22d directed a sudden and vehement attack on his left flank. On hearing the sound of firing, McPherson rode towards the scene of action, but, coming unexpectedly on some skirmishers, was mortally wounded by their rifle-shots. Though barely 36 years of age, this officer was one of the ablest of Sherman's subordinates, and his loss at so critical a moment was a serious misfortune. General Logan was temporarily appointed to the command, and took measures against the threatening demonstration of the Confederates. The attack was being pushed with great spirit. The Union line was assaulted in three different places; several guns were taken, and the Southern cavalry, under General Wheeler, dashed into Decatur (Georgia), in the rear of the Union line, and nearly captured the wagon train. Some of the troops began to give ground, and it was for a time doubtful whether their line would not be cut in two by the furious advance of the Southerners. By special efforts, however, and by the concentration of reinforcements at the weak points, Sherman contrived, after an anxious interval, to restore the fortunes of the day.

With a view to isolating Atlanta, and cutting it off from all sources of supply, Sherman entered on a series of operations for the destruction of the neighboring lines of rail. To this end it was proposed to occupy East Point, a small town about five miles south of Atlanta, which forms the meeting-place of the West Point and Macon Railways. The movement was one involving some risk, for it was necessary to extend the right of the Union line round Atlanta, so as to reach the junction from which it was desired to operate. Two bodies of cavalry were sent out on this service; the larger commanded by Stoneman, the smaller by McCook. Both expeditions ended disastrously. Marching by different routes, the two columns were to meet at Lovejoy's Station, on the Macon Railway; but, owing to some mistake, the coalition was not effected. Each body was encountered by a superior force of Confederates (McCook's on the 29th, Stoneman's on the 31st) and entirely defeated. Large numbers of prisoners were taken, and the Union army was appreciably weakened with respect to its cavalry.

THE SIEGE OF ATLANTA: CONFEDERATE ATTACK ON LOGAN'S CORPS.

The Army of the Tennessee, now under command of Howard, who had succeeded to McPherson, was occupying a high ridge which crossed one of the principal roads leading from the Chattahoochee to Atlanta, when a large body of Confederates poured down on their uncompleted breastworks. The engagement lasted from noon until four o'clock P. M.; but, after six assaults, the attacking force withdrew. Hood's object in ordering this movement was to draw away that portion of Sherman's army which was being extended towards the right. Herein he failed, and Sherman, having strengthened his position by extensive and elaborate entrenchments, was enabled to advance his line to within three miles of East Point. Nevertheless, he could not touch the railways, which Hood protected by a counter-movement. Engagements were constantly taking place; the loss of life on both sides was lamentable; but at the close of July nothing of importance had been done. Atlanta was now being bombarded, and the miserable inhabitants shrouded themselves in the vaults of churches and the cellars of private houses. But as yet there were no signs of yielding, and Hood thought he could relieve his own communications by threatening those of his enemy. He sent a body of 4500 cavalry, under Wheeler, to act against the railway running from Marietta to Chattanooga—the line by which Sherman maintained his intercourse with the North. Portions of the rail were for a time destroyed; cattle and stores were captured; and Sherman was obliged to take special measures to provide against the danger. Yet no permanent injury was effected; the garrisons at the several stations maintained their positions; the lines were speedily repaired; and when Steedman marched against Wheeler from Chattanooga, the Confederate was glad to escape into Eastern Tennessee, and ultimately into Northern Alabama. His services were thus lost to Hood, who had soon cause to regret his mistake.

Stoneman had been captured in the unfortunate affair of July 31; but his place was supplied by Kilpatrick, who, though still far from cured of his severe wound, received before Resaca on the 13th of May, had heroically returned to his post, and in the early part of August was busily engaged in the task of reorganizing the Union cavalry, which had been much reduced by the recent operations, and by the surrender of so many of its number. On August 18, Kilpatrick was despatched to operate against the Southern railways, which he was not merely to injure, but, if possible, to destroy. In executing this commission, he was attacked both by cavalry and infantry, and only with difficulty succeeded in breaking through the opposing hosts. He then returned to Decatur, which he reached on the 22d, after having made a complete circuit of the enemy's position. Very little had resulted from this incursion, and Sherman saw that, if he would produce any decided effect on his antagonist's communications, he must strike with nearly the whole of his army. Reverting to his favorite method of outflanking the adversary, he formed a plan by which, while leaving behind him one corps for guarding his rear, he hoped to draw Hood from out his entrenchments, and compel him to stake his fortunes on a decisive battle, unless he should be able to retreat. In the prosecution of this scheme, Sherman would be obliged to enter the very heart of the enemy's country, and to endanger his own communications with the North; but he had confidence in his ability to carry out the movement, especially as the absence of Wheeler's horsemen allowed him to employ his cavalry with but little fear of opposition from the Southerners. Preparations for this momentous enterprise were rapidly pushed forward. The wagons were loaded with fifteen days' provisions, and on the night of the 25th two corps, occupying the extreme left, moved quietly out of their entrenchments, and marched in a southwesterly direction. Other corps followed on succeeding days, and the West Point Railway was soon destroyed. For twelve miles the ties were burned, and the rails twisted out of all ordinary shape. Large gaps were made in the earth, which were filled up with the trunks of trees, with rocks and other foreign matter intermingled with torpedoes, so placed as to explode should any attempt be made to remove them. With the exception of the 20th corps, the Union army was now out of sight of Atlanta, and the people of that city, perceiving the abandoned lines, issued forth under a false impression that the danger had been entirely removed. Hood, having but little cavalry at his disposal, was unable for several days to ascertain the whereabouts of his opponent; but, on discovering that his rear was menaced, he despatched the corps of Hardee and S. D. Lee, under the chief command of the former, to Jonesborough, a few miles south of East Point, on the Macon Railway. He was even then ignorant that nearly the whole of the Union army was severing his communications, and considered that a portion of his force would be sufficient for encountering what he regarded as a detachment of the enemy. Howard, marching due east from Fairburn, on the 30th arrived within half a mile north of Jonesborough on the evening of that day, when, finding the two Confederate commanders entrenched outside the town, he proceeded to throw up entrenchments of his own at a little distance. He was attacked on the 31st, but without being dislodged from his position. On the contrary, the Confederates were obliged to retire; and, as the Union troops were reinforced by successive divisions during the action—Sherman himself being now on his way to Jonesborough—the position of the Southerners became extremely critical.

It was important to divide the corps of Hardee and Lee from that which was still left in Atlanta itself. To accomplish his design, Sherman ordered Schofield to move rapidly along the Macon Railway, which he was entirely to destroy; at the same time, Howard, with one corps of Thomas's army, was to engage Hardee in front, while the cavalry vexed his flank and rear. The plan failed in some of its particulars, but was so far successful that a lodgment was effected within Hardee's lines before nightfall on September 1. Darkness coming on Hardee was enabled to fall back seven miles south to Lovejoy's Station on the Macon Railway, where he fortified himself in a strong position. The feeling of consternation in Atlanta itself was now extreme. It had become known during the day that the main body of the Union army lay between the city and Hardee; and Hood perceived that he would no longer be able to hold the position. His left flank had been completely turned; his communications with the south had been intercepted; and he feared that Hardee and Lee would be overwhelmed, and that the large body of prisoners at Andersonville, amounting to no fewer than 44,000, might be released by the Union cavalry, and form an army for the devastation of Georgia. It was imperative, therefore, to abandon Atlanta with all speed. A large proportion of the army stores was rapidly packed in military wagons; the rest was burned, or distributed to the people; and by the light of vast conflagrations, which reddened the sky for many miles, Hood's soldiers, accompanied by several of the citizens, marched out of the city, and made their way towards Lovejoy's Station. The explosion of ordnance trains was distinctly heard by the Union forces at a great distance; and it was evident from this circumstance, and from the widespread glare of the flames, that Atlanta had been relinquished in despair. General Slocum, from his position on the Chattahoochee, sent out a heavy reconnoitering column at daybreak on the 2d. Meeting with no opposition, the Northern troops entered the city at nine o'clock A. M. The mayor shortly afterwards made a formal surrender of the place, and the stars and stripes were raised over the Court House to the throb of martial music. On abandoning Atlanta, Hood directed his course west, and succeeded in forming a junction with Hardee and Lee at Lovejoy's Station. On September 2 Sherman, marching from the north, appeared before the entrenchments of Hardee, but, hearing of the capitulation of Atlanta, did not consider it worth while to risk an attack on the now reunited Confederate forces. He accordingly led his army by easy marches towards the captured city; and on the 8th the Army of the Cumberland encamped round Atlanta, that of the Tennessee above East Point, and that of the Ohio at Decatur.

The capture of Atlanta placed in Sherman's grasp a city not very remarkable in itself, but valuable as forming the connecting point of several lines of rail linking together many wide and productive districts. It was a centre from which the power of the Union could radiate in various directions, and which it was therefore important that the Union forces should gain, and grievous that the Confederates should lose. The great fact was known at Washington on the very day when it occurred, and Lincoln despatched an expression of the national thanks to Sherman, his officers and soldiers, for the distinguished ability, courage, and perseverance which had been displayed throughout the campaign. September 11 was appointed a day of solemn thanksgiving for the successes of Sherman in Georgia, and of Farragut at Mobile. On arriving at Atlanta, Sherman determined that the place should for the present be appropriated exclusively to military purposes, and orders were issued for the departure of all civilians, except those employed by Government. A truce of ten days was proposed in a letter from Sherman to Hood, and accepted by the latter, though not without a strong protest against the contemplated measure of his victorious adversary, which he denounced as transcending in studied and ingenious cruelty all acts ever before brought to his attention in the dark history of war. The Mayor of Atlanta likewise sent a petition to Sherman, imploring him to reconsider his decision, and painting in vivid hues the misery which it would cause to large numbers of women, children and infirm people. Sherman replied to both these representations; vehemently attacking the whole policy of the South in his answer to Hood, and with greater moderation arguing with the mayor to the effect that war is inevitably cruel, that the necessity of re-establishing the Union was paramount, and that his military plans were such as to make Atlanta a place totally unfit for noncombatants.

An extension of the truce was obtained, as a concession to the unfortunate people who were compelled to remove. In the result, 440 families, counting 705 adults, 860 children, and 470 servants, were moved south, together with the furniture and household goods of each family.

Hood exhibited great ability in withdrawing his corps from Atlanta, and effecting a junction with the rest of the army on the Macon and Augusta lines. In this way he was still able to cover the main roads to the South, and, as his numbers were far from contemptible, was in a position, even after his great defeat, to present a formidable front to the enemy. Sherman considered it prudent to fortify Atlanta against any possible attack.

He also strengthened the entrenched posts on the line connecting his army with Chattanooga, and, having provided that place and Rome with efficient garrisons, despatched Schofield to watch over the conquests that had just been made in Eastern Tennessee. In the interval between his late exploits and those which were to follow, it was a sad but necessary duty to count up the cost of what he had already won. His loss was estimated at 30,400 men; but it was probably more. The Confederate loss was set down at 42,000; but it may have been less. The campaign had been skilfully and valorously conducted by both combatants; but it had proved the immense superiority of the Union over the Confederation—a superiority which every month was making more overwhelmingly apparent. Sherman, it is true, was in a position of some danger; but his forces were being constantly augmented by conscripts from the North, while the Southern army could hardly be maintained at its original strength. Thus did matters stand in those desolated regions during the autumn days of 1864; and the feeling of exultation at the North found its natural counterpart in an extreme depression at the South, which even the steady self-reliance and unflinching purpose of Jefferson Davis could scarcely counteract.

Alarmed by the defeat of Hood and the fall of Atlanta, Davis determined to investigate for himself, by personal examination and inquiry, the real state of affairs at the South. Although his presence was needed at Richmond, and the distance from that city to Hood's headquarters on the Macon Railway was very considerable, he made his way to the neighborhood of Jonesborough. There he found much to inspire him with grave anxiety; but Hood was full of confidence in his ability to retrieve the misfortunes of the Southern army. He proposed to Davis to assume the offensive by attacking Sherman's lines of communication. It was a bold and hazardous plan; but nothing else of an equally practical character remained open to the harassed Confederates, and Davis gave his sanction to the scheme. With astonishing want of prudence, however, he made a speech at Macon, in which the main features of the contemplated operations were revealed. The address was reported in the Southern journals, and soon got into those of the North; so that in a very little while Sherman was well informed as to the blow that was being prepared against him, and took his measures accordingly.

Davis' imprudence was not confined to his intimation of what it was intended to do in the future. In his querulous outbursts of disappointment, he divulged the fact that Hood's army was very much weakened by desertions, and made the success of the proposed operations dependent on the return of the absentees. The grievance was in truth very serious. Governor Brown, of Georgia, had just withdrawn from Hood's command the whole body of the State militia, on the ground that the men had been called out for the defence of Atlanta, and that the fall of that city released them from any further obligations. Such was the true Southern idea of patriotism—an idea purely local, circumscribed within the narrowest limits, and entirely disdainful of nationality. This was a matter in respect to which Davis was constantly at issue with Governor Brown. He perceived the necessity of establishing some species of strong central government in place of that which he had helped to overthrow; and the safety of the Confederation was with him a more important matter than the convenience of particular citizens, or the exaggerated independence of certain States. But to many of the Southerners, and to the Georgians especially, such ideas were the expression of pure tyranny. The year

1864 abounded in complaints against the Richmond Government for transcending its powers, and aiming at despotic predominance. Yet if ever a political body had reason to remember the fable of the bundle of fagots, that body was the Slave Confederacy of America in the dwindling days of its existence.

Having determined on their plan, the Southerners were prompt in their endeavors to carry it into execution. Even before Davis' ridiculous speech at Macon, Forrest had made a movement against the communications. He crossed the Tennessee on September 20, and captured Athens, in Alabama; then, turning northwards, he attempted to cut the railway which passes from Nashville to Chattanooga. But the incursion was speedily repelled by the skilful combinations of the Union troops and Forrest escaped with difficulty to the neighborhood from which he had started. The forward movement of Hood and his colleagues commenced on October 1, when they crossed the Chattahoochee, and marched on Lost Mountain, lying to the west of Marietta. Detachments were sent out in various directions to destroy the rail, and to threaten the Union troops in many places at once; but Sherman knew that his adversary had passed the river very shortly after the event occurred, and he had already made arrangements for resisting an attack to which he might be exposed. Desirous of learning a little more as to the enemy's plans before he made any important move, he remained in the neighborhood of Atlanta until the 4th; but on that day, having ascertained beyond a doubt that a large force was in his rear, he marched with five corps to Kenesaw Mountain, in the immediate vicinity of the elevation on which Hood had drawn up the main body of his army.

By this time, Colonel Tourtelette, with the men under his command, was threatened at Allatoona Pass, one of the military stations by which Sherman guarded his rear. The troops at that post stood in great danger of being overwhelmed by French's division of Stuart's corps; and Sherman, dreading the consequences, sent word to General Corse, at Rome, to go with the whole of his division to the assistance of Tourtelette. A portion of this force was at once moved up; but the rest was delayed by an accident on the railway, owing to the damaged condition of the line. Even with the reinforcement, not more than 2000 troops could be brought together; and to these a whole division was opposed. The Union forces were drawn up on both sides of a deep railway cutting, and were protected by forts from sudden assault. A vigorous attack, however, was made on the morning of October 5. Advancing along the railway track, and at the same time operating against the heights, the Confederates struck with vigor and effect, and the feeble ranks of their opponents were driven from fort to fort until they reached the last of the defences. Supplies to a large amount were stored up at Allatoona; and for this reason alone it was most important that the position should be retained, to say nothing of its value as one of the links in the chain which bound the invaders to their military bases. During that anxious day, Sherman was standing on the crest of Kenesaw Mountain, where, though he was 18 miles off, he could see the smoke from the guns at Allatoona, and hear some faint reverberation of the discharges. The electric wires along the railway had been cut; but a less rapid mode of communication still existed in the form of signal-posts, by means of which Sherman was able to send orders to the commander at the pass. It was a great relief to him when he learned by the same method that General Corse, with a portion of his command, was at the scene of action. He knew that that officer was one on whom the fullest reliance could be placed; that he would hold out to the last, even against superior numbers. Such proved to be the fact. In the progress of the struggle, Corse was wounded, and for a time insensible; but on recovering consciousness he urged his men to renewed efforts, and about four in the afternoon the Confederates, being once more repulsed, and having lost a large proportion of their number in killed, wounded and captured, thought it prudent to retire. Their retreat was hastened by a report that a large body of Union troops was marching against them; in truth Sherman had sent to the relief of his beleaguered detachment the corps under General Stanley which had been stationed at Pine Mountain.

Disappointed with the result of French's attack on Allatoona, Hood pushed rapidly northwards, crossed the Etowah and the Oostenaula, and made for Resaca, at the foot of the Rocky Hill Ridge. Sherman followed on his track, and, proceeding through Allatoona Pass on October 8, reached Kingston three days later. On the 12th, the Confederates summoned the garrison of Resaca to surrender, but, being met by a refusal, moved on towards Dalton, the hills round which were occupied by Hood on the 14th. A demand for the capitulation of the fort was at first rejected, but not for long. The position was held by a colored regiment, under Colonel Johnston, who, finding himself surrounded by the whole bulk of Hood's army, considered that defence would be impracticable. All this while, the Southern forces were tearing up the rails behind them; but the work was so ill performed that Sherman, as he pursued his way, was able roughly to restore the line without much difficulty. After the fall of Dalton, Hood passed through Tunnel Hill, and for a few hours took up a position near Villanow. Sherman was close at his heels; but some dispositions which he made, in the hope of bringing his adversary to bay, and cutting off his retreat, were foiled by the rapid movements of the Southerners. Fighting with his rear-guard, Hood escaped on the 15th into the valley of the Chattanooga, and, turning southwest, entered Alabama, where he took up a position at Gadsden, between the spurs of Lookout Mountain and the river Coosa. The northern advance had been a failure, and Sherman was relieved of anxiety with respect to his communications. He followed his enemy as far as Gaylesville, where he halted, and sent out strong working parties to effect a complete repair of the railways. The work was done with remarkable rapidity, and in a very few days trains were running as usual between the several towns which had been threatened by Hood's adventurous campaign.

Hood was now to some extent superseded by Beauregard, who on October 17 assumed command of the Military Division of the West, and issued an address to the troops, in which he said:—" The army of Sherman still defiantly holds Atlanta. He can and must be driven from it. It is only for the good people of Georgia and the surrounding States to speak the word, and the work is done." Notwithstanding the appointment of this officer, Hood retained his special command, subject to the supervision and direction of Beauregard. After remaining some time at Gadsden, Hood moved, about November 1, towards Warrington, and thence to Decatur, on the southern bank of the Tennessee, where he was enabled to menace the Chattanooga and Atlanta Railway. He was somewhat puzzled at the inactivity of Sherman, and did not know what schemes were being revolved in that commander's mind. It was obvious to Sherman that Hood, though possessing an army capable of endangering his communications, was unable to meet him in open fight. He considered that to follow him would be simply to waste his strength in vain attempts to overtake an active and constantly retreating enemy, and would necessitate the abandonment of Georgia, with all the great results which the retention of that State would render probable. A further prosecution of the advance seemed therefore the most advisable course to pursue. Sherman had previously suggested to Grant a plan which amounted substantially to the destruction of Atlanta and of the railway track to Chattanooga, followed by a march through the heart of Georgia, with a view to capturing one or more of the great seaports. "Until we can repopulate Georgia," he wrote to Grant, "it is useless to occupy it; but the utter destruction of its roads, houses, and people, would cripple their military resources." He felt confident of his ability to reach Savannah, Charleston, or the mouth of the Chattahoochee, and dwelt on the advantage of compelling Hood to guess at what he meant, instead of being obliged himself to guess at what his adversary designed. While staying at Gaylesville, Sherman renewed these proposals, with certain modifications, but at the same time insisted on being left free to adopt one of the three alternative routes, in which case he could follow so eccentric a course that no one could guess at his objective. Grant authorized the proposed movement, but indicated his preference for Savannah as the objective, and fixed Dalton as the northern limit for the destruction of the railway.

Towards the end of October, Sherman detached Stanley's and Schofield's corps to Chattanooga, where they were placed under the orders of Thomas for the protection of Tennessee. Preparations for the great march were now being actively hurried forward. By moving like a devastating storm across Georgia, from Atlanta to the sea, Sherman hoped to cut the Confederacy in two, and thus to hasten its death. He had ardently desired that Hood, in retreating after his ineffectual attempt to sever his communications, would retire west-

SHERMAN'S GREAT MARCH THROUGH THE HEART OF GEORGIA.

ENTERING BLACKVILLE, CROSSING THE SOUTH EDISTO

CROSSING THE SAVANNAH

277

ward into Alabama, instead of southward to the vicinity of Jonesborough. When the event proved that the Confederates had done the very thing wanted, Sherman saw that his opportunity had arrived. He threw out strong reconnoissances in the direction of the enemy, so as to induce in him the idea that future operations would be towards the west; but at the same time everything was being arranged for an eastward march. For the present, however, the design was kept a profound secret from all but the corps-commanders, and the head of the cavalry, General Kilpatrick. Nearly 70,000 men were brought together, and these were divided into two columns; the right under Howard, the left under Slocum. The garrisons were withdrawn from Kingston, Rome, Resaca, and Dalton; all troops north of Kingston were concentrated in and around Chattanooga; the railways south-east of the Oostenaula were completely destroyed; and the country about the Chattahoochee was reduced to the condition of a desert. Sherman had determined to relinquish his former bases of supply at Chattanooga and Nashville, and to live entirely on the fertile regions through which he was about to make his way. On the evening of November 15, Atlanta was fired, and continued burning all that night. The glare of the conflagration filled the heavens, and the roar of exploding shells and magazines was heard at intervals, as the rear-guard of Sherman's army marched in a south-easterly direction, to join the more advanced divisions which were already on their road. When Sherman ordered the removal of non-combatants from that unfortunate city, and told the mayor that his military plans rendered such a step necessary, he was doubtless contemplating this event, and the great march to which it was a preliminary.

Beauregard and Hood were at Tuscumbia, south of the Tennessee River, with a view to the invasion of the State. The former had for some time been moving in an opposite direction to that which Sherman was now pursuing. He had never for a moment suspected the great design of his opponent, and both he and Beauregard were much surprised when they heard that Sherman had burned Atlanta and struck into the heart of Georgia. It was too late to overtake him, for he had by this time got the start for more than 250 miles. The Confederate leaders therefore determined to conduct a series of operations against Tennessee and Kentucky, in the hope that Sherman would in that way be drawn back to the defence of the imperilled States. At the same time, arrangements were made for harassing the rear of the invading force, and for bringing into the field as many troops as possible for opposing the onward march. Alabama and Mississippi were required to aid Georgia to the utmost of their power; but the resources of the South were now nearly exhausted, and only a very small army, as compared with that of the Northern commander, could be collected at the bidding of Beauregard. This poverty in the material of war was well known to Sherman, and was one of the elements in the general situation on which he had based his calculations. Had the forces under Hood been in front of Sherman, a better show of resistance might have been made; but they had been cleverly manœuvered out of the way, and Georgia lay at the mercy of the Union advance.

Sherman's army moved in four columns, forming two principal wings. The direction followed was between Macon and Augusta, so as to compel the Confederate general to divide their forces for the protection of both those towns. The habitual order of march, whenever practicable, was by four roads, as nearly parallel as possible, and converging at points which were indicated from time to time. No general train of supplies had been provided; but each corps was accompanied by its ammunition and provision train, and the army had permission to "forage liberally" on the country. To the corps-commanders was entrusted power to destroy mills, houses, cotton-gins, &c.; but no such destruction was to take place in districts where the army was unmolested. "In all foraging, of whatever kind," said Sherman's order laying down the details of the march, "the parties engaged will refrain from abusive or threatening language, and may, when the officer in command thinks proper, give written certificates of the facts, but no receipts; and they will endeavor to leave with each family a reasonable proportion for their maintenance." The high military genius of Sherman will not be questioned by any, nor can the honesty of his intentions be for a moment impeached; but his greatest admirers must admit that in the accomplishment of his designs he was remorseless. The ends attained, he had probably not a thought of revenge; but no considerations of mercy ever softened the rigor of his will, or the iron temper of his disposition.

The movement from Atlanta commenced on November 14; but Sherman did not leave until the 16th, when he started with the left wing. Howard was at the head of the right wing, which was ordered to proceed due south, and to destroy the Macon Railway at various points. The left was under the immediate command of Slocum, who was to menace Augusta, and tear up the Georgia Central Railway. The Confederate forces opposed to this immense invading host consisted principally of militia, under the command of Howell Cobb, who had been Buchanan's Secretary of the Treasury and had traitorously used his authority when in that office towards the furtherance of secession. At the utmost, he had not more than 10,000 infantry under his orders; and Wheeler's horsemen, by whom he was supported, were few in comparison with the well-appointed cavalry of his antagonist. Very little resistance, therefore, could be opposed to the torrent of invasion now pouring through the land. Passionate appeals to the citizens were, indeed, not wanting. On the 18th, Beauregard, from his headquarters at Corinth, Alabama, put forth an address to the people of Georgia, which promised success as the speedy result of vigorous efforts. " Obstruct and destroy all the roads in Sherman's front, flank, and rear," he said, " and his army will soon starve in your midst. Be confident; be resolute." The Georgian Senators in the Confederate Congress, writing on the same day from Richmond, told their fellow-citizens:—" You have now the best opportunity ever yet presented to destroy the enemy. . . . . Every citizen with his gun, and every negro with his spade and axe, can do the work of a soldier. You can destroy the enemy by retarding his march." Governor Brown ordered a levy *en masse* of the whole of the free white population of the State between the ages of sixteen and forty-five, and offered pardon to such convicts as would volunteer. Very little, however, came of all these efforts. A few skirmishes occurred now and then, but they were without effect in checking the advance of Sherman's legions. Bridges were burned, but speedily repaired; and roads which were broken up by the retreating troops were soon put once more into a practicable state by those who followed. Milledgeville, the capital of Georgia, was occupied on the 21st and 22d. When the expedition started from Atlanta, the Legislature was in session at Milledgeville. On hearing that the Union forces were approaching, Brown, the State representative, and several officials, fled in panic to Augusta; two days after, the Union scouts dashed into the town, which was at once surrendered by the mayor. It was plundered and partially destroyed;

large numbers of slaves were set free; and the army swept on.

At the beginning of the campaign, the cavalry under Kilpatrick had been sent towards Macon, in order to distract the enemy's attention; and 800 horsemen, with four cannon, made a feigned attack on East Macon, two miles from the chief city, but, after an animated combat, retired in the direction of Griswoldville, destroying several miles of rail. The demonstration against Macon was resumed on the 22d, when very severe fighting took place between a large body of Union troops and a Confederate army of 5000 troops. The Southerners, who made six desperate assaults upon the breastworks which their opponents had constructed, were ultimately compelled to retire, and Macon itself might have been taken, had it formed any part of the Union scheme to do so. Kilpatrick's cavalry afterward joined the right wing at Milledgeville, in accordance with previous arrangements. The plan of the campaign was carried out with the utmost regularity and success, and the Confederates, not knowing where the blow was principally to fall, were distracted with anxiety and apprehension. Augusta was now hastily garrisoned, and Hardee obstructed the roads towards Savannah by as many defences as he could improvise. Sherman's advance, however, continued with inexorable steadiness. On November 24, the right wing of the Union army, marching from Milledgeville and Gordon, arrived at the Oconee River, which they immediately prepared to cross. Being edged with swamps, through which many creeks ran in winding courses towards the main stream, the Oconee seemed easy of defence, and difficult for an invading army to pass. The Georgian militia, under General Wayne, endeavored to hold the line; but the troops got across with little trouble, and the Confederates retreated without any serious attempt at fighting. Kilpatrick entered Waynesborough on the 27th, and, after tearing up the railway which connected that town with Augusta, escaped towards the left wing of the advancing army; though not without a sharp action, in which his regiments were very nearly surrounded and taken prisoners. The left had by this time crossed the Ogeechee, and, on the 28th, Louisville was entered by that division of the invading force.

Sherman's troops were now approaching the sea, and the arid soil and wiry pine-trees of Eastern Georgia had succeeded to the richer forest lands and cultivated fields of the interior portions of the State. Sherman, with the center corps of his army, was at Millen on December 3, from which spot he made demonstrations against Augusta and Savannah, that the Confederates might be kept in doubt as to what point would be attacked. He then moved down the peninsula formed by the Ogeechee and Savannah Rivers, and thus approached the object of his march through the swamps and rice-fields by which it is encompassed. Deluging rain had come on; the marshy soil presented great difficulties to the masses of heavily-armed troops, with their artillery and baggage-wagons; and it was necessary in many places to construct the roads over which the army was to pass. Felled trees, field-works, and other defences were now encountered by the invaders; but by the 10th, the Southern troops had been driven within their lines, and Sherman's entire army was massed in front of Savannah, after a march of more than 300 miles, which had been accomplished in about 25 days. The Union losses during this great military operation had been very few, and all the divisions were in excellent condition when Savannah rose before them over the flat and watery landscape. The men would gladly have assaulted the town at once; but the walls were mounted with heavy guns, and Sherman had brought with him nothing stronger than field-artillery. He therefore refrained from a general attack, and trusted to the effect of time in starving out the city and its garrison. The fleet under Dahlgren was lying not far off; but it was no easy matter to communicate with the naval force, owing to the guns of Fort McAllister, which commanded the mouth of the Ogeechee. It was necessary in the first instance to capture that work, and this was effected, after a hot and gallant contest on the 13th, by General Hazen's division of the 15th corps, which carried the position by assault.

The fleet was thus enabled to operate with the army. Arrangements were made for a supply of ammunition and heavy guns from Hilton Head, and Sherman sent instructions to General Foster, commanding the Union troops in that department, to occupy the railway between Savannah and Charleston, so as to complete the environment of the former city on the side where alone any gap existed in the investing force—viz., the side towards the north. The surrender of Savannah was demanded on the 17th, but refused by Hardee, who apparently relied on his ability to defend the position. Preparations were made for a bombardment and assault, while on the other hand, the Confederate batteries, as well as the gunboats on the river, kept up a constant fire, which seemed to promise a desperate resistance on the part of the besieged. But Hardee had in fact made up his mind to abandon the city to its fate. It was considered that the army would be of much greater use in other quarters than in a town where it was shut up within walls, and exposed to the certainty of capture, if once the defences were overcome. The Confederates still had command of the Savannah River, and across that stream they escaped during the night of the 20th. Having reached the farther shore, they threaded a little-known road through the swamp, and made their way to

South Carolina. Sherman entered the city on the following day, and despatched a telegram to President Lincoln, in which he said:—" I beg to present you, as a Christmas gift, the city of Savannah, with 150 heavy guns, and plenty of ammunition; also about 25,000 bales of cotton." A good deal of Union feeling seemed to be latent among the citizens. They behaved with civility towards the soldiers, and made no attempt to destroy cotton or any other kind of property. On the 28th, a meeting was held at the requisition of the mayor, at which certain resolutions were unanimously adopted with a view to a complete submission to the Union, and the laying aside of all differences; and under the considerate rule of General Geary, the commandant appointed by Sherman, the city enjoyed a period of repose and of comparative prosperity.

Reckoning up the results of the campaign, in the official report which he afterwards sent the War Department, Sherman wrote:—" I estimate the damage done to the State of Georgia and its military resources at $100,000,000, at least $20,000,000 of which have been used to our advantage, and the remainder is simple waste and destruction. This may seem a hard species of warfare; but it brings the sad realities of war home to those who have been directly or indirectly instrumental in involving us in its attendant calamities." Sherman's wonderful success had been accomplished at a cost of not more than 567 men in killed, wounded and missing. The almost total collapse of the South had been made manifest by the facility with which he had conducted his legions from Atlanta to the sea; and the transport of enthusiasm at the North was all the greater in consequence of the previous feeling of anxiety. The news of Sherman's triumph came like a burst of sunshine to brighten the departing year, and those who had been most doubtful now acknowledged that one of the greatest achievements of the war had been accomplished, and that the subjugation of the Confederacy at no distant date was thenceforth assured.

During the progress of these events in the South, Hood was conducting that series of operations in Tennessee which ultimately proved his ruin. His army was of respectable dimensions, consisting of nearly 30,000 infantry and artillery, with about 12,000 cavalry; and the forces of Thomas, to whom the defence of Tennessee had been confided by Sherman, were, speaking roughly, about equal to those by which he was confronted. The Union base of operations was at Nashville, where, while awaiting the arrival of some additional regiments, Thomas formed his plans of resistance to the threatened attack. Hood began his forward march on November 21, shaping his course along the road between Florence and Nashville; and the outlying Union divisions were either concentrated at Chattanooga and Murfreesboro', or withdrawn across the Duck River in the direction of Nashville. Forrest, in command of the Confederate cavalry, crossed the river a few miles above Columbia on the night of the 28th, and Schofield, who had command of the Northern armies in the open country, was nearly cut off from his line of retreat. The Southerners were actually on the flank of one of Schofield's divisions; Confederate reinforcements were advancing from other directions; and had an attack been made at once, it seems almost certain that a great success would have been achieved. But the Confederate officer, General Cheatham, let his opportunity slip by. He awaited the arrival of Stewart, and, after that officer had reached the spot, still hesitated to engage the enemy. The two armies were so close that even after nightfall the march of the Union regiments could be distinctly seen by their adversaries; yet Cheatham forbore to attack. Thomas now ordered

Schofield to entrench himself in such a position as would enable him to defend the approaches to Nashville from Columbia. This he immediately did; but, before his works could be completed, he was furiously assailed by Hood.

Schofield had thrown up his entrenchments in front of the small town of Franklin, situated on the Big Harpeth River, 18 miles south of Nashville; but he was somewhat encumbered by a long train of wagons, which had not yet got over the river extending in his rear. If, therefore, he could be defeated in this position, he would probably be overwhelmed, and one great obstacle to Hood's plans would be removed. The Confederate force was divided into two columns, one of which was to attack Franklin in front, while the other was to move down the stream, to cross it some distance east of Franklin, and thus

GENERAL SCHOFIELD.

unexpectedly to approach the Union rear. At four in the afternoon of November 30, Hood's main column advanced to the attack. The contest was prolonged and sanguinary; entrenchments were taken and retaken; but Schofield, at the head of 15,000 men, held his positions until nearly midnight, when, ascertaining that he was in danger of being outflanked by the column that had crossed the river, he ordered a retreat. This was continued during the night, and on December 1 Schofield had reached a point seven miles south of Nashville, where General A. J. Smith's corps was posted. Hood had suffered very severely in the action, and confessed to a loss of 4500 men, including a large number of general officers; but, as the Union troops also had suffered grievously, and were dispirited by the necessity of retreating, the Confederate leader did not hesitate as to the expediency of pursuit. He followed closely on his adversary's track, and Smith, finding himself hard-pressed, fell back to the outer line of the Nashville entrenchments, which were situated three miles from the town.

The consternation in Nashville was extreme when it became known that the outlying armies had been defeated, and that the enemy was near at hand. Large numbers of civilians were hurriedly armed; Thomas's forces were drawn up in line of battle outside the town, and additional troops were brought up by rail from Chattanooga. Hood arrived in front of Nashville on the 2d, and, throwing up strong works and counter-batteries, made preparations for a siege. Forrest, in command of a body of cavalry and infantry, was despatched towards Murfreesboro', to summon the garrison to surrender; but a portion of this detachment behaved ill, and the army before Nashville was weakened by the absence of so large a contingent. Thomas, on the other hand, was being continually reinforced, and by the middle of the the month felt himself strong enough to deliver a powerful assault on the beleaguering hosts. In the early morning of the 15th, a feint was made on Hood's right, and a real attack on his left, which ended in the capture of several redoubts and guns, and in the complete discomfiture of Hood, who was forced from his chief position on Montgomery Hill, and compelled to retreat a distance of some miles. Next day his troops were again attacked, and, after an action of varying fortunes, driven in confusion towards Franklin. The division which misbehaved itself at Murfreesboro' had once more given evidence of deficiency in fighting qualities.

GENERAL GEORGE H. THOMAS.

Its dismay was communicated to other divisions, and only one corps preserved its organization and self-respect. The retreat of the main body necessitated the withdrawal of Forrest from before Murfreesboro'; but, owing to the swollen condition of the rivers, his detachment had great difficulty in joining the regiments that had fled from Nashville.

The pursuit was vigorously pressed by Thomas, and Hood's defeated legions, pouring over the Duck River, and in time obtaining the support of Forrest, who rejoined the army at Columbia, made for the Tennessee, which was crossed on the 27th. The Confederate Army of the West was completely shattered. In the two days' battles before Nashville, 54 guns and 4460 prisoners had been captured by the Union forces, and the entire loss of the Confederates during the whole campaign was stated at 13,189 in prisoners alone, including several general officers, and 1000 others of lower grades. During the same period, more than 2000 deserters came into the Northern lines, and 72 pieces of artillery passed from the defeated to the victorious army. The Union loss was about 10,000 in killed, wounded, and missing; but the authority of the Union in Tennessee was saved by a series of actions in which Hood had done little more than demonstrate the weakness of his resources, and his own want of commanding ability as a general. Shortly after his withdrawal into the northern part of Alabama, he was relieved of the command, at his own request, and was succeeded by General Taylor, who was transferred from the Trans-Mississippi Department.

Sherman rested at Savannah only long enough to prepare for that further advance of his armies which he from the first judged to be necessary. To penetrate northwards through South Carolina, to enter North Carolina, and in due time to combine his forces with those besieging Petersburg and Richmond, seemed to him the most likely way of terminating the war. Grant desired that the whole of Sherman's army should at once be transported by sea from Georgia to the banks of the James River; but the hero of Savannah considered that it would be far better to march through the intervening country, reducing it to submission by an overwhelming display of force. The land, it is true, presented in many parts great difficulties to the progress of a hostile body; but the Confederate Army was now so reduced in numbers, and so broken in spirits, that little active opposition was to be feared. In January, 1865, Beauregard was at Augusta, on the Georgian side of the Savannah River, endeavoring to scrape together from various localities a force to resist the further measures of Sherman. But his attempts of this nature were not very successful, and he found himself at length in command of only a few thousand men with which to confront the serried legions of his adversary. He wished to augment his scanty divisions by abandoning Charleston and Wilmington; but these measures were not then sanctioned by the Confederate Government.

Beauregard had the assistance of General D. H. Hill, and also of Wade Hampton, who commanded the cavalry. The want, indeed, was not in generals, but in men, so that little could be done to protect the roads by which Sherman would move towards the more northern States. On the completion of his preparations at Savannah, that commander found himself at the head of 60,000 infantry, 10,000 cavalry, and artillery in proportion. A detachment of his force he left at Savannah, and with the rest set out for Goldsborough, in North Carolina. To deceive the enemy, demonstrations were to be made against Charleston to the right, and Augusta to the left; and, while these were in progress, the main body was to push forward along the causeways by which the marshes of the coast are traversed. The advance did not fairly commence until February 1st, when the several divisions set out on their northward march, and entered on a dreary tract of flooded lands, where the Confederate cavalry had done their utmost to impair the roads and destroy the bridges, and where therefore it was necessary to conduct many engineering operations before the troops could pursue their course. In South Carolina, as in Georgia, houses, barns, agricultural produce, and even large woods, were set on fire, and the invaders, as they passed over the country, left behind them a blackened desert, stripped of everything which could support the life of man or beast.

The Confederates held the line of the Salkahatchie, but, on their positions being forced, fell back behind the Edisto at Branchville, where they burned two bridges. Sherman's forces, however, crossed the stream, and advanced towards Orangeburg, which was occupied on February 12th. Wade Hampton was now compelled to fall back on Columbia, the State capital, situated north of the Congaree River. The bridge in front of the town was burned by the retreating Southerners; but the Union troops, on reaching the banks of the Congaree, early in the morning of February 16, passed the river by means of extemporary bridges, and received the surrender of Columbia. The place was consumed by fire on the night of the 17th; but Sherman charged this fact on Wade Hampton himself, who, it is alleged, applied the torch to a large quantity of cotton and lint stored up in the town, blazing fragments of which were carried by an unusually high wind in many directions. Hampton denied the accusation, and vehemently asserted that the city was fired by Sherman's men. The left wing, under Slocum, reached Winnsborough on the 21st, and was followed by the cavalry of Kilpatrick. The latter then moved upon Lancaster, so as to foster the impression that Sherman intended a general march on Charlotte, North Carolina, to which city Beauregard and all the Confederate cavalry had by this date retreated from Columbia.

At the same time, Hardee evacuated Charleston, it being considered that to retain 11,000 troops within the defences of that city, when they were so much needed to oppose the advance of Sherman, would be a grave mistake. Thus, the original proposal of Beauregard was now adopted; but the time had passed when it was capable—if it was ever capable—of producing the desired effect. The abandonment of Charleston was attended, on the night of February 17, by the burning of the city, which was fired by the Confederates themselves, in order that the Northerners should have little but a mass of ruins as the reward of their long endeavors to take this stronghold of rebellion. The Government stores, the railway depôts, and the ironclads in the harbor, were burned or blown up; the guns on the ramparts were burst; and the rear-guard of Hardee's army left by rail for the north-west, in the midst of an infernal glare and clamor of destruction, which the Union troops were for the moment powerless to prevent. Gillmore's troops entered the flaming city on the morning of the 18th, and, hoisting the national colors once more over the remnants of the forts, proceeded to subdue the conflagration. But only a small portion of the city could be saved. Charleston, the cradle of the rebellion, had perished in fires of her own kindling—a fit type of that rapacious and cruel oligarchy which would wreck where it could not rule, and which knew no medium between the insolence of domination and the despair of baffled crime.

Wilmington, in North Carolina, was also abandoned. The reduction of Fort Fisher, on January 15, had greatly diminished the value of the position; and in this instance, as well as in the case of Charleston, it was thought better to add the garrison to the scanty forces then in the field under the direction of Johnston, who had been restored to command as one of the most capable of the Southern leaders, notwithstanding the series of defeats which he had suffered at the hands of Sherman in Georgia. During the depth of winter, the 23d corps, under Schofield, had been transported from Clifton, on the Tennessee River, to the vicinity of Wilmington, that it might aid in the capture of that city, and, when the main object had been effected, might assist the designs of Sherman by marching on Goldsborough. The siege operations against Wilmington were so vigorously prosecuted that both the outer and the inner line of defences were outflanked in the course of February, and on the 22d of that month the Confederates under Hoke destroyed the steamers, cotton, and Government stores, and, retreating on Goldsborough, where Johnston was concentrating his forces, abandoned Wilmington. Schofield then determined, as soon as his arrangements should be complete, to advance in two columns from Wilmington and Newbern to Goldsborough. But means of transportation could not at once be obtained, and the first week of March had nearly closed ere his movement began.

After quitting Winnsborough, Sherman turned eastwards, and directed his columns on Cheraw, a small town situated on the Great Pedee River, at the termination of the line of rail running from Charleston. His supplies were getting short; the solitary lands where he now found himself yielded but little for the support of his regiments; and it became imperative to open communications with the sea. Progress was fatiguing and difficult. Heavy rain was frequently falling, and the roads were so rotten with mud and ooze that it was often necessary to make long causeways of felled trees across some desolate stretch of watery soil. The labors of the men were prodigious; yet their advance was not seriously delayed.

Sherman pushed on to Fayetteville, and while there learned that the fragments of an army that had left Columbia under Beauregard had been reinforced by Cheatham's corps from the West, and by the garrison of Augusta; that Hardee had succeeded in getting across Cape Fear River; and that the whole of the Confederate forces, under Johnston, made up an army superior to his own in cavalry, and not contemptible either in infantry or artillery. Sherman was quick to see that the real difficulties of his enterprise were about to begin, and that his further operations must be characterized by extreme caution.

On the 15th, he resumed his forward march, and on the 16th discovered Hardee strongly entrenched at a point where the road branches off towards Goldsborough, by way of Bentonville. He was immediately attacked and defeated by the Union left wing, and during the ensuing night the whole body withdrew in the direction of Smithfield, where Hardee effected his junction with Johnston. Another battle was fought on the 19th near Bentonville, where Slocum's column sustained a temporary check. Johnston had moved from Smithfield with great rapidity, and without the encumbrance of many heavy guns, hoping to overwhelm his opponent's left flank before it could be relieved by the co-operating columns; but Sherman had expected such a movement, and was prepared for it. The action continued the whole day, and Slocum's forces repulsed no fewer than six attacks, delivered by the Confederates with their accustomed energy and enthusiasm. The Union troops had hastily entrenched themselves, and, being reinforced during the night, were in a position of comparative security on the morning of the 20th. The two armies then confronted one another from behind their respective breastworks. The battle was resumed on the 21st, when, after many hours of heavy fighting, the Southerners were driven towards Smithfield, and, Sherman, who had by this time been joined by Schofield, remained master of the situation. Schofield's advance had been delayed by the vigorous opposition of Hoke's forces, with whom some severe actions had been fought. On the 21st the Union columns entered Goldsborough, where Sherman left his army under Schofield, while he proceeded alone to Grant's headquarters, which he reached on the 27th, and then for the first time learned the general state of affairs, of which he had been ignorant since the end of January. The main Union armies were now in such a position with reference to one another that they could readily combine for the prosecution of any campaign which might be considered advisable in the spring. The great object of the march had been obtained, and the two Carolinas, as well as Georgia, were all but lost to the Confederacy.

CHAPTER VIII.

THE CLOSING BATTLES IN VIRGINIA.

WHEN, in March, 1864, General Grant was invested with the command of all the armies, he found himself at the head of 770,000 troops, provided in the most ample measure with the resources of modern warfare. To this immense army the Confederates could only oppose much scantier legions (Lee's veterans who fell in the awful charge of Gettysburg could never be replaced). The North could now depend on the services of tried and able officers; and in Grant was found a directing mind which would not fail in energy or intelligence. His idea was that active and continuous operations by all the troops that could be brought into the field, regardless of season and weather, were necessary to complete and speedy success. The armies of the East and of the West, he perceived, acted independently of each other, and without concert; while the enemy, taking advantage of his interior lines of communication for transporting troops from one point to another, was enabled to reinforce any army that might be particularly pressed, and also, during seasons of Union inactivity, to furlough large numbers of men, who were then at liberty to return to their homes and assist for a few months in reproductive labors. Grant determined to use all the troops practicable against the armed hosts of the Confederacy, thus preventing his opponents from using the same force at different seasons against first one and then another of the Northern armies, and allowing them no possibility of repose for refitting, or for the production of fresh supplies. He resolved to strike continuously against the forces of the enemy, until "by mere attrition, if in no other way," nothing should be left them but submission.

To crush out the rebellion by simultaneous operations on a vast scale was Grant's scheme. He proposed to march against Richmond with the armies of the Potomac and of the James River, while Sherman, in command of the three armies of the Cumberland, Tennessee and Ohio, was to move towards Atlanta, in Georgia. For the protection of Richmond, Lee had less than 58,000 men of all arms. In other parts of the Confederacy, the armies of the South were formidable rather by the fighting qualities of the soldiers, and the ability of the generals, than by positive numbers; but altogether the assemblage of armed men, when we consider both sides, was probably greater than any one nation has ever set in hostile array. If to the forces of the North already referred to we add 222,000 for those of the South—and this appears to be a probable estimate—we reach a total of nearly a million men. The much larger population of the Northern, as compared with the Southern States, enabled the Government to put such gigantic armies in the field, and, after repeated losses of the most appalling character, to be ready with fresh legions for yet grander enterprises. Even more remarkable, however, was the ability of the South to bring forward a force of more than 200,000 men, after their separation from the Western and the border States.

WILDERNESS (May 5, 6, 1864).—The new movements of the Union armies were to begin as early in May as possible. The Potomac army now consisted of three instead of five corps. These were wielded by Hancock, Sedgwick and Warren, while Meade continued as principal commander, under the general directions of Grant. On May 4, 1864, the Army of the Potomac crossed the Rapidan, driving in the Confederate pickets, and advancing through the dense shades of the Wilderness in a south-easterly direction. Burnside, with the 9th corps, remained for a while at Warrenton, north of the Rappahannock, to protect the line of communication with Washington.

Lee's forces were also divided into three corps, commanded by Longstreet, Hill and Ewell, and occupied a position round Orange Court House, south-west of Fredericksburg. Lee ordered the larger part of his army to march towards the advancing foe, while with the rest he watched the fords of the Upper Rapidan, that he might guard against a flank attack on his left. Early on May 5, the vanguard of Ewell's corps came into collision with the Union troops. After a fiercely-contested action, in which success seemed to incline first to the one side and then to the other, the Confederates remained in the most favorable position, although their brilliant courage and lavish expenditure of life had enabled them to do little more than check the Union advance. The battle lasted all day and was distinguished by the utmost valor and resolution on both sides. Grant sought to outflank his enemy on the right, so as to get between him and Richmond; but in this he failed.

The struggle began again next morning. The Union Army was drawn up across the Orange and Fredericksburg road—the right, under Sedgwick, covering Germania Ford; the center, under Warren, posted at Wilderness Tavern, and the left, under Hancock, drawn up to the south-east of Chancellorsville. The reserve, under Burnside, which had crossed the Rapidan during the previous night, was stationed in the rear, with orders to support Sedgwick, if he needed it; or in the event of the worst happening to cover the retreat of the army towards its base. The Union line extended over five miles, and was involved in tangled woods. The trees were so thick the cavalry could not be employed, nor could the artillery make use of any complicated manœuvres. Hard hand-to-hand fighting was what lay before the combatants, and during the day they had plenty of it. Grant (who in the rear of the center was acting with Meade) ordered an advance of his whole line, and for some hours the battle swayed to and fro with changeful fortune. The Union left attacked with such irresistible force that the Confederates under Wilcox and Heath were scattered in utter rout, and Lee, for once, lost his equanimity as he saw the ruin that had overtaken some of his trusted divisions. Had it not been for the timely appearance of Longstreet with McLaw's division, the disaster would have been more extreme. Longstreet's arrival saved the right from a crushing reverse. The attacking force was driven back with the loss of many prisoners, and Grant then ordered the greater part of Burnside's corps to strengthen the line between the left and the center. Lee now directed a vehement attack on the Union positions. This was headed by Longstreet, who fell seriously wounded—struck accidentally, like Jackson at Chancellorsville—by a volley from his own men who, seeing some officers through the trees, mistook them for Unionists. Another Confederate general (Jenkins) was killed by the same discharge; and this started a feeling of confusion and dismay into the attacking force. Ultimately, after a great deal of hot fighting in all parts of the line, the Confederates were repulsed, and the Union troops in the main retained the ground.

SPOTTSYLVANIA (May 8–12, 1864).—It was thought

that the Union forces would retire back to the Rapidan. Grant, on the contrary, gathered up his army, and pushed towards Spottsylvania Court House. Longstreet's corps were sent thither, and were in possession when, on the 7th, a large body of Union infantry arrived. Lee sent up additional troops, and the fighting on the 8th resulted in the Confederates retaining their possession. Some unimportant fighting occurred on the 9th, when General Sedgwick was killed. Towards night Grant ordered another advance. The right wing crossed over the south bank of the Upper Po; but after an encounter with the opposing troops the Union forces withdrew to the northern side of the river. On the 10th, severe fighting again took place, and the Union losses throughout the day were estimated to exceed 10,000. The slaughter was great and without any commensurate gain. The Confederates were driven to their breastworks, but were not compelled to abandon their chief positions. The Confederates lost a large number in dead, wounded and captured on the morning of the 11th. Grant was satisfied with the progress he had made during the six days' struggle, and wrote to the Secretary of War, " I propose to fight it out on this line if it takes all summer." The 11th was a day of comparative rest. It rained heavily, and both sides were glad of any excuse for repose. Some fighting was done by Hancock on the 12th. Lee fell back a short distance on the 13th, but his hold on Spottsylvania Court House was not relinquished. Six days of comparative inactivity, varied by occasional engagements of a minor character, followed this tremendous series of battles. Torrents of rain had converted all the ways into so many muddy channels, and manœuvering was impossible until the weather should change, and the roads become more dry.

Up to this time, it cannot be said that Grant's plans

had been attended by any great measure of success. He vowed he would not turn back; but advance toward Richmond. He held his positions in front of Lee's army, and created a feeling of anxiety and watchfulness at the Confederate capitol. The Southern forces had been so well handled, so ably directed, and so expeditiously moved from one point to another, that they seemed more numerous than they really were.

COLD HARBOR, (June 3, 1864).—Grant concluded that he could not force his way through the Southern army, and he therefore proposed to outflank it, and compel its retreat towards Lynchburg, lying on the James River, to the south-west of the threatened city. He moved his immense army, and after a deal of manoeuvering and some severe fighting, Lee slipped into the entrenchments of Cold Harbor. Heavy rains prevented an attack on June 2, but on the 3d the advance was begun. Hancock attacked with his usual vigor, and Breckenridge was driven back; but the success was short-lived. Hancock's men were repulsed with great slaughter to their former lines, and in other directions the Confederates held their ground against the utmost endeavors of the Union forces. Lossing asserts that, " in 20 minutes, 10,000 Union soldiers were killed or wounded." Lee's army, sheltered behind its works, suffered but little.

Grant telegraphed, "We have driven the enemy within his entrenchments at all points, but without gaining any decisive advantage. Our troops now occupy a position close to the enemy." Grant's new movement had been as unsuccessful as his first; but it must be borne in mind that Lee had done nothing more than hold his own, and had been totally unable to drive off his adversary. On the evening of the 3d, the Confederates suddenly attacked Smith's brigade and Gibbon's division, but, after a furious combat of half an hour's duration, were completely repulsed. On the following morning, Lee's left wing, in front of Burnside, was found to have been drawn in during the night; yet for the most part the opposing lines continued close to each other.

Grant had arranged for three co-operative movements to divide the strength of the Confederate army. Sigel, with 10,000 men, was to advance up the Shenandoah Valley and threaten the railroad communications with Richmond. He was totally routed at NEW MARKET (May 15). Hunter, who superseded him, defeated the Confederates at PIEDMONT (June 5), but pushing on to Lynchburg with about 20,000 men, he found it too strong, and prudently retired into West Virginia. Sheridan likewise had been defeated by the cavalry of Wade Hampton and Fitzhugh Lee.

In the second week in June, Butler, with 30,000 men, ascended the James River, under the protection of gunboats, and landed at Bermuda Hundred. After some trifling successes, he was surprised in a dense fog by Beauregard, and driven back into his defences with considerable loss. Beauregard could get no reinforcements from Richmond, so the entrenchments in front of Butler were secretly evacuated, and the men added to the scanty forces still holding desperately to Petersburg.

The operations against that city were now being pushed with great energy. Grant marched his army over the James River, and fell upon Petersburg; but here again he was confronted by his indomitable antagonist, and the works could not be forced. Grant, therefore, threw up entrenchments. The campaign now resolved itself into a siege of Richmond, with Petersburg as its advanced post. The campaign had cost the Union army 40,000 men and the Confederates 30,000.

It was proposed to run a mine under one of the approaches to the Confederate entrenchments before

Petersburg, and having created a gap by its explosion, to surprise the town by capture in the crisis of confusion and alarm created by the catastrophe. The plan was adopted, though reluctantly. More than three weeks were consumed in the construction of the mine. Eight thousand pounds of powder were placed in the chambers. The explosion occurred in the early morning of July 30. It resulted in the formation of a cavity 200 feet in length, 60 feet wide, and 20 feet deep. The defenders of the parapet were struck with consternation, and began to retire into the town; but Lee and Beauregard were soon on the spot, and restoring the self-reliance of their men, ordered their batteries to reply to those of the Union works, which opened fire immediately after the explosion. Owing, perhaps, to this unexpected opposition, the assault was made with but little spirit, and the attacking force, instead of dashing over the aperture, simply occupied it. The men sought cover, and fired over the edge of the crater, without attempting to advance any farther. The Confederates, now calm and collected, sent their shells in great numbers into the crater, inflicting terrible slaughter on the unfortunate men huddled together in that ghastly hole. No commander of high rank was present to give directions such as might retrieve the failure of the first assault; and long before night closed on that disastrous day the Union loss in killed, wounded, and captured was more than 4000 men. A long series of misfortunes had received another dismal addition, and Grant had to consider once more how he should conquer that success which was so long in coming.

Invasion of Maryland.—The exposed condition of the Shenandoah Valley consequent on Hunter's retreat, and on the large concentration of troops before Petersburg and its vicinity, invited attack during the summer, and the Confederates took advantage of their opportunity.

General Early resolved to advance from the Valley, and enter the Northern States, and in this way draw off a portion of Grant's army which was giving so much trouble to the forces of Lee, Bragg, and Beauregard.

On July 2, Early forced Sigel to evacuate Martinsburg, with the loss of some of his stores. Early continuing to advance, Sigel fell back across the Potomac, and took up a position on Maryland Heights. This movement of the Confederates was a dangerous one, for a successful blow might be struck before Union reinforcements could be sent to repel the invasion. Scattered bodies were seen in various places, and Pennsylvania was entered, as well as Maryland. Whole neighborhoods were laid waste, in revenge for what had been done by Hunter in the Valley; and the rich people were compelled to ransom their dwellings and property by the payment of large sums of money. To meet this invasion Lincoln called for 12,000 militia from New York, Pennsylvania and Massachusetts. On the evening of July 8, General Wallace, in command of a hastily raised force, was attacked. His ill-disciplined troops soon gave way before the vehement assault to which they were exposed, and fled towards Baltimore, pursued by cavalry. This disaster produced consternation in Washington. Reinforcements were hurried up and a corps of Grant's army was despatched from before Petersburg. Early next attacked Rockville, Maryland, a little town about 14 miles west of Washington. Some of his troops got within five miles of the Capital, where they siezed prisoners, horses and cattle, and inflicted a large amount of damage. Intoxicated by his success, Early appeared before Washington on July 11, and engaged the batteries of Fort Stevens, one of the outworks of the metropolis. Reinforcements had by this time reached the city, and in the evening a body of men under General Auger sallied forth to drive away so troublesome and humiliating an enemy. A sharp skirmish ensued, and the Confederates were speedily compelled to retreat, leaving 100 dead and wounded on the field. The invaders retired up the Potomac to the western side of the Shenandoah. Early established his headquarters at Winchester, and successfully resisted an attack by General Averill, who was obliged to seek shelter behind the works at Harper's Ferry.

On July 29, Early once more crossed the Potomac into Maryland and advanced on Chambersburg, Pennsylvania. Gilmor's cavalry demanded $200,000 in gold, which the people declined to furnish. The city was accordingly given to the flames, and Averill, on arriving for its relief, found it fiercely burning. The Confederates retreated, and contrived to elude the Union troops sent to intercept them, and again to reach in safety the southern shores of the Potomac. Grant, before Petersburg, determined to unite in one the three departments of Western Virginia, Washington, and the Susquehanna; and placed the direction of this large area under control of General Sheridan, who found himself at the head of more than 40,000 men. Early had only about 13,000 troops with whom to maintain his position round Winchester; yet Grant refused to sanction any offensive movement on Sheridan's part, fearing the disastrous consequences of a defeat. At length, he gave his consent, but only on the understanding that the Valley of the Shenandoah should *be completely devastated, so that nothing might be left to invite any further invasion.*

On September 19, Sheridan attacked Early with complete success. 2500 prisoners and five pieces of artillery were captured. Gordon and Rhodes of the Confederate army were killed. The Union forces were themselves great losers, for the Confederates fought well. Sheridan made another attack on the 21st, when

Early was again defeated and forced to withdraw farther into the Valley. A division of Longstreet's corps reinforced Early, but Sheridan's divisions were too strong to be seriously menaced.

GENERAL PHILIP H. SHERIDAN.

Sheridan carried out only too well the instructions he received from Grant; and a scene of desolation was produced in one of the most fertile and beautiful valleys in the land. These frightful excesses were much condemned.

On his return down the Cedar Creek Valley in the direction of the Potomac, Sheridan was closely followed by a large force of Confederates. A collision took place on October 5, ending in the repulse of the Southerners; and ten days later a more important action was fought on the banks of Cedar Creek. The Union troops were entrenched on the north bank of that stream (which runs into the Shenandoah), when, in the early morning of the 19th, they were unexpectedly attacked by the Confederates. Sheridan had gone to Washington, leaving General Wright in temporary command; while his adversary was preparing for a powerful and well-directed blow. The assault, when it came, was delivered simultaneously against the front and the rear. Most of the pickets were captured; the rest of the troops, suddenly aroused from sleep, were thrown into confusion, and driven back tumultuously on the road to Middletown. Eighteen of the Union guns were seized by Early, and turned on their late possessors; and for a time it seemed as if the Union troops would be utterly overwhelmed. Wright succeeded in restoring order to the ranks, and in checking the advance; the Southerners, scattering themselves through the abandoned camps, began drinking and plundering; and when Sheridan arrived from Winchester—" thirty miles away"—and ordered a vigorous attack, the opposing troops gave way in unreasonable panic, abandoning the guns they had captured in the morning.

Sheridan's reputation was greatly advanced by this affair, and the President, on November 14, promoted him to the rank of major-general, as a reward for his "personal gallantry, military skill and just confidence in the courage and patriotism of his troops." He had in truth saved the Union cause from a crushing reverse, and had inflicted on Early a blow which made his forces stagger. On the morning of that memorable October

SHERIDAN AT THE BATTLE OF CEDAR CREEK.

19, the Union troops had fallen back in dismay; in the evening, it was their adversaries who were in flight, and who, smitten with dread, blocked the roads with the scattered remnants of an army which only a few hours before had almost attained the summit of victory. A charge by the Union cavalry, as dusk was setting in, completed the ruin that had already been commenced; and from that hour nothing but terror and despair prevailed throughout the Confederate ranks. Early bivouacked at Fisher's Hill during the night, and next day retreated beyond Woodstock, followed by the cavalry. He did not consider himself safe until he had taken up a position on Mount Jackson, near the southern extremity of the Great North Mountains, where, counting up his losses, he found that 22 of his guns had passed over to the enemy, together with most of his stores and camp-equipages. The Southerners were extremely disappointed at the result of his movement. They had not only lost a large number in killed, wounded and captured, but their operations in the Valley had been injured beyond the hope of redemption. The superiority of the Union troops in that locality was now so clearly established that Grant felt he could safely recall to the army before Petersburg those detachments which he had sent a few months earlier to guard Washington. It had been hoped at Richmond that the alarm at Washington would be so great as to induce Grant to transport the major portion of his army northward for the protection of the Government; but Grant, refusing to be influenced by the fears of the timid, only despatched a comparatively small contingent and retained the bulk of his forces for the prosecution of the task he had in hand. Lee, therefore, had been but slightly helped by Early's bold incursion. Great courage and ability had been shown by the Southerners, who had at one time carried the utmost dismay into

Washington; but their divisions were not strong enough to meet the superior forces of the North, and the Shenandoah Valley, after being desolated in turn by the hostile operations of both armies, remained as the prize of the Union troops, and throughout the further course of the war was not again threatened by the Southern armies.

While these events were proceeding on the banks of the Shenandoah, Grant continued to watch his adversaries at Petersburg and Richmond, in the hope that he should be able to discover some weak point through which he could strike effectually at one or both of those cities. His lines, strongly fortified, covered a length of nearly 30 miles, starting from near the Weldon Railway on his left, and, after crossing the James River, terminating in the vicinity of Newmarket on his right. During the autumn and early winter, he made many attempts to turn the Confederate flanks; but Lee accommodated his own movements to those of his opponents with so much skill and address that nothing could be effected. The army under Lee consisted of veterans, who had had experience of almost every kind of war, and whose steadiness was certain not to desert them under any circumstances, however adverse; but their numbers were few in comparison with those of Grant, and, what was worse, the population of the Confederate States seemed to have lost all heart in the struggle, and to be increasingly disinclined to furnish the recruits who were now so sorely needed. "The rebels," Grant wrote, "have now in their ranks their last men. The little boys and old men are guarding prisoners, guarding railroad bridges, and forming a good part of their garrisons for entrenched positions. A man lost by them cannot be replaced. They have robbed the cradle and the grave equally to get their present force. Besides what they lose in frequent skirmishes and battles, they are now losing from desertions and other causes at least one regiment per day. With this drain upon them, the end is not far distant, if we will only be true to ourselves." These statements were substantially correct. The desperate game of the Southern Confederacy was almost played out, and it was merely the determination of a few able and adventurous men that prevented the immediate submission of the people to a power which they might dislike, but which it was obvious they could not withstand. The consciousness of this fact strengthened Grant in that tenacity of purpose which was one of his most distinctive characteristics. Another might have given up the attempt on Petersburg and Richmond after so many failures; Grant, on the contrary, held to his position, and did not suffer himself to be discouraged by incidental reverses.

The weakening of Lee's force by the despatch of divisions to the assistance of Early, appeared to offer an opportunity for an offensive movement. The approaches to Richmond from the north-eastern side of the James River were believed to be guarded by not more than 8000 men; and Grant accordingly sent a strong detachment, under the general orders of Hancock, up that stream to Deep Bottom. The troops, however, disembarked with so much slowness that Lee had time to concentrate his regiments on the menanced point, and, after a good deal of fighting, the Union forces were obliged to retire. This was a movement against the left flank of Lee, to repel which it had been necessary to draw away the greater number of the defending army from the opposite extremity of the line. Grant, being aware of the fact, struck in that direction also. The commander of the expedition against the Confederate right was Warren, who took with him the 5th corps, and succeeded in obtaining a position beyond the Weldon Railway. Although Lee had only a few troops in that quarter, he

CAVALRY FIGHT BETWEEN THE FORCES OF SHERIDAN AND STUART, NEAR RICHMOND, VA., MAY 11, 1864.

assailed his antagonist with great spirit, and achieved a temporary success; but the Union forces, on being reinforced, recovered the ground they had abandoned, and proceeded to fortify themselves against further molestation. An attack by the Southerners, on August 21, met with no success, and on the same day Hancock reached the Weldon Railway at a point four miles south of Warren's entrenchments. On the 25th, an action took place between Hancock and Hill, which resulted in the Confederates obtaining possession of Reams' Station, and in the retreat of the Union forces. Nevertheless, the latter still held the Weldon Railway, and succeeded in connecting it with the center of the army in front of Petersburg. All this while, that city was shelled by the Union troops, and the Confederate batteries on the James River were revenging themselves by firing on the Union gunboats.

Grant now ordered Meade to conduct a feigned attack against Lee's right, while he sent two corps under Butler, to make an attempt against the Confederate works north of Chaffin's Bluff, opposite Drury's Bluff, on the James River. It was believed that only a small force of Southerners occupied the works on the north side of the river, and it seemed therefore not improbable that a sudden movement and rapid advance in that direction might ensure the capture of Richmond. The inhabitants of the city were apprehensive for their safety, and, being threatened at so many points, feared that at some one the circle would be broken through, and all would be lost. Even should the movement fail, it was anticipated that the withdrawal of a large part of the Confederate force from the southern to the northern side of the river would materially aid the Union forces in their operations against Petersburg; and it was therefore considered by Grant that the venture would be worth the cost in life it would demand. The movement was commenced on the night of September 28, when General Ord, with the 18th corps, was directed to cross the James at Aikin's Landing, eight miles above Deep Bottom, and at daylight to advance quickly against the enemy's works in his front. At the same time, General Birney, with the 10th corps, was to move on Bermuda Hundred, and cross the river during the night. These two detachments were to obtain possession of the Newmarket road, and to form a connection in front of Richmond. The design was carried out without any accident, and the outer line of Confederate defences was soon in the hands of the two Union commanders. The inner defences at Chaffin's Bluff were now before the assailants, and preparations were made for carrying them. Before these preparations could be completed, reinforcements had reached the garrison, and the assault, when at length it came, proved unsuccessful. The troops employed on this service were negroes, of whom only a small proportion succeeded in reaching one of the forts. These behaved with much gallantry, but were unable to take so formidable a position. All who were not killed were captured, and it was found necessary to abandon the attack. On the 30th, further portions of the enemy's lines were seized by the Union troops, and an attempt to recapture the works, on the same day, was wholly without result. On October 7, the Confederates made a partially successful endeavor to turn the right flank of their opponents, but were repulsed. Other encounters took place on subsequent days, without materially altering the position of the beligerants towards one another ; and Grant, considering it important to keep what he had gained, extended his lines from opposite Dutch Gap to the Newmarket road. Meade's simultaneous movement against the right of the Confederate line ended, after an engagement of three days' duration, and a heavy loss in men, in the Union forces acquiring a position across the Squirrel road parallel with the Weldon Railway; whereupon the Confederates retired within their main entrenchments.

Another attempt to capture Petersburg followed these operations. Meade was ordered to occupy the Boydton road and the Southside Railway, both lying to the south-west of the town; and this movement was accomplished by Hancock on the 27th. The march was performed with great secrecy, and without being discovered by the enemy. The 2d corps passed round the Confederate flank, and was proceeding to execute other portions of the concerted scheme, when Hancock received orders to halt. The 9th corps, under Warren and Parke, had been directed to engage the adversary in front; but Parke had been unsuccessful in capturing the works against which he was sent, and Warren was accordingly instructed to form a junction between Hancock's right and Parke's left. This, however, could not be effected, owing to the density of the forest, the mazy character of the roads which intersected it, and the want of proper maps. Hill, who commanded the Confederates in that direction, conceived that the proper time had arrived for making an attack, as the Union corps were now separated and confused. Hancock and Warren were simultaneously assailed, and night closed in over an undecided combat. Next day, the Union troops, perceiving that their design had been a failure, withdrew across Hatcher's Run, a stream crossing the Boydton road, and with some difficulty got back to their own lines. At the same time, Butler attempted a similar manœuvre on the north side of the James River; but his operations entirely failed, and it was with a loss of nearly 1500 men that the Union troops returned to the point whence they had started. This terminated the active operations of the year in front of Petersburg and Richmond. Both sides were getting sick of the struggle. From both armies there were many desertions; but the Union army could suffer this depletion of their ranks much better than the Confederates. Grant's numbers might have been called overwhelming, but that they did not overwhelm; the Confederates, on the contrary, presented a daily diminishing host to their adversaries, and could ill afford any further reduction of their meagre legions. Yet, although his forces were so numerous, Grant was deeply impressed with the necessity of filling those gaps which the progress of the war had inevitably made. He communicated his views to the Government, and the call for 500,000 men, issued by the President on July 18, was ordered to be carried into effect on September 19, and succeeding days. Grant, writing to the Secretary of War, gave it as his opinion that "prompt action in filling our armies, will have more effect upon the enemy than a victory over them. They profess to believe, and make their men believe, there is such a party North in favor of recognizing Southern independence that the draft cannot be enforced. Let them be undeceived." To the same effect, and on the same day, wrote Sherman from Atlanta; and as by this time there was evidence of the Confederacy giving way on all sides, the probability of an enthusiastic response to the draft was considerable.

The last two months of 1864 were not characterized by any events of importance on the Potomac or the James River. Grant had failed in all his active operations, but he had obtained a position in close proximity to his antagonist, from which that antagonist was unable to expel him. The Union lines were fortified so strongly as to defy successful attack, and Butler was engaged in cutting a canal through Dutch Gap (a peninsula formed by a great bend of the James River), in the hope of facilitating the passage of the troops, and of turning the Confederate batteries at that part of the channel. The Southern armies in Richmond and Petersburg were getting short of food and clothing; yet the soldiers manning the works still fought with resolution, and repelled with spirit whatever attacks were directed against their lines during the early winter; and it is impossible not to admire the courage and self-reliance exhibited by these men at a time when everything was tending to their defeat. Fort Fisher covered the harbor of Wilmington (North Carolina), one of the great resorts of the blockade-runners; and, until it could be reduced, Wilmington was secure from attack, together with the vessels which preyed on our commerce. In the early winter, a detachment of 6500 men, under Butler, was sent to act in concert with Admiral Porter. The fort was defended by rather less than 1000 men. The assailants were in every respect much stronger than the assailed; but it was not proposed to take the fort by storm. A plan was formed for destroying the work, by blowing up a powder vessel beneath its walls, and 215 pounds of the explosive were placed on board the steamer *Louisiana*, which, under pretence of being a blockade-runner, was anchored within three-quarters of a mile of the fort. The attempt turned out a failure; for, although the powder exploded, it did not take fire simultaneously, and the effect was thus dissipated. The boat was fired on the morning of December 24, but the detonation was productive of but trifling results. It was followed on the same day by a tremendous bombardment of the fort. The fleet was extremely powerful; but, although the roar of the guns was terrific, and the garrison, expecting immediate death, crowded into the bomb-proof galleries, very little damage was effected. The attack was renewed on the following day, when a detachment of more than 2000 men, commanded by General Weitzel, landed beneath the walls, and took up a position for ulterior operations. The bombardment from the fleet still continued; yet Weitzel found he could do nothing. He reported to Butler that it would be butchery to order an assault, and under these circumstances it was determined to abandon the attempt. The troops were re-embarked, and conveyed to Fortress Monroe. Fort Fisher was scarcely injured, and its garrison was now strengthened by the arrival of troops from Richmond. Butler was removed from command, and the proceedings at Fort Fisher were made the subject of an inquiry, which resulted in Butler being acquitted of blame.

A second expedition against the fort was sent out almost immediately after the failure of the first. On the departure of the army, Porter withdrew his fleet to Beaufort, in the confident expectation that the troops would soon be ordered back again. He had not long to wait, for on January 2, 1865, General Terry, commanding a division of the Army of the James, was ordered to proceed to Fort Fisher with the soldiers who had been employed in the former attempt, and an additional brigade of 1500 men. Having arranged a plan of operations with Porter, Terry made his way to New Inlet, by which Cape Fear River is approached from the Atlantic. While the ironclads and monitors shelled the fort, the disembarkation of the troops was effected on January 13. The works were presently bombarded by all the vessels of the fleet, and the garrison were able to make scarcely any reply, owing to the inferiority of their guns. Bragg, who was at Wilmington, sent on some reinforcements; but little could be done against so terrible and concentrated a fire. The small gunboats got in very close on the 14th, and, firing with great accuracy, dismounted some of the guns on the land-face. Preparations were made for an assault on the following day. The walls were beginning to show signs of serious injury. The rampart was overthrown, the palisades were torn away, and communication with the mines was cut off. Early in the afternoon, three brigades, under General Ames, were sent against the north-eastern rampart, while a party of sailors and marines, who had landed on the beach, made a feint against the sea-face. The Confederates fought with much resolution, and the two principal commanding officers were severely wounded; but the determination of the Union troops was equal to that of their enemies. From one position to another the defenders of the fort were driven back; the whole work was at length abandoned; and the garrison, flying to the extremity of the neck of land on which the fort was built, threw down their arms in despair. The feint against the sea-face had been badly managed, and resulted in a somewhat precipitate retreat of the sailors; but the main attack had been successful in the highest degree, and, now that Fort Fisher had fallen, Wilmington lay at the mercy of the conquerors. For the present, however, it was not attacked. The other works at the entrance to Cape Fear River were abandoned by the Confederates, and the stream was entered when the torpedoes had been removed. A few days afterwards, the ironclad squadron which had recently been built at Richmond, and launched on the James, made an attempt to destroy the pontoon bridges and transports by which the Union troops were supporting their operations in that quarter. On the night of January 24, the Confederate vessels tried to force their way through the obstructions. One of the ironclads passed a boom which had been drawn across the channel; but three larger vessels grounded, and in the early morning, when the shore batteries opened fire, the flotilla was compelled to withdraw.

Peace negotiations of a formal character were opened

FORTRESS MONROE.

in January. Three commissioners—one of whom was Alexander H. Stephens, Vice-President of the Confederacy—were charged with power to arrange with Union agents the terms on which peace might be concluded. These discussions ended in nothing but a more complete manifestation of the inability of the two sides to find any common ground of agreement. Lincoln went in person to Fortress Monroe and met the commissioners. Nothing was effected. Lincoln would not recede from his inflexible demand of absolute submission on the part of the South; the commissioners were not empowered to make any such terms. The conference was held on February 3, and it was the last attempt on the part of the Confederacy to obtain peace together with independence. The game was very nearly played out, and the South was shortly compelled to accept peace on any terms it could get.

"The man," Davis remarked, "who should go before the Southern people with any proposition which implied that the North was to have a voice in determining the domestic relations of the South, could not live here a day. He would be hanged to the first tree, without judge or jury."

We now approach the final series of operations which proved the ruin of the Confederacy. The state of affairs at Richmond was now very critical, the troops had been on short rations throughout the winter, and, as the Northern forces tightened their grip on the devoted city, it was evident that the prevalent distress would become still greater. If anything more was to be done, it must be done at once. Lee accordingly determined to strike a heavy blow at Grant, such as might possibly compel his withdrawal from Petersburg and Richmond, and enable the Confederate forces of that locality to unite with those under Johnston for ulterior operations against Sherman and Schofield. The point of attack was Fort Steadman, the second work from the extreme right of the Union defences in the neighborhood of Appomattox. The position was most formidable. Works of a very elaborate character, strongly built and heavily armed, stretched for a distance of 30 miles from the north side of the James to Hatcher's Run, on the south side. These lines had the Appomattox in front during the greater part of their course, and between them and the river were the opposing works of the Confederates. The attack on Fort Steadman was made at dawn on March 25. The assailants were led by General Gordon, and the garrison was so completely surprised that the place was captured with but little difficulty. Gordon then proceeded towards Fort Hascall, forming a portion of the second line of defence; but the attempt to carry this position was an utter failure. Baffled and discouraged, Gordon retired to Fort Steadman, where he was furiously attacked by the 9th Union corps, and, after a sanguinary fight, was compelled to yield what he had acquired with such delusive facility. Losing a large proportion of their number by death and capture, the Confederates retreated to their own works, followed by the victorious Union troops who established themselves in a position beyond that which they had occupied when the day's operations began. It was two days after this event that Sherman arrived at City Point, on the James River, to consult with Grant on the future conduct of the campaign. The two commanders, together with Meade, Ord and President Lincoln, subsequently met in conference in front of Petersburg, and debated on the measures necessary for the final subjection of the Confederacy. The great object was to keep the forces of Lee and Johnston from effecting a junction, and thus prolonging the struggle over an indefinite period. To frustrate this design, Grant proposed to take the initiative and to make so overwhelming an attack on Lee as to prevent the union of the two armies. March 29 was fixed upon for the renewal of active operations. The plan embraced a simultaneous attack on many scattered points of the Confederate position about Petersburg. For resisting this combined assault, Lee had only a comparatively small body of troops; but those troops were seasoned veterans, and Lee himself was a commander of the highest ability. The approaching contest, therefore, seemed likely to be the death-grapple, and each side summoned up all its energies for the prosecution of the task which lay before it.

The movement began on the 29th, when the 2d corps, under Humphreys, and the 5th, under Warren, arrived before the Confederate breastworks in the vicinity of Hatcher's Run. That night Grant communicated with Sheridan, and directed him to act in conjunction with the main army, instead of simply operating against the enemy's lines of communication, as had been originally intended. Violent rain on the 30th prevented any active measures; but the Confederates in the meanwhile concentrated several of their brigades opposite the corps of Humphreys and Warren. On the 31st, Lee considered himself strong enough to anticipate his enemy's blow by striking a blow of his own. A portion of Warren's force was driven back with great slaughter; but the success was only temporary, and was followed by a recoil when other troops were encountered. Lee then turned on Sheridan, who had taken up a position in front of Dinwiddie Court House, at the Five Forks—a meeting of cross-roads, three of which run towards the Southside Railway. The attack was made with so much impetuosity and vigor that Sheridan's men were for a time driven back, and seemed likely to be entirely defeated. The troopers, however, retired behind a breastwork of logs and earth which had pre-

CAPTURE OF THE WORKS AT PETERSBURG.

viously been erected, and after a while the combat was renewed by two brigades of Union cavalry, who attacked the Southerners in flank, and checked their farther advance. Towards night, the Confederates were forced to yield the ground they had won at an earlier period of the day, and this was at once occupied by their antagonists, who in some directions pushed their line beyond the points which they had held at the beginning of the action. A detachment from Warren's corps was sent on the night of the 31st to the support of Sheridan; and when these troops arrived at daybreak on April 1, they beheld the rear of the opposing cavalry in rapid retreat. Sheridan now felt in a position to assume the offensive, and a murderous conflict again ensued, ending in the total discomfiture of the Confederates, who retreated in disorder towards Petersburg.

On April 1, Grant opened a furious bombardment along his whole line, and directed the corps of Wright, Parke, and Ord, which had not as yet been employed in this series of operations, to attack Petersburg next morning. The assault commenced at daybreak. The three corps appointed to the work dashed across the narrow belt of land separating their own from the Confederate lines, and, attacking with irresistible spirit and enormous concentration of power, swept like an immense wave over the entrenchments which had so long resisted the Union advance. At the same time, Humphreys, whose corps was on the left, beyond Hatcher's Run, assailed the works in his front, and drove back the defenders into the inner fortifications. Magnificent efforts were made by the Confederate generals to retrieve this dire misfortune; but the troops were fast losing their organization, and there was too much reason to apprehend that panic would presently succeed to confusion. The less determined were seeking the rear; the more self-reliant were desperately striving to retain such positions as still remained within their grasp; but the case was hopeless, and at the utmost nothing more could be done than to delay the Union progress, and cover the retreat of the army, so as possibly to avoid the humiliation of a complete surrender. Fort Gregg was held for some hours by a small body of devoted men, who in the midst of general consternation retained their coolness and their courage. The garrison of Fort Alexander also stood firmly to their guns. Repeated onsets were made by Gibbons's division; but it was not until half-past two in the afternoon that Fort Gregg surrendered, with the small handful of men, 30 in number, who alone remained out of the 250 forming the garrison that morning.

The day was Sunday; and while Davis was at worship, a message from Lee was handed to him which must have cast an additional shadow upon that worn and weary face. Lee announced that his outer lines had been forced, that he could resist only a few hours longer, and that Richmond must be immediately evacuated. In the course of the morning, however, Lee was enabled to rally his troops behind the inner defences, and so far to restore their confidence as to undertake the offensive on his own part. Hill, one of the most distinguished of the Confederate commanders, was directed to attack the enemy's 9th corps, and executed the movement with so much skill and daring that they were for a time staggered. But in this heroic effort Hill was slain, and his troops were ultimately obliged to recede. Field's division of Longstreet's corps, however, was at the same time so vigorously handled as to keep the Union troops in check; and during the night of that disastrous day the Southerners evacuated Petersburg, without further molestation from their opponents.

They retired on Amelia Court House, to the northwest of Petersburg; and on this point were concentrated the forces that had previously been north of the James. Great fires were kindled in Richmond, where the Confederates applied the torch to the Government offices, the great storehouses on the banks of the river, and other buildings. Davis, the members of his Cabinet, and all the citizens of importance, departed for Charlotte, North Carolina.

The evacuation of Richmond became known to General Weitzel—who occupied the Union works north of the James—at three o'clock on the morning of April 3. At daylight he moved his men forward, and, meeting with no opposition, entered the city. He found much suffering and poverty among the population. The rich as well as the poor were destitute of food; and, whatever their political sympathies, it must in some respects have been a relief that the long and arduous struggle was over. The great news was at once telegraphed to Washington, and on the following day President Lincoln arrived at Richmond, and occupied the house belonging to Davis, which was now used as the headquarters of the Union garrison. Martial law was for the present proclaimed in the city, and the people were requested to remain quietly in their houses, and to avoid all public assemblages, or meetings in the streets. At the same time, strict orders were given for restraining the victorious soldiery from acts of plunder and outrage, and from the use of insulting words or gestures towards the citizens. To have obtained possession of the Confederate capital was a great triumph for the Northern cause; yet the Confederation itself, though pierced and mortally wounded in many places, had still some life remaining, and was capable of resistance in the field. Lee had effected his escape at the head of an army not contemptible in numbers, and eminent for valor: and to the crushing of that force, wherever it might be found, Grant immediately directed his attention.

Breaking down the bridges over which he passed, Lee pursued his way in a westerly direction, and was presently 16 miles ahead of his adversaries. The fear was lest he should unite with Johnston, in which case he might still have offered a formidable resistance in the open country. To prevent such a result, every nerve was strained; and as early as the evening of the 2d the cavalry under Sheridan, and a number of infantry, were marching in the direction of the Southside and Lynchburg Railway. Lee was then retreating along the southern bank of the Appomattox; and at Amelia Court House the forces from Richmond joined those from Petersburg on the morning of the 4th. Lee hoped to have an opportunity of taking some of the Union columns in detail, and beating them one by one; but the commissariat stores which he had ordered to be collected at that spot had by some error failed to reach the depôt. It has been said that they were sent by mistake to Richmond, and that they perished there in the conflagration. The disaster, however arising, was one of an overwhelming character. The Confederate troops carried with them rations for not more than one day; the country was in such a state that it could not supply them with food; and it was no longer possible to perform the long and difficult march by which alone Lee could combine with Johnston. On the afternoon of the 4th, Sheridan cut the rail to Danville between Amelia Court House and Burkesville, and, entrenching himself strongly, awaited the arrival of the main army. The Confederates were now exhausted, depressed, and out of heart; desertions were numerous, and many permitted themselves to be captured. An attempt to escape towards Lynchburg, on the night of the 5th, was defeated by the able combinations of the Union troops, and next morning the advance-guard of Ord's army was planted across the roads by which Lee was marching. The obstruction was for the moment swept aside after a sharp encounter; but the Confederates were by this time reduced to such terrible extremities that they were compelled to feed on the young shoots of trees. The horses and mules were in an equally bad state with their masters, and the soldiers were utterly broken down by want of sustenance, and the fatigue of constant marching. It was so evident that all was over, that large numbers of guns and wagons were destroyed, to prevent their falling into the hands of the enemy, and the records and papers belonging to the army were burned. Most of the baggage shared the same fate, and it was now only a question of how soon the inevitable collapse would take place. Meanwhile, the pursuit was kept up with remorseless rigor. Lee's rear was attacked by Sheridan, and by the infantry of the 2d corps, on the 6th. In the first instance, the men fought with the fury of despair; but, on finding every avenue of retreat cut off by the converging columns of the foe, they threw down their arms, and surrendered. Lee pushed on, at the head of 10,000 men, conceiving that he might even yet reach Lynchburg, where supplies had been collected. General Pendleton expressed to him the opinion of himself and his fellow-officers that surrender was now unavoidable; but, clinging to his desperate hope, he refused to admit it. A few scattered actions still took place, and the attempts of the Union troops to bar the road of retreat were repulsed with amazing valor; but the end was by this time a foregone conclusion. Submission might be delayed for a day or two; but in the very near future it stood before those vanquished and starving men, a fact inevitable as death, inexorable as fate.

On April 7, Grant addressed a letter to Lee in which he said:—"The result of last week must convince you of the hopelessness of further resistance on the part of the Army of Northern Virginia in this struggle. I feel that it is so, and regard it as my duty to shift from myself the responsibility of any further effusion of blood by asking of you the surrender of that portion of the Confederate States Army known as the Army of Northern Virginia." Lee replied on the same day, and, while remarking that he was not entirely of the opinion expressed by Grant as to the hopelessness of further resistance, reciprocated the desire of that commander to avoid useless bloodshed, and therefore, before considering his proposition, asked the terms he would offer on condition of the army surrendering. Grant wrote on the 8th, demanding that the men surrendered should be disqualified from taking up arms against the Government until properly exchanged, and adding that he would meet Lee, or would designate officers to meet any officers named by him, at any point that might be considered desirable, for the purpose of arranging the terms upon which the surrender would be received. But Lee was still disinclined to entertain the proposition. He desired a personal interview with Grant, that the restoration of peace might be talked over; and proposed a meeting between the picket lines. If by this species of equivocation Lee hoped to effect any arrangement by which the war could be terminated, and the Confederacy at the same time recognized, with whatever limitations or under whatever conditions, he deceived himself. Grant told him, in a letter written on the 9th, that peace might be had at once on the South laying down its arms; and by that time he must have fully understood, as regarded his own army at least, that no other course was possible. His forces had sustained another severe defeat early on the morning of the 9th. Sheridan had cut off the line of retreat. Four trains laden with provisions, which were approaching along the line from Lynchburg, were captured. A last despairing attempt to cut through the opposing ranks was baffled; and as Sheridan was preparing to charge the staggering masses of the Confederates, a flag of truce was seen approaching, with the information that hostilities had been suspended, in order to arrange terms of surrender. Lee had at length requested an interview with Grant in accordance with the offer contained in the letter of the previous day; and the preliminaries were on the point of being arranged.

The two great rivals met during April 9, in a small dwelling near Appomattox Court House. The terms of surrender were, that the officers were to give their individual paroles not to take up arms against the United States until properly exchanged; that each company or regimental commander should sign a similar parole on behalf of the men; and that the arms, artillery, and public property, should be made over to officers appointed by Grant to receive them. This last condition was not to embrace the side-arms of the officers, nor their private horses or baggage. On these stipulations being complied with, the officers and men would be allowed to return to their homes, and would not be disturbed by the authority of the United States, so long as they observed their paroles, and the laws existing where they might reside. The surrender was to include all the forces operating with the Army of Virginia on April 8, and these auxiliary troops speedily laid down their arms.

The conduct of Grant and of his officers was in the highest degree considerate and kind, and the Union soldiers shared rations with their famished antagonists, now their antagonists no longer. Next day General Lee issued a farewell address to his army. "After four years of arduous service, marked by unsurpassed courage and fortitude, the Army of Northern Virginia has been compelled to yield to overwhelming numbers and resources. I need not tell the survivors of so many hard-fought battles, who have remained steadfast to the last, that I have consented to this result from no distrust of them; but, holding that valor and devotion could accomplish nothing that could compensate for the loss that would attend the continuation of the contest, I have determined to avoid the useless sacrifice of those

THE HOUSE WHERE GENERAL LEE SURRENDERED.

whose past valor has endeared them to their countrymen. By the terms of agreement, officers and men can return to their homes, and remain there until exchanged. You will take with you the satisfaction that proceeds from the consciousness of duty faithfully performed;

and I earnestly pray that a merciful God will extend you His blessing and protection." On that same day —April 10—Lee went with an escort of Union cavalry to Richmond, where he visited the quarters of Longstreet, and afterwards took leave of his staff, previous to departing for his own home.

The number of officers and men who surrendered on this occasion is not exactly known; but it has been estimated that Lee's army on evacuating Richmond, consisted of nearly 30,000 men. Probably it was not so large as this, but it was large enough to make the loss to the Confederacy one of the most crushing disasters that the Southern League could undergo in its then exhausted condition. Even before the surrender, many of the rebel soldiers had abandoned the army, and returned home, seeing the utter hopelessness of a struggle where the resources on one side were practically illimitable, and those on the other incapable of renewal or repair. The number of muskets given up by Lee scarcely exceeded 10,000, and the pieces of artillery were thirty. The total captures of artillery during this series of battles, and the pursuit that followed, amounted to 170 guns, while of wagons about 350 were yielded to the conquerors. On receiving news of the surrender, the War Department at Washington issued an order to the effect that a salute of 200 guns should be fired at the headquarters of every army and department, at every post and arsenal in the United States, and at the Military Academy at West Point. The Northern people were transported with delight at the great intelligence which reached them from Virginia. It was true that the army under Johnston, and the armies of the West, still kept possession of the field; but there could now be not the slightest question as to the final issue of the war. The slaveowners' rebellion was virtually at an end; the

GENERAL LEE BIDDING FAREWELL TO HIS SOLDIERS.

authority of the Union was on the eve of being restored throughout the length and breadth of the Republic. A tremendous price had been paid for this supremacy of the Federation over its turbulent members; but the result was nearly achieved. It was no longer possible for unfriendly critics, in England or elsewhere, to say that the American Government was one which naturally tended to disunion, that the model Republic was a bubble, that the commonwealth established by Washington, by Adams, by Jefferson, by Franklin, and by many worthy peers, had a natural tendency to fly into discordant fragments, to relapse into chaos, and to end in ruin.

With the surrender of Lee, the last hope of Southern independence vanished. As he rode back from his interview with Grant the troops crowded around him in transports of grief and enthusiasm. He said, "Men, we have fought through the war together. I have done the best that I could for you." There can be no question that he had.

On April 15, 1865, President Lincoln was shot while attending a theatre; and Andrew Johnson, the Vice-President, was inaugurated President three hours after Lincoln's death.

The surrender of Lee was the last great event under the Presidency of Abraham Lincoln. The first great event under the Presidency of Andrew Johnson was the surrender of the Confederate leader opposed to Sherman. Sherman had conducted his forces in safety to Goldsborough, in North Carolina, and Johnston, after vain attempts to bar his progress, had retreated to Smithfield, a few miles distant on the same line of railway. For some time, no active operations took place between the principal opponents; but, in the final days of March and early days of April, a detachment of cavalry marched to and fro in various directions, destroying railways and bridges, burning depots of stores, and so interfering with the lines of retreat of all the Confederate forces in that part of the country as to make their position even more desperate than before. At the same time, General Wilson, with another body of cavalry, rode through Alabama and a part of Georgia, defeating Forrest, capturing Selma (a place containing an arsenal, an armory and large depots) on April 3, and threatening other points. Mobile was surrendered to General Canby on April 12, after a short siege, and when Davis arrived at Johnston's camp it was apparent that the Confederacy was doomed.

On April 10, Sherman advanced in force against Johnston. Marching in two columns in a westerly direction along the northern bank of the Neuse River, and overcoming with but little difficulty the slight opposition of the Confederate rear-guard, he entered Smithfield on the 11th. Here he found that his adversary had crossed to the southern bank of the stream and escaped him, but he also learned that Lee had surrendered, and he saw that if Johnston could be brought to the same pass, the war would be virtually at an end. That he might move with greater quickness, he abandoned his trains, baggage and other impediments and pushed rapidly forward to Raleigh. Finding the enemy still in advance, he bent towards the South, crossed the Cape Fear River, and made for Greensboro', whither the Confederates were now retreating. But Johnston was not disposed to abide the shock of battle any further. He saw how fearfully he was overmatched; he knew that succor was impossible; he perceived that his troops would soon be destitute of the very means of life; and as Lee had done under similar circumstances, he negotiated for a surrender.

On April 26, it was agreed that the Confederate Army of the Tennessee should be surrendered on the same terms as those which had been granted to the Army of Virginia. The men laid down their arms and returned to their homes. A few of the cavalry escaped to Mississippi, and some other members of the same force accompanied Davis in his renewed flight towards the south, whence he hoped to escape by some port on the seacoast. With these exceptions, the Confederate soldiers under the command of Johnston ceased to be an army, and returned to their original capacity as civilians.

Jefferson Davis was captured on May 10, at Irwinsville, Georgia. He was taken to Fortress Monroe as a prisoner, and remained there till May 13, 1867, when he was released on bail, and departed for Canada; and after further postponements of his trial and enlargements of his bail the prosecution was dropped on February 6, 1869. The leniency of the Government towards their traitorous citizens was most remarkable, and conferred on the nation the highest honor it could receive.

General Grant became the eighteenth President on March 4, 1869, and was re-elected for a further term of four years on the expiration of his first term of office.

The Civil War was one of the most destructive on record. During the four years of its continuance, on the Union side, 2,656,533 men were called into service; 1,400,000 were in actual service; 60,000 men were killed in the field, 30,000 mortally wounded, and 184,000 died in hospital or camp. The Confederates, it is supposed, lost an equal number, while on both sides a large number were more or less disabled for life. Nor was the expenditure of money less lavish. In August, 1865, three months after the close of the war, the debt of the Union was $3,000,000,000, and if we include the whole nation, the actual cost of the war must have been over $6,000,000,000.

www.ingramcontent.com/pod-product-compliance
Lightning Source LLC
Chambersburg PA
CBHW021151230426
43667CB00006B/352